W

Yael Helfman-Cohen

Producer & International Distributor
eBookPro Publishing
www.ebook-pro.com

WILD IDEAS
Yael Helfman-Cohen

Translation from Hebrew: Sarah Winkler
Editor: Evan Gordon

Contact: yael@naturecode.co.il

ISBN 9798326908131

WILD IDEAS

*How Nature Inspires
Groundbreaking Innovations*

YAEL HELFMAN-COHEN

Contents

Part IV: WHERE?

FURTHER VIEWING

Various mechanisms from nature are discussed over the course of the book. To bring the explanations to life and to experience the described mechanisms in an experiential and clear manner, references to videos are included at different points in the text.

In the back of the book, on page 369, you will find QR codes that correspond to the numbers assigned to the further reading material. A quick scan of these codes will lead you through the text straight into 'nature' – as close as is possible – to the living and natural source.

The videos will enrich your reading experience and elucidate the mechanisms described in the text.

Sometimes one video is better than a thousand words!

Happy viewing.

How to read the codes

The codes are black-and-white squares embedded with links. Most smartphones today can read QR codes with their built-in cameras and sometimes you need to download a QR scanner app.

Aim your camera at the code to read it. The built-in scanner will scan the code and you will then be directed to the appropriate site. If you are using an app, a small window will appear once you scan the code. Touching the window will lead you to the link. If your camera does not come with a QR scanner, you can download one in the app store.

PREFACE

Human subtlety will never devise an invention
more beautiful, more simple, or more direct than
does nature because in her inventions nothing is lacking,
and nothing is superfluous.

Leonardo da Vinci

When I was a child in the 80s, I received a book as a gift called *Bionics: Nature's Patents*.[1] It was a spectacular album of nature photos paired with descriptions of technologies inspired by nature. I recall thinking that the idea that there are patents in nature is remarkable. The book remained on the shelf. I would leaf through it from time to time, and eventually forgot about its existence. I had many books in my childhood as well as elaborate and curated collections of various kinds, but they all disappeared over the years. Only this book survived, as though quietly waiting for the day I would realize that it foreshadowed my career in adulthood.

The years passed, the book gathered dust, and in the meantime, I studied nature through other means. I was not the kind of girl who grew up in the wild and breathed nature all her life. I was a city girl from Haifa who found nature in the asphalt cracks of the parking lot.

I was raised in the Carmel region among the shade of pine trees. During my childhood, I would spend many hours searching for small pine nuts on the ground. Some of them were coal black while some were lighter in hue, as though their worn appearance revealed how long they had been lying there waiting for me. These were years of reaping and harvesting, in which I would come home with blackened hands and a pure heart, years of expertise in finding the proper stone for cracking pine nuts and drafting recipes for my pine nut cookbook. During all these hours alone with the pine nuts, I never felt lonely. The small black seeds gave me my first experience of flow state, an experience of harmonious presence while losing sense of time. I was immersed in the activity and got sucked into it in an intense way.

As a soldier, I got the chance to officially work with nature. I was an education officer, and my duty was, among other things, to bring soldiers closer to the natural environment and introduce them to the flora and fauna. That is where I fell in love. In my wanderings around the Ramon Crater, each encounter with flora and fauna amidst the vast nothingness of the desert was particularly thrilling. I was exposed to the unique adaptations of plants and animals in the desert, to nature's miraculous strategies for solving challenges.

When I was released from the army, I continued to keep in touch with nature and worked as a tour guide around the country, but when choosing a career path, nature did not come up as a serious job option. I reserved it as a hobby and as a source of temporary income while studying, and when I began my graduate life as an industrial and management engineer, nature had once again become a space for me to travel and breathe. Even though my professional life took me away from nature, it brought me closer to the world of entrepreneurship and innovation: in the early years, I worked at a medical start-up and got to see how a patent written on paper becomes a product. I learned what entrepreneurship is and how to create value through innovative thinking.

As such, I collected the elements of everything I do today: nature, technology, entrepreneurship, and innovation.

In 2006, I discovered the existence of the field of biomimicry, which addresses innovation inspired by nature. It was during this time that I was involved in an ecological project that sought to promote sustainability and environmental values. As the project was developing, I realized that if anyone knew what sustainability is – it is nature – and that the connection between nature and sustainability has already been made and is recognized in the world through the field of biomimicry. Here again, the door was being flung open for me to the wonderful world of nature – only this time, as an engineer in awe of the rare knowledge inherent within it. The passion was rekindled.

In Israel, this field was virgin territory. The term "biomimicry" was unknown. In those years, a Google search in Hebrew for the word "biomimicry" yielded zero results. The idea that one can learn from nature was definitely not foreign, but it did not reach the level of awareness that exists today, where the concept has already developed into an accepted field of knowledge in the academic and business worlds.

Together with a partner, Daphne Haim-Langford, we decided to establish the Israeli Biomimicry Organization in 2008 and begin spreading the word. First, we went wherever we could – we lectured about the field and scattered seeds of biomimicry in the direction which the wind blew. The seeds began to germinate, and a small and young ecosystem of biomimicry lovers was born. It was as diverse as nature – consisting of planners, engineers, designers, biologists, managers, entrepreneurs, educators, and environmentalists. They all feed from the same soil: the soil of curiosity and passion for nature and its wonders.

At the same time, different ecosystems around the world were maturing and developing. In the United States, the Biomimicry Institute, a nonprofit organization founded to share nature's lessons with changemakers, became the cornerstone of the field on a global enterprise level, while Europe, and particularly Germany, became its beating heart on the academic front.

I was already full of passion for the field at this point and decided to get my PhD in it, from a place of great intellectual curiosity and a desire to establish a solid knowledge base on the subject here in Israel, as well. The task of finding a supervisor was not easy. The subject was not regarded as a field of research in any academic institution in Israel. Naturally, there were niche studies combining biology and engineering, but I was searching for the big picture and wanted to explore what a process of innovation inspired by nature would look like. It was clear that I needed to find an unconventional supervisor, one with a different mindset who was up to the challenge, and he was found: Yoram Reich from Tel Aviv University. We embarked on a fascinating journey together that lasted several years, which will also be described in this book.

***

For the past decade, I have been living and breathing biomimicry. I have developed professional courses and educational programs, and am leading innovation processes inspired by nature in organizations. I work to integrate nature into the equation of every design process and also as a way of life. Learning from nature does not simply amount to one technological solution or another, but to understanding the laws and qualities of nature, which act as a mirror for our life processes. You can read about this in my first book, *Ha-Teva She-ani* (The Nature that I Am [Hebrew]).[2]

This book, *Wild Ideas*, was born out of a desire to share my knowledge and great passion for nature and its wonders, and it combines solid professional knowledge with insights I gained along the way, which were packaged, expanded, and designed anew within the prism of innovation and environmental thinking. The book is based on more than a decade of teaching the field in academia and industry to thousands of people, as well as on my experience in leading practical innovation processes inspired by nature.

Wild Ideas is an invitation to enter my home, which is also home to you: Nature. In it you will find the best tools and methods I have learned and am still using today in practice, alongside fascinating research, case studies, and many diverse examples. This is my opportunity to answer the questions I have been repeatedly asked over the years, to share my awe of nature, and to provide the keys to nature's inventions to as many people as possible. One can find many stories of innovation inspired by nature online, but for the book, I wanted to build the foundation, the skeleton into which the stories can be poured and their meaning understood. This foundation will help you observe the field from a bird's-eye view, make sense of the concepts, and understand the map as you journey toward nature's inventions.

In Part I, we will address the question of 'what': What is biomimicry, anyway? What is the difference between biomimicry and related fields? We will ask: when did it all begin, when did humans discover the reservoir of nature's inventions and start learning from it, and when did the field become a scientific discipline? We will also address the worldview, values, and ethos that underlie the field of biomimicry and dictate the process of imitating nature, as well as the limitations and barriers of the innovation process.

In Part II, we will address the question of 'why': Why learn from nature at all? We will tackle the connection between the field of biomimicry and innovation and sustainability, to understand how the biomimetic innovation engine works based on analogies and an interdisciplinary nexus. Similarly, we will examine the difference between solutions of nature and that of technology, a difference which beckons application of an alternative design paradigm in the field of technology.

In Part III, we will address the question of 'how': How does one find a solution in nature? How can we analyze and apply it to create innovation? Here you will receive the operating instructions of the biomimicry engine that concerns imitating nature's inventions.

In Part IV, we will address the question of 'where': Where does one engage in the field of innovation inspired by nature? Following a glimpse into the corporate world, we will expand on stories of companies involved in biomimetic innovation processes. We will then demonstrate how to sow the seeds of biomimicry into pedagogical processes in the education system. We will also cover academia and present actions being taken there, how individuals are trained to work in the field, and which employment opportunities will be available in the future.

The book invites you to befriend the field and to begin observing nature with fresh eyes. It is intended for anyone who is curious about nature and wishes to see its reservoir of inventions and understand how to access it. Whether you are engineers, planners, designers, architects, managers, entrepreneurs, educators, or environmentalists, or whether you are simply nature lovers – this book was written for you.

One famous quote by Leonardo da Vinci is: "Human subtlety will never devise an invention more beautiful, more simple, or more direct than does nature because in her inventions nothing is lacking, and nothing is superfluous." With every passing day, I feel as though I understand this quote more and more, and if there is nothing lacking and nothing superfluous in nature's inventions, then they are inventions that deserve to be studied and recognized.

PART I

WHAT?

WHAT IS BIOMIMICRY — AND WHAT IS IT NOT?

The biggest innovations of the 21st century will be the intersection of biology and technology. A new era is beginning.

Steve Jobs

One of my favorite childhood series was *Steve Austin – The Six Million Dollar Man*. The hero of the series was decorated with many titles: a helicopter pilot in the United States Army, a fighter in the Vietnam War, a NASA astronaut – but there was one title that was unique and unforgettable: The Bionic Man. Austin was injured in an accident and almost lost his life. In an operation that cost millions, he was implanted with an artificial arm, legs, and eye that transformed him into a cybernetic organism: an entity containing biological and artificial components.

His performance was legendary and thrilling. He ran at a speed of 100 km/h, his arm had tremendous strength, and his bionic eye could see far, even in infrared. It was a classic science fiction series that evoked immense excitement among its viewers, especially young children, in the face of the unattainable and unrealistic. The series was created in the 1970s, when the concept "bionic" was already commonly used in the engineering world, but fiction has become reality since, and the bionic are indeed worth millions.

Imitating Life

The term "biomimicry" first appeared in 1982. It was preceded by the terms "bionic," "bionics," and "biomimetics," which all have similar meanings. Biomimicry was defined as a multidisciplinary field of nature's inventions that focuses on the research and learning of nature's solutions and their imitation at the level of structures, processes, or the system, in order to provide solutions for human challenges in innovative and sustainable ways. The term "biomimicry" primarily became widely known following the publication of a book by Janine Benyus, the co-founder of the Biomimicry Institute, in 1997, titled *Biomimicry: Innovation Inspired by Nature.*[3]

When I mentioned the term at the beginning of the journey, I was often met with raised eyebrows and the recurrent question – bio-what? The foreign word did not roll off the tongue. But when you break down the word into its components, the meaning is easier to understand. Bio = life; mimicry is derived from the word *Mimesis*, which means imitation. Aristotle, who coined the term, spent a great deal of time observing nature and saw it as a source of imitation and representation. The meaning of the word *biomimicry* is therefore the imitation of life – the imitation of the knowledge and insights found in the living world, the world of nature.

Nature is an enormous library of ideas, structures, materials, and processes; it is a source of inspiration, learning, and emulation. The premise is that many of the challenges that preoccupy humanity have actually already been solved in nature, so instead of "inventing the wheel," we are invited to imitate the solutions that exist in nature. In recent decades, scientists and engineers have begun looking at nature with new eyes – as a reservoir of solutions and inventions. Technology, which deals with the search for practical solutions in response to human needs, has also begun working with nature to transform the world into a new and unexpected place.

Another beautiful definition which alludes to the field's essence is Benyus's description: "the conscious emulation of life's genius." When engaging in biomimicry, the observation of nature is conscious and aimed at identifying its inventive solutions.

I have often been asked if imitating non-living mechanisms from nature is considered biomimicry. Though the answer is not according to the term's literal definition – imitating life – one can actually learn a great deal from emulating non-living natural elements, such as crystal and mineral structures and geological formations.

For example, the Eden Project – a huge greenhouse that serves an ecological institute in England and is built from a system of domes. The greenhouse design was influenced by soap bubbles. It was built on an active quarry site, and the final surface area was unknown. Therefore, it was necessary to find a structure that can gently adapt to any shape, similar to how soap bubbles settle neatly on any surface. The domes themselves were constructed in the shape of hexagons – shapes which characterize various structures in nature, including non-living systems such as minerals and crystals. One way this hexagonal structure excels is in its ability to preserve energy and material. It was translated into an economical and sturdy steel construction, without the need for internal column reinforcement. Imitating these structures led to particularly impressive efficiency: it turns out that the air trapped inside the domes weighs more than the domes themselves.

In general, nature comprises both living organisms and non-living objects, and all of them follow the laws of nature. One can learn from everything that identifies with and operates in the natural environment.

I am also often asked if biomimicry includes imitation of systems occurring in the human body. Steve Austin holds the answer to this. Bionic organs are designed to mimic the function of natural organs. We are part of nature, and the human body is a natural system. Imitation of the body's processes and mechanisms is identified with the field of biomimicry.

Brinker Technology, for example, which was sold to Seal-Tite in 2013, led innovation inspired by the human body's coagulation system and developed the Platelet Barrier Technology® to seal leaks in water transport systems.[4]

The technology was developed by an engineer and lecturer from the University of Aberdeen, who got a paper cut while reading a scientific paper on the challenges of the water industry in England related to leaks. He noticed that the natural coagulation system is activated quickly to close the incision, and wondered if the way the body stops bleeding could be applied in the water industry. Apparently, the connection between the paper cut and the content of the article he was reading led to the innovative solution. The challenge he was faced with was that approximately 30% of the water transported via various water systems was getting lost due to old infrastructure and poor maintenance. In addition to losing this valuable resource, the repair process would be expensive and cumbersome, and would involve shutting down the pipeline for several months, digging into the leakage area, and repairing it from the outside. In comparison, a cut in the human body gets sealed from the inside. The platelets accumulate at the site of the cut, clog it like a cork, and release several substances to complete the clotting process. This inspiration shattered a mental fixation of sealing leaks from the outside thanks to this innovative concept of sealing them from within. Once a leak is detected, PLATELETS® – small particles made of polymers – are inserted into the water system. The particles are carried through the water current to the leak site where, due to the pressure difference created by the leak, they stick to the crack and clog it from the inside. The breach is repaired within hours and at much lower costs. The company that developed and marketed this solution calls themselves 'Brinker,' after the Dutch boy who, according to legend, plugged a breach in the dam with his finger.

Life Science versus Life Imitation

Biomimicry is concerned with imitating nature's solutions for various challenges, solutions identified with systems in the animal and plant world. So, what role does biology have in the process? Classical biology deals with learning about nature, while biomimicry deals with learning from nature. The difference is essential. Biologists study form, structure, behavior, and interrelationships in the animal and plant world in order to better understand nature. Engineers that work in biomimicry study nature with a different motivation: they focus on the solutions of challenges in nature with the aim of making this knowledge practical.

Take the pine tree, for example. Biologists will learn its

scientific name, identify its geographic distribution, lifespan, and the fact that it belongs to the group of pyrophytes, which regenerate after fires. Engineers will look at pine trees and see mechanisms that can be gleaned: how to extract energy from the sun without using toxic substances; how to transport water vertically without investing energy; how to produce strong yet lightweight structures.

Another example can be seen in one of the fields studied in biology: the field of adaptation, in which researchers study how organisms adapt to their environments. Biologists will study the adaptation and be able to identify it. They will recognize, for instance, the correlation between leaf dispersion over an area and their ability to harvest more energy. Engineers will ask: What can be learned from this adaptation? Where is this function needed in the world of engineering-technology? They may consider, in this case, a similarly designed system of solar panels.

The difference between biologists and engineers clarifies the need for collaboration:

Biologists open the door to the biological world and provide the knowledge, while engineers make it practical. It can be said that biomimicry is the engine that propels us on the road to innovation, while biological knowledge is the fuel that feeds this engine. Every engine needs fuel to operate.

Inspiration versus Imitation

The word 'imitation' mentioned in the context of biomimicry may arouse objection. Imitations are viewed as inferior to their original counterparts. But here, we do not mean blindly copying without any special thought or attention. The intention is to identify a solution in nature, study it in depth, and extract its essence – an essence that can transform into a spark and often even a large flame to help find the required solution.

In the creative world, imitating ideas and presenting them as our own would be considered a misdeed, while being inspired is seen as sacred and is associated with the spark of creation. In the world of biomimicry, we have license to imitate nature, and the choice of how much to imitate is ours alone. The greater the similarity between the natural invention and the technological-engineering invention we develop, the more it is considered imitation over inspiration.

Nature's inventions can inspire a solution, provide a direction at the level of a spark, kernel, idea, or design principle. But they can also serve as a broader model, referring also to the operation of the natural system, its structures, materials, and the parameters that determine its operation. One can find a wide range of inventions in the realm of innovation from nature, some of which more closely meet the definition of being inspired by nature, while others more closely imitate nature.

Inspiration from Nature – Bioinspiration

The Israeli company, Cyvera (now owned by Palo Alto Networks), which worked in the field of cybersecurity, based its solution on inspiration from nature. The human body is exposed to viral and bacterial attacks on a daily basis. At the beginning of its journey, the company's founders consulted a microbiologist, an expert in viruses, and learned how the human body counters viral attacks. One of the principles they learned is that the body alters the virus's receptor, thus preventing its attachment. They applied this principle and developed a solution that alters the location of the attack targets within the operating system, analogous to changing the receptors in our body, and replacing this location with a type of trap. This is an example of a design principle that was gleaned from nature and inspired a technological solution.

Imitating Nature

The Canadian company WhalePower manufactures wind turbines that imitate the structure of tubercles on the fins of humpback whales. Humpbacks belong to the group of 'great whales.' Its length can reach 15 meters and its weight 27 tons. Despite its size and massive body, comparable to the dimensions of a bus, whales swim weightlessly through water. The tubercles on the tips of their fins forge lanes in the water and prevent the formation of whirlpools. The solution was implemented in an innovative wind turbine – the front edge of the blade, i.e., the part of the blade that makes first contact with the air (the leading edge), was also designed with tubercles. What works in the water also works in the air. The result is a quiet and stable wind turbine that harvests about 20% more energy compared to wind turbines of a standard design – undoubtedly a dramatic improvement given the modest engineering change that was implemented. This is an example of a development that imitates a mechanism in nature, on the level of structural parameters.

Piping Hot – Bioconvergence

Bioconvergence is one of the hottest fields of the past decade, especially in today's world of innovation. It refers to the combining of the biological fields with those of engineering, including electronics, artificial intelligence (AI), genetic engineering, nanotechnology, materials science, and more. This merging is a worldwide trend that strives to connect and integrate technological breakthroughs that have emerged separately in recent years in the fields of engineering and biology. Bioconvergence is considered the source of 21st-century innovation. Even the Israel Innovation Authority has recognized the great potential inherent in the bioconvergence trend and has developed a platform to promote the field through grants, collaboration, locating opportunities, and building a community.

The one who predicted this trend was Steve Jobs, who posited that "the biggest innovations of the 21st century will be at the intersection between biology and technology. A new era is beginning..." Anyone who has attended innovation events in recent years feels this trend strongly. There is almost no event about innovation I have attended where the prefix "bio" is not mentioned in one way or another. Scientific knowledge in general and biological knowledge in particular is growing at an exponential rate.[5] The next leap forward in biology lies in its connection to other fields, turning biological data into practical knowledge. The field of biomimicry is part of the bioconvergence trend.

Fields Closely Related to Biomimicry but Differ from It

Biomimicry differs in a number of aspects from several related fields also containing the "bio" prefix:

• **The transfer of knowledge from biology to technology and not from technology to biology:** Bioengineering applies engineering knowledge in the design of medical and biological systems. For example, the development of heart-lung or dialysis machines that support organs with damaged functions, or advanced robots that can move within the body with precision and efficiency to perform minimally invasive surgeries to support and repair damaged organs. In biomimicry, the direction of knowledge transfer goes the opposite way: knowledge is learned from the biological world and transferred to the technological-engineering world.

• **Learning from nature and not using nature:** Biotechnology uses biology in practice. For example, life processes in biological systems are used as systems of production, such as with bacteria. In biomimicry, one does not use nature, but learns from it. The attitude toward nature is one of study and not exploitation. The solution in nature is observed, investigated, and applied to the technological world, but the organism itself, its body, and products are not used for solving the issue – with the exception of the research and study phase. For example, spider webs themselves are not used, but research is conducted to investigate their structure and the secret behind their strength, allowing them to be produced artificially; molecules possessing unique properties are not used themselves, but their structure is imitated and synthesized under laboratory conditions.

Sometimes we wish to imitate a natural process, but in the absence of technological alternatives, nature itself is used during actual implementation. In this case, the invention combines biotechnology and biomimicry. For example, a constructed wetland is an artificial system of marshes that strives to imitate purification processes that occur in natural wetlands. In nature, plant roots in swamps form substrates for rich bacterial populations, which break down pollutants and use them as a source of energy. Although we literally use nature (plants) in constructed wetlands, the system is still considered bioinspired, as it is built according to principles learned from nature.

• **Functional and non-aesthetic learning**: Biomorphism is the integration of natural patterns and shapes into artistic or architectural designs, with the goal of providing a natural appearance to the object of design, while evoking an emotion in the viewer. For example, there is a fish-shaped restaurant in Japan designed by architect Frank Gehry. It is safe to assume that it is a fish restaurant, and its unique design attracts visitors and may even hint at the menu, but there is clearly no planned functional value to the fish-shaped restaurant other than the desire to garner interest and attraction via the design gimmick.

On the other hand, Mercedes-Benz imitated the fish shape

for functional purposes in a biomimetic process. An aquarium of fish served as the source of inspiration for the company's engineers in the designing of a new vehicle. One of the fish that caught their eye was the clumsy-looking Yellow Boxfish with its box-like body. They probably would not have chosen it as a source of inspiration for a car design based on intuition, but a closer look revealed its impressive maneuverability, despite the fact that its body is almost square, like the space of a car meant to house people. Research has revealed that the contours of the fish are streamlined, such that drag is significantly reduced. The engineers proposed a concept vehicle designed according to the contours of the fish. The functional value they aspired to mimic was indeed achieved – the drag was reduced, as was the fuel consumption. However, the car was not developed beyond the conceptual stage and did not reach the market. It turns out that the customer base did not like its appearance.

Technologies that Parallel Nature

Not every product of engineering technology that is also found in nature was inspired by it. There are technologies that were developed in the field of engineering and it is known for certain that they were not learned from nature. Sonar, for example, was developed many years prior to its discovery in nature. Its original purpose was to locate glaciers. The development of sonar was accelerated following the sinking of the Titanic in 1912. In 1915, the French physicist Paul Langevin invented the first device based on sonar, and his work influenced future sonar designs that were used in World War I.

In nature, bats are able to orient themselves in space despite their limited vision, found especially among insectivorous bats. In experiments, bats were placed in a small room with many transparent wires hanging from the ceiling to the floor. The bats did not collide with the wires nor with each other. It became clear that bats "see" in a different way, using echolocation. They produce clicking sounds (signals) from their throats that spread throughout space, encounter obstacles, and return. Using the difference in time between the outgoing and returning signals, the bats decode a spatial image of the environment, allowing them to move around safely. Echolocation in nature (biosonar) was only discovered toward the 1940s, first in bats and later in dolphins, many years after engineered sonar systems were developed.

Another technology that was developed in the field of engineering regardless of its existence in nature is jet propulsion. In a classic jet engine, Newton's third law is applied: the air thrusted in one direction is generated by a jet propulsion ejected with equal force in the opposite direction. Jet propulsion also exists in nature. Sea creatures such as squids, octopuses, and jellyfish locomote similarly: they squirt jets of water from their bodies, causing them to move in the opposite direction. The rapid release of the water allows them to accelerate underwater impressively. As mentioned, the development of the jet engine was not inspired by the jet propulsion found in nature.

It seems that the question of awareness is key in identifying whether an invention is biomimetic. Was the process of imitating and learning from nature a conscious one? The difference between biomimicry and other inventions that have advanced humanity throughout history is the conscious attempt to study biological mechanisms and imitate them.

Biomutualism
Robert Full is a biologist who has been studying geckos. In a successful TED talk,[6] he described an unconventional aspect of the field of biomimicry, which he calls biomutualism: "the

association between biology and another discipline, where each discipline reciprocally advances the other." Just as engineering benefits from biology, biology in turn can benefit from joint research and capabilities in engineering.

Full was a co-developer of the Stickybot, a robot that mimics the gecko's adhesion mechanism and is able to climb vertical surfaces. He learned from his engineering partners in the project that the robot would fall without the tail. They asked him if geckos also use their tails while climbing walls – a question that he, as a biologist, never thought to ask. The joint study gave rise to a new research question, and as a result we learned that the gecko's tail plays a critical and active role in climbing: in the event of a fall, it helps the gecko flip over in the air to land on its feet, similar to a cat.

Another example of biomutualism is a robotic fish called SoFi – The Soft Robotic Fish – developed at the Massachusetts Institute of Technology (MIT) for the purpose of conducting ecological research without disturbing the environment.[7] It was designed to be the size of a real fish and has swimming patterns and behavior similar to those of a real fish. It integrates naturally into the coral reef environment and allows for close-range observations, without the presence of humans threatening the fish. This development is an interesting example of biomimetic innovation that learns from nature in order to "give back" to nature. Its research may contribute in the future to the preservation of species diversity and natural habitats. In biomimicry, biology indeed serves as a source of knowledge for engineering, but biology also often benefits from the process, when it receives valuable engineering insight for biological research in return. Mutualism at its best.

A Journey through Time

A person must read from the book of nature
and walk among its pages.

Anonymous

Imagine a world without the written word, without books, without the internet, without the ability to travel beyond walking distance, a world with very little human interaction. In such a world, nature becomes the primary source of knowledge, a meeting of stimulating and instructive interactions. In such a world, it is natural for people to read from the book of nature and walk among its pages. Humans live and walk inside a large reservoir of solutions, and it is likely that many of the solutions to life's challenges have come from observing nature.

In the distant past, invention processes went undocumented. They were spontaneous and emerged as needed. They were invented by the creative individuals who conceived them, likely through a process of trial and error involving adjustments and improvements, and examining the latter during use. During the transition era between nomadic behavior and permanent settlement – around 10,000 years ago – humans began searching for ways to minimize their dependence on luck. This necessity almost certainly led to the development of tools that meet the basic needs in life – food, water, and security. Naturally, the development process of these tools went undocumented, and no one actually knows precisely when they were invented, but it is clear that a large similarity exists between the basic tools we use to this day and the solutions found in nature, and one can reasonably assume that the sources of inspiration were solutions that humans observed in nature.

For example, tongs resemble – both in shape and function – bird beaks, crab pincers, and even the gripping motion we make with our thumb and forefinger on our way to grab something. Wire fences are similar in form and function to the thorns adorning bushes and protecting tree trunks. Fishing nets used to catch fish are similar to spider webs woven to catch prey, and the form of liquid-storing bottles – containers with narrow openings – resemble a breast and nipple in both function and design.

We also find human cultural developments associated with nature observation. For example, Japanese and Chinese calligraphy was first created 5,000 years ago as a result of deep nature observation. The graphic symbol representing a tree contains roots, from an understanding that without roots, there is no tree. The symbol representing rain includes depictions of the sky, a cloud, a cloudburst, and water coming down – similar to the water cycle in nature. Later on, with the formation of abstract concepts, symbols from nature were chosen to represent them. This is why, for example, a flower makes up part of the symbol expressing change or transformation. Even in Hebrew, we find evidence of the letter symbols being touched by nature. The letter *aleph* (א) originates from the word *alif* which means 'bull,' and its shape evolved from the shape of a bull's head.

Mimesis

The concept of "imitation" with regards to nature, is attributed to Aristotle, who lived at around 300 BC and coined the word "mimesis," which means imitation or a representation of reality. Aristotle claimed that humans are imitators by nature and feel the need to produce art that reflects reality. During this ancient era, mimesis was primarily expressed in artistic form reflecting qualities of nature and representing the symbolism and emotion evoked from observing an object in nature.

Over the years, when engineers began viewing nature as a source for technological solutions, mimesis expanded from mimicking nature's features to artistic expression, to mimicking functional mechanisms for engineering development. While Aristotle's mimesis focused on the emotion, beauty, aesthetics, symbolism, and vitality of nature; technological mimesis focuses on function, structure, processes, systems, and design principles.

Take the snake, for example. Aristotle's mimesis will perceive a symbol representing evil, something frightening, and therefore, a statue of Apollo killing a serpent is seen as an expression of Apollo's heroism. On the other hand, functional mimesis will look at the snake from an engineering-technological perspective and will focus on functional mechanisms identified with it. An example of a development derived from this type of perspective is a robot snake. Such a robot was developed at the Technion – Israel Institute of Technology, led by Alon Wolf of the Biorobotics and Biomechanics Laboratory and in collaboration with the Administration for the Development of Weapons and Technological Infrastructure. The developers observed the mechanism of snake locomotion and constructed a robot made up of vertebrae that looks and advances like a snake. A camera connected to its head transmits images in real time, intended for intelligence and military operations on future battlegrounds, in bunkers and tunnels, and even to locate survivors under collapsed buildings. The robot was even presented to President Obama during his 2013 visit to Israel.

Learning from Nature in the Bible

The idea of learning from nature appears in the Jewish scriptures, as well. Rabbi Joseph Albo said that "humans can become educated about individual values from animals"[8] and Rabbi Na-chman of Breslov made the connection between observing na-ture and innovation, saying: "By observing nature and the work of genesis, humans merit innovation."

Rabbi Kook summarized the idea of imitating nature in one sentence: "All the wonderful talents found in animals, which we often regard in awe, and man will not be able to reach and imitate them unless after a great and long study."[9] The quote explicitly references the features of the imitation process: the bi-ological model associated with the wonderful talents found in animals, the process of awe that directs our attention to these talents and to the imitation process, all mentioned in one breath with the need for prolonged research and study.

Buddhism, particularly in the school of Zen, also largely refer-ences nature and imitates its qualities. This is how, for instance, in *The Book of Tao*, water is mentioned as having the ability to take on any form; plants and herbs are described as flexible when alive and dry and brittle when dead; and seas and rivers as complementing each other without competition. So in con-trast to the engineering perspective, which examines functions in nature, Zen's observation of nature is more oriented toward imitating the qualities and properties of nature.

The Father of Biomimicry

In the drama series, *Da Vinci's Demons*, there is a beautiful scene where you see Leonardo da Vinci walking to the local market to purchase birds. After buying them, he freed them, observed them, and drew them in flight. For him, the sketch served as a tool for imitating the principles of aviation in nature, but this is only one of his secrets.

Da Vinci (1452–1519), as we know, was a Renaissance man. He was an artist, painter, sculptor, architect, and engineer, but when he decided to mimic nature, he was industrious and went to learn zoology with the goal of strategically merging the knowledge bases of engineering and biology. Da Vinci dedicated many hours a day to contemplating, researching, and sketching various aerial animals in the wild, like flying fish, bats, dragonflies, and more, with the aim of developing a flying contraption. He investigated the principles of natural flight, but was unsatisfied with mere observation and data collection, so he strove to implement it.

Da Vinci also deeply observed the human form as well as the animal and plant world. He presumed that the moment we know how the human body and forces of nature work, we will have a foundation for machines that can imitate nature. For this purpose, he explored and identified repeated patterns in nature, in different behaviors and circumstances.

This is how, for instance, da Vinci discerned the "Rule of Trees," according to which the sum of the cross-sectional area of all branches above a certain branching point is equal to the cross-sectional area of the trunk below the branching point: If we were to lift up all the branches and bunch them together, the tree would look like one large trunk with uniform thickness from top to bottom.[10]

In one sense, nature and engineering deal with the art of creating products, of processes and of systems, and provide a solution for specific needs. Da Vinci regarded nature's creations, such as the human foot, as creations that combine engineering and artistic masterpieces. He strove to decipher the interrelationships between the cornerstones of the creative processes of both nature and engineering: form, structure, material, and function.

Man has observed nature since the dawn of time, but da Vinci strove to complete the strategic design process which begins with investigating nature and ends in implementation. While da Vinci did not succeed in his mission and did not develop the first aircraft, he did lay the foundations for the field of biomimicry, and is therefore considered the father of biomimicry.

Today, we understand the great potential inherent in studying nature. Da Vinci understood this hundreds of years ago when he said: "Human subtlety will never devise an invention more beautiful, more simple, or more direct than does nature because in her inventions nothing is lacking, and nothing is superfluous." It is incredible that his presence is felt even after 500 years. Perhaps because he was someone who emanated infinite creativity, someone who had come close to the secrets of the universe and nature – secrets that had become his own. It seems as though humans have always been intrigued by riddles and secrets, and that their charm has not diminished over the years.

The 19ᵗʰ Century and the 20ᵗʰ Century

Toward the end of the 19th century and over the course of the 20th century, many inventions and icons of design were invented that were inspired by nature and changed the world.

• **The invention of the telephone:** The invention of the telephone in 1876 was based on Alexander Graham Bell's work with the hearing impaired and his deep understanding of the ear's physiology. Until then, communication was telegraphic and based on the cumbersome and slow Morse code, and there was a need for faster communication that allowed for the transmission of sound waves. One of the suggestions that came up was to disassemble a sound wave into separate frequencies, transmit them in parallel lines, and reconnect them in a receiver. But Bell realized that this complexity was unnecessary. One device can convert all the sound frequencies into an electrical signal. The idea for the solution came from observing a biological device: the ear. Bell was a professor of vocal physiology in Boston. He noticed that the eardrum was actually a thin membrane that was able to translate sound frequencies into different neural signals. The eardrum is a single device capable of handling all sound frequencies at once. Its back and forth vibrations move the bones of the middle ear, and the movement is transferred using the inner ear fluid. He understood that if a membrane as thin as paper can control the movement of bones, which relative to the membrane are huge in size and weight, then surely a much larger and thicker membrane will be able to move a piece of iron before an electromagnet. This paved the way for the invention of the telephone which was based on transforming mechanical vibrations into electrical vibrations.

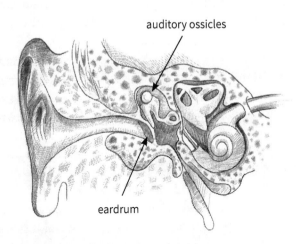

auditory ossicles

eardrum

• **The Eiffel Tower:** Behind the Eiffel Tower, which was erected in 1889, hides a beautiful tale of inspiration from nature. It was constructed for the World Fair in Paris. Leading up to the Fair, a competition was held among architects who submitted proposals for monuments to be showcased. A young French architect named Gustave Eiffel decided to participate in the competition. It is said that Eiffel flipped through the anatomy book that rested on his desk until he stopped at a chapter that caught his attention; it described the anatomy of the femur. The femur is the longest bone in the body and at its end is a spherical joint. It is characterized by a structural hierarchy composed of fibrous tubes called osteons separated by air cavities, where each tube is further composed of tubes and cavities. Tubes and cavities within tubes and cavities. The structure boasts great strength and light weight, and is designed to bear loads and pressure efficiently. Eiffel was very impressed with this form and turned it into the design concept for the Eiffel Tower, whose structure very much resembles that of the bone. When I present the structure of the femur during lectures and ask which famous architectural construction it reminds them of, many recognize its resemblance to the Eiffel Tower without ever having even heard of the inspiration story. The Tower is built from a system of trusses within trusses separated by air gaps located and designed according to the bone model in a way that reinforces the Tower. It is said that competing architects argued that the Tower would collapse due to its weight, but it has remained a known Parisian icon to this day. Years after it was built, mathematical models of the femur showed its similarity to the Eiffel Tower's system of trusses and reinforcements.

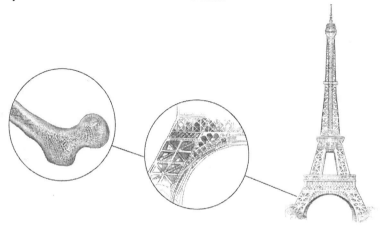

• **Flight:** Humans turned to nature and observed birds to fulfill their age-old dream: ascending to the skies. As a child, Otto Lilienthal was fascinated by storks and tried to understand how they learn the craft of flight. In adulthood, he discovered the advantage of a convex wing over a flat wing in generating lift. He was the first to design and build a hand glider that could carry a person: himself. In the summer of 1894, Lilienthal built an artificial hill near Berlin that rose to a height of 15 meters, from which he used to jump with his hand glider before the astonished viewers who came to watch the incredible spectacle of the "Flying Man." Unfortunately, the best show in town ended tragically when Lilienthal crashed his hand glider during one of the runs. His last words were: "Small sacrifices must be made." His legacy and contributions live on in the book he wrote in 1889, *Birdflight as the Basis of Aviation*, which was also used by the Wright brothers a few years after his death. The Wright brothers also spent a long time observing flying birds, especially pigeons, and tried to incorporate the principles they learned into the prototype of the airplane they designed. In 1903, their first flight, which lasted twelve seconds, was recorded in the pages of history.

• **Velcro:** One of the famous tales of biomimicry is that of the invention of Velcro, which was developed in the 1940s and inspired by the mechanism of seed distribution in nature. In everyday life, we often need to fasten and join different items together, particularly in the textile industry. Before the invention of Velcro, most separation and attachment was done using buttons, buckles, and zippers, but the notable disadvantages of these are the motor skills required for closing them, the relatively long time it takes to close them, and the recurrence of malfunctions.

In 1941, a Swiss engineer named George de Mestral went on a hunting trip with his dog and noticed the spherical burrs of the burdock plant clinging to his dog's fur. Every time he removed them to clean his dog, they would stick again. Instead of thinking about the bath, he would have to give his dog at the end of the trip, he noticed how incredibly easy it was to separate and reattach the seeds. Millions of others encountered this phenomenon before him but regarded it a nuisance. De Mestral was the first person to place the burrs under a microscope and discovered a system of hooks that bind to the loop-like fur of passing animals. The burrs of the burdock plant bind to various types of fur, in any climate, quickly, and at different angles to ensure their distribution. These seeds inspired de Mestral to invent a fastener accessory based on hooks and loops: a closure system comprising two opposing strips of nylon fabric; one of the strips is covered in tiny hooks that mimic the structure of the seed and the other is covered in tiny loops that mimic the structure of fur. Once the strips are brought together, the hooks get caught in the loops, and the strips remain attached. They can be separated by pulling by hand and releasing the hooks. De Mestral overcame the technological difficulty of producing loops on fabric, registered a patent, and opened a company that began manufacturing Velcro. Velcro achieved commercial success and can be found in every home. It is convenient, easy, and quick to use. It is less susceptible to malfunctions, serves as a substitute for zippers and buttons, and is better adapted for use by people with disabilities. Following the success, it is said that de Mestral would advise the company managers: "If any of your employees ask for a two-week holiday to go hunting, say yes."

Main Trends in Biomimetic Technological Developments

Velcro is not where the journey ends and perhaps even marks the beginning of a new era, one where biomimicry is a scientific discipline. Since the development of Velcro until today, three main trends in the development of the field have been identified.[11]

• **The morphological trend – developments based on the connection between structure and function:** This is the oldest trend, which began developing at the end of the 19th century and deals with the connection between biological forms and structures and their functions. It is based on the fields of biology, zoology, and botany, which are heavily engaged in the study of structure and function. The inventions described here – the telephone, the Eiffel Tower, the airplane, and Velcro – belong to this trend and are essentially based on the study of structures that provide different functions.

• **The biocybernetics, robotics, and sensing trend:** This trend began developing in the middle of the 20th century, and it is based on fields that are far from biology, such as electrical engineering and cybernetics (the study of communication processes, and control and computation systems). Knowledge from these areas led to the study of biological mechanisms whose functions are not necessarily related to structure or form but to processes of communication, control, and sensing. The biomimetic developments identified with this trend are found in the fields of robotics, mobility, and sensing. For example, a sensor for long-distance fire detection. Most creatures flee from fire, but fire-chaser beetles detect forest fires and move in their direction. They fly en masse toward the fire, mate in the burning forest, and the females lay eggs in the newly scorched bark. There, inside the hot trunk, which is neutralized from defense mechanisms of living trees such as resin, develops the next generation. The amazing thing is that the beetles can detect fires from 80 kilometers away! It turns out that their thorax contains extremely sensitive infrared receptors that detect heat, and they are even capable of discerning between different types of smoke being emitted from different types of trees. This sensing mechanism has been studied with the aim of developing biomimetic sensors to approach that of the fire-chaser beetle's sensing abilities.

• **The nano-biomimetic trend:** This trend began to develop toward the end of the 20th century following microscopic discoveries that enabled the study of structures on a tiny scale. It deals with the study of natural mechanisms on the level of tissues, cells, and molecules, and even on a nano level. For example, imitating shark skin. Shark skin only appears to be smooth when in reality, on a nano scale, it is covered in tiny, diamond-shaped teeth called dermal denticles, separated by grooves. The denticles are distributed on the shark skin in positions and angles that affect the fluid dynamics, reduce turbulence, and minimize drag – the opposing force to the shark's movement. Thanks to these surface areas, sharks invest approximately 10% less energy during locomotion compared with similarly sized fish with smooth skin. In the Sydney 2000 Olympic Games, an unusual swimsuit stood out in the swimming pool. Many swimmers wore an innovative suit developed by Speedo called Fastskin, which imitated shark skin and incorporated denticles. Swimmers who wore this swimsuit gained an advantage that also translated into performance. Around 80% of the swimmers who earned medals wore this suit, and many world records were broken by swimmers who wore it. Later on, advanced generations of similar swimwear were developed, until their use was finally banned in 2009, due to the technological advantage they provided. Today, shark skin technology is used to coat ships and aircraft in order to reduce drag and improve efficiency in mobility. An additional development that mimics shark skin are antimicrobial surfaces. It turns out that those tiny denticles also interfere with bacterial adhesion, and the shark skin remains biofilm free (biofilm is the accumulation of bacteria on a dense surface area).

A necessary application is the production of antimicrobial surfaces for the medical world, which battles bacteria in hospitals. The American company, Sharklet, developed tiles for operating rooms and coatings for medical equipment bearing a shark-skin effect that fights bacteria in a sophisticated way through its smart structure.

Technology as an Accelerator

Biomimicry as a process of observing nature and learning from it is as ancient as humanity itself. Along with the advancement of technology, humans developed the capacity to explore, understand, and imitate mechanisms in nature. From awe-inspiring contemplation that led us to simplistic solutions, observation has become exhaustive, bypassing the limitations of the human eye, and reaching unprecedented levels. Biological knowledge that accumulated over the years grew in parallel with technological progress that enabled investigation and imitation of nature's solutions for the first time, in a way that was not possible before. Below are examples of some of these technologies:

• **Microscopy:** An electron microscope is capable of magnifying the object being examined 10,000,000 times its original size! The electron microscope only came into use in the middle of the 20th century, opening the door to an exciting encounter with the world of micro and nano in nature. To illustrate the power of magnification, the ratio between a nanometer and the diameter of a tennis ball is like the ratio between the diameter of a tennis ball and the diameter of the Earth. Today, electron microscopes are found in many laboratories and allow researchers to examine biological structures and characterize the surface area of many materials. This technology accelerated the development of the biomimetic nanotechnology trend.

• **Satellites:** In 2007, the largest beaver dam in the world was discovered, which reaches 850 meters in length. This construction is a particularly impressive undertaking that was carried out over several generations of beavers, through strenuous work which requires collaboration. The structure was so massive that it could be discerned from space. The beaver dam was discovered in northern Canada, in an area that was inaccessible from the ground, by a Canadian ecologist who identified it using a Google satellite... Just as the electron microscope gives us the opportunity to zoom in and bring us closer to the nano world, so too satellites allow us to zoom out on natural phenomena and expose us to the macro, to the ecosystem, to the broader picture.

• **Photography:** Louie Schwartzberg, a nature photographer, dedicated his life to making the invisible visible – and revealing the mysteries of nature. He has been photographing nature for 30 years using a unique photography technique which allows us to see movements that are too fast or too slow in nature, ones that cannot be viewed with the naked eye. When one glimpses the invisible, the imagination never stops working. The Spanish photographer, Xavi Bou, who has a strong passion for birds, also uses a unique photography technique that allows him to capture the invisible forms birds produce in flight in a single frame. If a paintbrush were attached to the legs of birds and the sky was a huge canvas, what sort of painting would we get? The answer can be found in Bou's incredible pieces. The work of Schwartzberg and Bou demonstrate advanced photography techniques that did not exist before. These techniques, which develop the world of creation and art, also accelerate scientific research. These photography methods, along with advanced image processing capabilities, are currently being used to study natural phenomena, which in the past were difficult to investigate (*see 1a and 1b).

For example, researchers at the University of Berkeley studied the hummingbird,[12] which excels in its impressive aviation and hovering ability. It hovers over a flower steadily for a long time and sucks its body weight in nectar every hour. The hummingbird moves its wings in rapid movements that the human eye has difficulty seeing. The researchers put a hummingbird in a wind tunnel and photographed it using a special camera that can capture 1,000 frames per second. Using this photography technique, they were able to decipher its unique flying shape: while most birds flap their wings up and down, hummingbirds move them backwards and forwards in a figure eight movement, similar to how insects fly. As a result, a lifting force is generated that reduces the energy required for stable flight over time, even in wind and rain. This model may have different applications, for example aerial refueling mechanisms, stabilization systems for drones carrying cameras, and more (*see 2).

• **Modeling:** When nature offers us models as gifts, especially those that are difficult to achieve mathematically, we require modeling capabilities, ones that allow us to take natural models and convert them into computerized ones. Over the years, such modeling capabilities have been developed; they refine natural models into parameters for designing analogous engineering systems. An example of the use of these capabilities can be found in the story of the Japanese railway, which is described in detail in the chapter titled "Stages of the Process." The locomotive was redesigned according to the spatial model of the kingfisher's beak, and gained the functional value of this model: noise reduction.

• **Three-dimensionality:** 3D printing is an incredible manufacturing technology that began developing toward the end of the 20th century and disrupted the rules of the game in the manufacturing world. Suddenly it was possible to print complex structures with curved contours, and to design shapes and textures at a high resolution, even when the design surfaces are internal and not external. This description is immediately reminiscent of structures in nature. Structures in nature are characterized by curvilinear contours, functional surfaces, and complexity in design. With traditional manufacturing technologies, such as metalworking, where design is based on subtracting material from a solid block, it is very difficult to imitate complex natural structures, to design and manufacture in the "exact" manner nature does. 3D technology makes it possible for the first time to imitate these complex structures, and it accelerates processes of imitating natural structures.

Growth

Over the years, observing nature has become methodical and is recognized as a clear means of solving challenges in an innovative way. It began taking shape as a distinct field of knowledge at the end of the 20th century, and then arose the need to call it by a separate name. Today, the field of biomimicry is growing globally and is recognized as a scientific discipline. It is taught at universities, and there are research grants, registered patents, academic journals dedicated to publications in the field,[13] as well as professional literature. There is also extensive activity in the education system and industry, and the field is growing and emerging.

There is even a biomimetic standard from the International Organization for Standardization (ISO),[14] which I had the privilege of being involved in the writing for. The first thought that entered my mind when I joined the standardization committee was: why does the field even need a standard? To me, a standard is defined as having qualitative and measurable processes. Is it possible to treat innovative production in the same way? Later on, I understood that a standardization process is actually one of documenting knowledge. Approximately 40 experts from different counties sat around one table who discussed foundational issues related to biomimetic innovation processes, with the goal of creating a solid infrastructure of knowledge to serve the industry. The standardization committee is an integral part of the formulation of the field of biomimetics as a firm scientific discipline.

In light of da Vinci's work and him being the father of biomimicry, a biomimetic index was developed in his name. The Da Vinci index tracks the growth rate of the field by collecting data such as the number of publications, patents, research grants, and their financial value. The index was created, maintained, and published by the Fermanian Business and Economic Institute and shows a significant growth rate over the years, which indicates an expansion of the field.[15]

According to a business report published in 2013 forecasting the economic growth of the biomimicry field,[16] it is expected to contribute around 1.6 trillion dollars to global GDP by 2030 and around another 65 billion dollars, due to reduced resource depletion and pollution, with the transition to bioinspired technologies which are more efficient. An additional report, which focused only on the fields of medicine and robotics, predicted that these sectors will reach 18.5 billion dollars by 2028 with an annual growth rate of 10%.[17]

BIOMIMICRY AS A WORLDVIEW

*"Destroying rainforest for economic gain is like burning
a Renaissance painting to cook a meal."*

Edward Wilson

The Bombardier beetle is a small beetle with an unusual defense mechanism. Their name may be amusing, but it is absolutely justified. Whenever they feel threatened, they eject a noxious spray at a temperature of 100°C, rapidly and at high pressure, while producing a distinctive sound. In this way, they deter predators that are much larger than them, as they are unable to fly and escape. The beetles' bodies are able to produce liquids at an extremely high temperature and control the direction and speed of its spray (*see 3). Their spray mechanism was researched and inspired the construction of a specialized rig, two centimeters in length, that is capable of spraying liquids up to four meters away or producing a spray cloud while in full control of the temperature, speed, and size of the liquid droplets. This spraying technology[18] can be the basis for many applications, from more efficient fuel injection systems to improved drug absorption processes. Let's assume for a moment that this mechanism can also assist in the development of weapons of mass destruction.

Mountain goats skip over steep slopes and dams easily, while clinging securely to the ground without slipping. What makes this spectacle so breathtaking and awe-inspiring are their precise movements and stability. How do they cling to steep, smooth slopes while moving about safely, easily, and quickly? The company Nike researched the structure of the mountain goat's foot, which combines a soft, flexible pillow with a stiff hoof, and developed hiking shoes for trekkers that offer better grip on the terrain. Sounds reasonable. But let's assume for a moment that these shoes were manufactured by 10-year-old kids from developing countries, employed under difficult working conditions that are inappropriate for their age. The reality is that at the end of the 20th century, Nike was indeed accused of employing young children as a labor force in third-world countries, although not necessarily during the manufacturing of this shoe.

The surface area of a lotus leaf is extremely water repellent (superhydrophobic). The repelled water droplets glide over the surface like tiny marbles, and even remove dirt along the way. Smart, dirt-repellent fabrics were developed inspired by this mechanism. A shirt made from such fabric simply refuses to get dirty; not a single thing can stick to it. But let's assume that the shirt was dyed in toxic colors in a process at the end of which water with toxins was released into the factory environment. Didn't something stick to the shirt?

These hypothetical examples reflect an ethos, level of trust, and core values that are not aligned with nature. Ethos meaning intention, responsibility, ethics, motives, and values that drive any behavior. Ethos also drives design processes. Does the designer have a holistic vision, one that seeks to do good for the entire system, or is the designer's vision narrow, striving toward a specific achievement? And in the context of biomimicry, one must ask: Does the system overall benefit from imitating nature's inventions, or perhaps are people and the environment being harmed by the process?

Janine Benyus described the tension well between engineering solutions found in nature waiting to be plucked and an imitation method that does not align with the spirit of nature: "If you make a bioinspired fabric using green chemistry, but you have workers weaving it in a sweatshop, loading it onto pollution-spewing trucks, and shipping it long distances, you've missed the point."[19] We can emulate solutions in nature, but if we implement them unsustainably, while polluting, using toxic and harmful substances, or wasting excessive amounts of material and energy resources, the emulation will be technical and will not reflect the spirit of nature.

Biomimicry as a World View

Biomimicry is not only an innovation method leading us to nature's reservoir of solutions while showing us how to conduct methodological imitations of its inventions. Biomimicry is also a world view, and ethos is a vital component of world views. Nature's ethos connects to a number of perspectives and values:

• **Purpose:** 'Products of nature' are not meant to destroy other products. While hunting and killing are a part of nature, they are proportionate and synchronize with the entire system's resilience and balance. Prey in nature preserves the delicate ecological balance between organisms. If more widespread destruction is caused by earthquakes, fire, or natural disasters, the entire system will undergo a new order and new balance. Therefore, a product whose purpose is widespread destruction – a spraying contraption for mass destruction, for example – which serves political, social, or other agendas, does not adhere to the ethos of nature. One day, I received a video showing a tree-harvesting robot. The robot both cuts and shaves the trees, and within seconds there is a pile of stripped tree logs, ready to be used. Along with admiring the engineering achievement, I couldn't help but wonder who in the world is operating this robot and for what purpose. Uncontrolled deforestation leads to habitat destruction and to a massive loss of wildlife species.

• **Holism – Perspective of the whole**: Organisms do not act separately and disconnected from their environments. They are part of a broader system, of a larger life cycle, and their existence depends on the well-being of the system, just as the well-being of the system depends on the activity of organisms. Organisms will not act in such a way as to wreak havoc in its habitat, the cradle of its development. It is actually human intervention, even out of good intention, that is likely to disturb this delicate balance. Last year, I hiked the Ramon Crater in the Negev Desert and saw onagers, Asiatic wild asses, for the first time. I encountered them twice in two days – an impressive and exciting frequency. The 11 onagers that they brought over from Iran in 1968 in order to return them to our country's landscapes turned into around 250 onagers roaming around freely today. But their successful integration into the local environment led to novel challenges: each onager eats roughly 8 kilograms of dry material a day, and the vegetation that was once a food source for deer and rodents is depleting. Local farmers are also suffering from the damage being done to their fields by the onagers.

The anthropologist, Gregory Bateson,[20] describes this delicate balance by defining the relationship between horses and grass. Horses feed on grass, but the grass in turn needs the horse's "grazing" services, their services of treading and crushing with their feet turning soil into turf (compressed and decomposed matter), and the fertilizing services of the horses that releases the organic waste from its body onto the grass. In fact, every organism is a key to visible or invisible connections within its environment.

Unlike the reductionist approach to design, which strives to minimize complexity and focuses on the design aspect itself and less on the consequences it has on the environment, the concept of design in nature is holistic. It views the entire array of factors in the ecosystem, the delicate balance of connections among organisms, their environments, and their subsistence resources. Shoe production, while harming the manufacturer; or fabric production while polluting the environment, are examples of jarring damage caused to the entire ecosystem. The folly of reductionism is beautifully articulated in a quote by Wilson, comparing the destruction of rainforests for economic gain to using a Renaissance painting as tinder. Viewing rainforests merely as profit-yielding resources is a narrow perspective, one that cancels out its value as the source of life to so many species.

• **Sustainability:** Living beings have learned to meet their needs without sabotaging the next generation's chances of continuing to exist. Even large and crowded populations of organisms thrive over time, despite subsistence resources being limited. At the 2002 UN Earth Conference, sustainability was defined succinctly: "enough, for all, forever." The Irish also harnessed their beloved potatoes to express the concept of sustainability in a proverb I once heard: "Don't eat today tomorrow's potatoes." Looking to the future is a necessary step in sustainable design.

Jane Goodall, a well-known researcher of chimpanzees, who observed them in nature over many years, tells how the ethos of sustainability is expressed in indigenous cultures that are close to nature. In a TED Talk titled *How Humans and Animals Can Live Together*,[21] she said: "Indigenous people around the world, before they made a major decision, used to sit around and ask themselves, 'How does this decision affect our people seven generations ahead?'"

Designs that do not consider sustainability values may deplete the subsistence resources in one fell swoop and deprive the future of these resources. In the spirit of this ethos, biomimicry is deeply connected to sustainability, and even studied primarily from the point of view of sustainability in many places in the world.

Toward a New Design Ethos

Observing nature invites a different way of thinking about how we design, produce, consume, and end the life of our products. Nature is not only a storehouse of materials, but also a source of knowledge and revelations, and its rich variety of animal and plant species offers an extensive platform for learning. Biomimicry, as a world view and as a philosophy of design, is leading to the formation of a new design ethos that is aligned with nature.

Undoubtedly, we have reached impressive technological achievements to date. The challenge today is to preserve these achievements and even reach additional technological breakthroughs, by helping humanity thrive without consuming the savings on which we rely. The role of the engineers, designers, entrepreneurs, and inventors is therefore to shape the new future, and the closer the new future is to nature and to expressing nature's ethos of sustainability, the more we will benefit from nature's resilience and wealth. And as Benyus concluded: "The more our world looks and functions like this natural world, the more likely we are to be accepted on this home that is ours, but not ours alone."[22]

LIMITATIONS AND BARRIERS

The natural structure provides a clue to what is useful in a mechanism. But maybe you can do it better."

Robert Cohen

One day, while Charles Darwin was hunting for beetles,[23] he recognized one that was extremely rare. Elated, he caught it in one hand. A moment passed and he saw a second rare beetle. A pleased Darwin caught that one as well with his other hand. A second later, he saw a third rare beetle that he couldn't let get away... what did he do? He shoved one of them into his mouth to free up a hand. But the beetle ejected an extremely pungent liquid that burned his tongue, so he had to spit it out, and in that moment, lost the other two beetles, as well. Even some bio-inspired processes are met with painful failure, ending with a beetle-less end result. Alongside the great promise of the field – to find innovative, effective, and beneficial solutions for the environment, to break through the blockade imposed on imagination and strive to do the impossible – are also limitations that are important to be familiar with.

One of the major frustrations awaiting those attempting to imitate nature's inventions is to see the promised land from afar, to know that it's there, but not to reach it. Due to the limitations and barriers related to the unique nature of this innovation process – the reality is that not every solution we find in nature can be imitated.

Scales

Solutions in nature occur on specific scales, suited to the size, weight, and system of forces operating on that scale. If we emulate a natural solution that works on a nano or micro scale and wish to apply it on a macro scale, it won't necessarily work. Function corresponds to the hierarchy from which it stems.

For example, a gecko, which weighs around 100 grams, can climb a wall while bearing a weight of roughly 3 kilograms. The question is whether this adhesion system can be imitated to carry much larger weights.

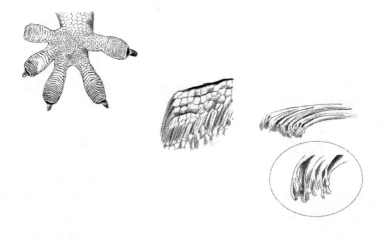

To this day, it amazes me to see geckos quickly climbing up walls, and especially across ceilings, without falling. They can walk on walls that are wet or dry, smooth or textured, clean or dusty. In the past, it was thought that geckos had vacuums on their feet, similar to snap buttons. As it turns out, geckos don't have vacuums or secrete mysterious glue. Each foot has around 500,000 hairs, or setae, 130 microns long and 100-200 nanometers thick – about one-tenth the thickness of a strand of human hair. The setae are bundled together in structures that gradually split apart to form a large contact interface with the wall. This adhesion mechanism is based on van der Waals forces, which operate at the atomic and molecular level and are considered the weakest forces in nature, but when you multiply them by, say, 500,000, you get a strong and powerful force.

When geckos peel their feet off from the side, attachment begins to fray, similar to adhesive tape on a wall that gets peeled off from the side rather than from the center.

To date, various attempts have been made to imitate this attachment mechanism. In 2005, a group at Stanford University developed the Stickybot, which can walk on walls and glass, albeit somewhat clumsily, but it demonstrates a solid attachment ability. In 2012, a group at the University of Massachusetts developed Geckskin, which can haul heavy weights even on surfaces as smooth as glass. This adhesive activates the imagination with all of its possibilities, from cleaning robots walking on houses, windows, or ships, to that childhood dream we all share – to walk on walls like Spider-Man, dressed in a gecko suit.

I was asked during a lecture one day whether this adhesive could lift up a lion. My response was that the answer depends on the weight of the lion. Fortunately, a CEO of a safari was in the audience who revealed that the average lion weighs less than 320 kg – the maximum load-bearing capacity of the Geckskin.[24] It therefore seems as though this adhesive will indeed be able to lift up a lion, but beyond this weight, the attachment ability of Geckskin is questionable. A Gecko's attachment mechanism works with small scales and weights, but a threshold exists beyond which the mechanism simply will not function.

Complexity

Biological mechanisms may be complex to a degree that makes it difficult to measure, quantify, and understand them – and hence imitate them. Even if we succeeded in the research and measurement stage, which is a much more challenging process when it comes to living versus inanimate objects, the challenge of decoding the complexity still lies ahead. Functionality in nature is found in different hierarchies. When viewing a structure through a microscope, functions can be identified at each level of magnification. Each level has its own laws, order, guidelines, and particular features. Each scale provides a different function, and sometimes the same function is expressed on different scales. This structural hierarchy causes natural systems to be efficient and intelligent, but also complex to comprehend, imitate, and produce.

When a natural mechanism is complex and difficult to understand, one can attempt to simplify it by isolating a certain parameter, for example, or by compromising on some of its resolutions, assuming that the function can be understood that way. It is also vital to remember that complexity is not always required for the application. Oftentimes designers only need to emulate some of the elements from the natural solution, especially when the mechanism bears a complexity that is unnecessary for the application and can pose a barrier to success.

A design that is good enough is one that meets the requirements. Sometimes the effort put into complex designing doesn't justify the derived benefit. Even nature has a preference for simple mechanisms. Nature doesn't produce elaborate and complex seeds that land like guided missiles at designated locations. It produces many simple seeds that spread all over and fulfill their purpose. The mathematician, Daniel Bernoulli, said, "Nature always tends to act in the simplest way." Nature's systems are simple and free of frills, but not overly simple. They are complex to the minimum extent required in order to provide the benefit.

Click beetles, for example, can rotate their bodies mid-jump. They only manage to do this 50% of the time, so they will keep jumping until they succeed. This somersault mechanism is simple and allows them to rotate in a reasonable amount of time. It also appears to be better than a complex mechanism promising 100% success on the first jump (*see 4).

In the same vein, an engineer working in the field of biomimicry at Rafael Advanced Defense System said: "It is important to note that the mechanisms found in nature are not necessarily perfect nor optimal, but nature stops once it is 'good enough.' Perhaps we too should stop when our systems are good enough."[25] Even if we "lose" some of the natural system's complexity when transitioning to its technological application, in most cases, we will still be able to provide the required functional benefit.

Technological Barriers

Sometimes the mechanism we wish to imitate is straightforward, but technologies supporting its imitation are unavailable. In such cases, only once the technological barrier has been removed, can imitation succeed.

• **The race to produce spider silk**: For years, the scientific world knew the exact structure of spider web protein, which gives the spider silk its wondrous and desirable properties, but they didn't know how to produce a synthetic material that mimics this structure in commercial quantities. Spider webs in nature appear thin and weak, but if we compare a strand of spider silk to steel fiber of identical thickness, the silk is as much as six times stronger than the steel and even more flexible and resistant to extreme temperatures. Spider webs are known for their strength and flexibility. There is a popular saying in Ethiopian culture that goes: "When spider webs unite, they can tie up a lion."

Scientists all over the world have embarked on the spider web race years ago to emulate their inherent potential for the benefit of humanity. Who will be the first research group to succeed in mimicking them? The potential application is enormous. Imagine a strong and flexible material suitable for medical uses, defense, the automotive industry, construction, and more.

Unlike the domesticated silkworm, whose cocoon silk is produced in commercial quantities, the spider is a territorial animal, and mass breeding it to produce a commercial quantity of silk is not possible. Therefore, we must find a solution that bypasses the need for a spider to spin a spider web. This solution will pave the way for the mass production of these unique fibers and enable their integration into various applications.

During the last two decades, a large number of attempts have been made to artificially synthesize the proteins that make up the dragline fiber from which spider webs are made using yeast, bacteria, plants, and even transgenic goats, i.e., goats containing foreign DNA – researchers genetically modified goats to possess spider genes and were able to isolate the web protein from the goat's milk in small, not commercial, quantities. These attempts were made possible thanks to technological advancements in genetic engineering. However, the properties of the fibers they managed to weave artificially were significantly inferior to the natural fiber.

The breakthrough occurred at Seevix Material Sciences, an Israeli company based in Jerusalem, that managed to produce fibers with identical properties to those of spider webs. Using the biological system and production processes developed by the company, spider web fibers are being produced at a fast rate and in commercial quantities for the first time. The fiber's extraordinary properties – strength, elasticity, durability, and low weight – allow the company to develop a wide range of high-end luxury products for various industries, such as the automotive, aviation, defense, and sport industries, which require strong and lightweight materials. Fiber is also in demand in the medical device industry due to the fact that it is a biopolymer with a preferred biocompatibility profile.

• **Touching the sun:** The sun is our life source, an infinite well-spring of heat, light, and energy. But we are still a long way from realizing its potential as a clean and non-biodegradable energy source. In the process of photosynthesis, plant chlorophyll cells absorb some of the solar energy that touches them and convert it into chemical energy that is stored as carbohydrates, which are organic compounds, within atomic bonds. The plant stores the carbohydrates for future use and they are the primary ener-gy source that enables life on Earth. Humanity currently knows how to produce photovoltaic energy, or thermal energy, from the sun, but storing these energies is complex. The day scientists manage to extract energy from the sun like leaves and store it for future use, humanity's energy problems will likely be solved.

This scientific field, called "artificial photosynthesis" is a hot topic and is fascinating. Scientists from all over the world are trying to imitate this natural mechanism. The mechanism is theoretically straightforward, but the challenge is technologi-cal. It calls for the design and construction of materials or mole-cules that know how to absorb the sun's energy as well as cata-lyze an efficient process in which this energy is converted into a different form of energy stored in stable chemical bonds of fuel such as hydrogen or sugar.

One of the breakthroughs was recorded in 2016 at the Tech-nion when a group of researchers led by Lilac Amirav identified particles that demonstrate record efficiency in utilizing sunlight to create negative charges (electrons) that will produce hydro-gen.[26] In 2020, the group found that hydrogen production can be directed to advance other chemical reactions in a way that closes an electrical circuit and facilitates the conversion of solar energy to fuel. Amirav summed up the magnitude of the achievement in simple terms: "With this research, we have transformed the process from photocatalysis to photosynthesis, that is, genuine conversion of solar energy into fuel." If they succeed, we will be able to produce fuel directly from solar energy, just as nature has been doing for millions of years. We can begin dreaming of enormous photosynthesis farms that will replace solar farms. There is still a long way to go, but if we don't dream – we won't get there.

Barriers to Production

Sometimes the biological structure is straightforward, but there is no production method that will allow its imitation. This barrier has been partially solved with the development of 3D printing technology, which enables the production of "growing" structures and complex forms.

• **Dynamic structures:** Biological structures are dynamic formations with diverse functions that adapt to needs, each originating from a single part capable of performing various functions. Natural structures are not carved from a single chunk, but are built from the bottom up, connecting different building blocks. What would a design made entirely out of one material look like? This question was asked by Neri Oxman, an Israeli-American designer working in the Media Lab at MIT. Oxman is known for her work in art and architecture where she combines design, biology, computation, and materials engineering. According to her, the assumption that a structure is composed of different elements that fulfill predetermined functions is an axiom imposed by the various industrial and technological limitations. Nature works differently. To produce a dynamic "growing" structure composed of one element providing a range of functions, Oxman incorporates 3D printing and manufacturing techniques in many of her projects. For example, a building exterior printed entirely in 3D that allows the flow of light, water, and even information (if fiber optics are involved).

Dutch designer Lilian van Daal has also harnessed 3D printing technology to create an elegant chair made entirely of one material with multiple functions and recyclability. Unlike traditional chairs made by assembling parts from different materials produced in different factories, this chair grew to its complete form already in the printing unit, similar to structures in nature that emerge as they grow into one whole. The chair is made of one material, in one manufacturing process, and in one factory. This process, of course, is much more sustainable – it produces less waste and pollution. Van Daal summarized the advantage of using 3D technology as the ability to grow structures that cannot be produced any other way.

• **Complex and curvature structures**: Flow systems in nature are complex systems, characterized by curvature lines, channels, and arteries that are not easy to produce using traditional manufacturing technologies of milling material, such as metalworking.

The American company Harbec, which manufactures plastic parts by injection molding, encountered the need to reduce the molding cycle time. Plastic material is injected into the mold and can only be removed once it has cooled. In the traditional cooling method, two straight cooling lines are machined into the mold. Does this design allow for optimal cooling? The company began investigating geometric principles of cooling systems in nature and examined the efficiency of heat and liquid dissipation in natural systems. Finally, they chose to focus on the vascular structure of dicot leaves and designed a pattern that mimics it. This structure enables faster cooling of the molded parts, increases the cooled surface area, provides cooling to the internal mold cavity, and leads to a 20% improvement in molding cycle times. The company would not have been able to produce this complex mold without the option to print it in 3D.

Decrease in Quality

In the process of imitating nature, something from the original quality might be lost. Execution can be disappointing at the end of the road. Oftentimes, the imitation is simpler than the complex model in nature. Sometimes it is certainly satisfactory and meets the defined engineering requirements and sometimes it does not.

For example, when I was exposed years ago to developments inspired by the lotus effect – coatings for self-cleaning surfaces – I thought it was incredible technology. I hoped someone would bring them to Israel and even suggested the idea to several suppliers. Finally, someone picked up the gauntlet and imported them. The coatings were intended for various surfaces: metal, wood, stone, fabric, and glass. To test the coating's effectiveness on glass, a pilot was conducted at the Ramat Gan Safari in the tigers' habitat that is enclosed by a glass fence. Given that the fence is near tigers, it is not easy to clean it often. The tiger fences were treated with the lotus coating, but unfortunately the results were unimpressive and the glass remained unclean. A variance was found in the effectiveness of coatings on different surfaces. It was actually the coating of stone surfaces that yielded the best dirt removal effect at the time. It should be noted that today, more effective coatings for glass already exist.

Perhaps it Could Be Done Better

There are inventions that were not invented in nature at all, probably due to various constraints. For example, the wheel, one of the most important inventions for human development, does not exist in nature. According to ethologist and evolutionary biologist Richard Dawkins, we consider the wheel an important tool only when compared to the limitation of our feet's movement. Nearly all large animals can move faster than we can using their feet. A horse with wheels? It seems that a wheel would only slow down a horse rather than speed it up. Due to various constraints, even designs in nature aren't always perfect. We are familiar with the blind spot in our eyes, an area in our field of vision that does not perceive via sense of sight. The blind spot is where the retina connects to the optic nerve, which transmits visual information from the retina to the brain. This nexus lacks photoreceptor cells, and as a result, the brain doesn't receive information about this area in the field of vision of both eyes. It seems as though an engineer who would have approached this issue from the beginning would have chosen to place the optic nerve elsewhere. One can only speculate that the current location of the optic nerve is due to various limitations and constraints in the evolutionary process of the eye.

Nature's solutions are subject to constraints that are not necessarily relevant for implementation. It is therefore possible to propose changes when applying engineering knowledge.

For example, cacti are covered with conical spines that produce a water-harvesting effect (condensation of water from the moisture in the air). Researchers examined what would happen if the conical spines were changed to square or hexagonal spines. Indeed, the results improved. The best water-harvesting effects were found with hexagonal spines. The production of square or hexagonal spines is unlikely to be the optimal solution in nature, but human production technologies can easily manufacture such structures and improve performance.[27]

Another example of engineering improving a natural model can be seen in the attempt to mimic biological muscle. Muscles are extraordinary organs that arouse great interest among engineers who are trying to develop artificial muscles to integrate them into a variety of applications in propulsion systems and robotics. Artificial muscles are tested on a number of performance metrics, such as the degree of contraction, strength per unit area, efficiency, and more. Biomimetic technologies come very close to the biological performance of human muscles, and even bypass them in some parameters.[28] "The natural structure provides a clue to what is useful in a mechanism. But maybe you can do it better." This was suggested by Robert Cohen,[29] an MIT engineer who works on biomimetic projects. Nature serves as a starting point for innovation, and the engineering world leads it to other places.

Cultivation and Funding

One day, I was called upon to help a company in the water industry that was facing a mechanical challenge. As always, I began the process with the following stages: understanding the challenge; identifying analogous, functional mechanisms in nature; and assessing their relevance. I conducted a comprehensive review that included approximately 15 strategies for solving the mechanical challenge using natural solutions, and identified a number of other biomimetic technologies that have already been developed that could be suitable as well.

The review was presented to the company's management and engineering teams and was received with great enthusiasm and interest. After a considerable amount of silence on their part, the CEO told me that he was unsure how to proceed from there. The company doesn't always have the knowledge or ability required to promote innovation within the organization. In such cases, external knowledge is needed to promote innovation. This is true of any innovation process, including innovation inspired by nature.

Nature presents magic, but doesn't generate magic. In order for the seed of invention to grow, it must be nurtured and developed, otherwise its potential will not be realized. The design principle gleaned from nature is only the beginning. One must work on its implementation just like any other project. In the absence of resources of time, knowledge, and funding – innovation will not succeed.

PART II

WHY?

WHY LEARN FROM NATURE?

*Look deep into nature, and then you will
understand everything better*

Albert Einstein

Years ago, I was exposed to Albert Einstein's quote: "Look deep into nature, and then you will understand everything better." This intriguing sentence raises questions for me: What will we understand better if we look at nature? Many scientists have elaborated on how they learn from nature. Jacques Cousteau, an ecologist and marine researcher, and father of modern diving and underwater photography, looked deep into the sea and tried to understand what was happening in there. In one of the famous quotes attributed to Cousteau, he says: "What is a scientist after all? It is a curious man looking through a keyhole, the keyhole of nature, trying to know what's going on." Keyholes are sometimes associated with voyeurism, but in this context, they relate to the curiosity that leads us to "peek into nature" and discover what is hidden within it. Keyholes might also elicit an image that arouses resistance, since they are associated with narrow vision, however I feel as though the meaning behind Cousteau's words simply reflect an attempt to understand the world through nature, and perhaps observing through a narrow hole actually focuses the vision and makes it possible to observe well, as Einstein suggested.

Scientists who observe nature have a better understanding

of how nature works. They detect the rules, order, and patterns revealed on nature's canvas. They recognize the language of nature as a mathematical language describing its wonders. Engineers and designers who observe nature view it as a model, measure, and mentor, as Benyus puts it, for solving challenges in innovative and sustainable ways.

Nature guides the way to a solution and provides strategic counseling on how to achieve it. Each of the millions of life species is a model for coping with life's challenges and demonstrates different principles, patterns, and strategies for solving them. One may view nature as a collection of models for solutions. For example, the contours of the Boxfish mentioned earlier is a hydrodynamic model that is difficult to achieve by purely mathematical calculations, and here it lies before us, inviting us to imitate its design down to the parameters, so that it can serve as a model for energy efficiency in movement. Nature is also a measure, one that presents a standard of sustainability and demonstrates how to design systems that are both sustainable and regenerative. Nature is also a mentor for a new design paradigm – design that is based on what we can learn from nature as opposed to what we can extract from it.

Nature as a Source of Inspiration

Even if we are not scientists, engineers, or designers who view nature as a model, measure, and mentor, nature is a big source of inspiration for all of us. In fact, any interface with nature has the potential for inspiration and learning. Any such interface can trigger sensory, mental, or emotional stimulation, which will turn on the light switch of inspiration. Inspiration is formed in the gap between the external and the internal, between the known and the unknown, between the possible and the impossible. In nature, too, flow occurs between poles that are formed, for example, between differences in height (waterfall), concentration (concentration gradient), temperature (lapse rate), or electric potential (voltage drop). Similarly, inspiration is a gradient of knowledge.

Inspiration is a wonderful state of mind, in which a stream of ideas flows through us. Sometimes I wake up in the middle of the night or just have trouble falling asleep because I'm full of ideas. Thinking about ideas increases levels of enthusiasm and excitement, like oxygen to fire. The more the idea is fueled with mental oxygen, the greater the fire, and the more intense the thoughts. This is the model of inspiration: a model that fuels itself. The only way I can go back to sleep is to get up, write down the ideas, and only after they are safe and secure, do I manage to fall asleep. Sometimes in the morning, when I revisit these recorded ideas, I find that they have lost their beauty that stood out only in the darkness of the night, and sometimes they are the spark that starts a new venture in my life.

The term "inspiring" is well used today; it is easily attached as an adjective to people, stories, organizations, and more. Almost everything today is inspiring. The way I see it, this overuse of the term simply indicates our strong human need for inspiration, for movement, for vitality, for "food" which is not necessarily tangible, but that nourishes us. The term also implies the existence of an external factor that sparks inspiration. There is something external that is responsible for our inspiration, which can be sensed by the Latin etymological root 'inspirare' which can be translated as 'breathe into.' Greek mythology depicts the nine Muses, the goddesses of creativity, arts, and sciences, who entertained the gods of Olympus by playing instruments, singing, and dancing, and whose main function was to inspire various artists, especially poets, musicians, and philosophers. In contemplating the qualities of nature in relation to these Muses, we find that nature is not a bad muse at all. It features the dance of leaves moving in the wind, the cooing of birds; it boasts vivid colors that burst forth with all their might before turning pale again; it embodies scientific laws, beauty, and aesthetics. In nature, there are many "spirits" that can enter us and awaken the flame of inspiration within us.

In the process of bioinspired innovation, we take responsibility for our inspiration and set out in active search for the cascade of knowledge. We do not wait for something in nature to inspire us, but venture out into nature alert and open to find this inspiration, or proactively seek it in nature's reservoir of inventions. And as is nature's way, it is up to us to infuse these ideas with oxygen, so that the fire in them does not extinguish. The onus is on us to contemplate, examine, investigate, and understand them, until they are refined and ready for transformation – to accept their new form in the world of technology.

Nature's Reservoir of Inventions

There are an enormous number of solutions in nature's reservoir of inventions that have been successfully developed and attempted over an unimaginable amount of time, solutions that provide a response to the constraints of life – sustainable, effective, and even patent-free solutions. These solutions dissolve mental fixations and offer potential for applications in a wide range of fields. Nature, which is traditionally perceived by many as opposing technology, is emerging as a reservoir of inventions, ideas, and solutions.

• **A wide reservoir of inventions**: Nature's reservoir of inventions is overflowing, and in fact, its size is unfathomable. Every species of life offers different patents for different challenges. How many species exist in the world today? The question is simple, but the answer is markedly less so, since no one really knows the precise number of species that exist today. There is life present in habitats that are inaccessible to humans, such as the depths of the oceans; there are animals that are too small to see with the naked eye, and there are those that live inside other organisms. Most species are insects, and many have not yet been identified.

In the 1980s, American entomologist Terry Erwin hypothesized the global number of insect species in an interesting way.[30] He sprayed pesticide over a tropical rainforest canopy in Panama. At least 1,200 different species of beetles fell to the ground, 163 of which grew on one specific tree. Assuming that each species of tree hosts a similar number of beetles, and assuming that beetles make up about 40% of insects, Erwin estimated that there are 30 million species of insects worldwide. Many scientists argue that this number is too high. Even the exact number of all species in the world, not only of insects, is debatable. If microorganisms are considered, the number increases by several orders of magnitude. The margin of error is wide, but one thing is clear: the titanic number of species offers endless potential for learning and innovation. Each of these species is a source of knowledge and wisdom. Here's another good and important reason to preserve species diversity: an extinct species is a lost model of solutions.

• **3.8 billion years of research and development**: Nature is an enormous laboratory with 3.8 billion years of research and development behind it, since the dawn of life. Years upon years of trial and error until convergence to tailored optimization. It is difficult to grasp this duration and its significance. A thinking exercise can illustrate where we are on the timeline: if we compress the age of the Earth (4.5 billion years) to one year, then the Industrial Revolution, the cradle of today's technological innovation, occurred merely two seconds ago (about 250 years on the real timeline).

I am not aware of any other R&D method that involves so

many trials. In reality, we are limited in the number of experiments that can be performed, and statistically, many attempts fail. In nature, progress is much slower and more gradual, and is not the product of one or two experiments, but of many experiments that have stood the test of time. Time is undoubtedly a critical factor in innovation processes – and nature refers us to a solution that already works. The immense experience of nature's laboratory, which is expressed in the wonders of creation, is a notable reason to learn from nature – to shorten development processes and learn from those who have already "done it" before us.

• **Addressing constraints**: Constraints are shaping forces in nature's laboratory. Amazing solutions can be found in extreme natural habitats around the world, where organisms deal with difficult life constraints. For example, desert organisms demonstrate solutions for water production. In the depths and utter darkness of the ocean, organisms astound in their ability to produce light. In predatory environments, the basilisk lizard (also known as the Jesus Lizard) escapes by running across the water. Most amazing of all is the solution of plants for their limitation in movement: the development of sophisticated mechanisms for seed distribution. The challenge of constraints is shared by humanity and nature, and the solutions in nature, which are the result of these constraints, are of great value to humanity.

• **Sustainable technologies**: Natural systems are built and operate sustainably. They are efficient when it comes to material and energy resources and offer holistic solutions that take the ecosystem into account, as well. In nature, one can find solutions to the core challenges faced in the environmental field, solutions in areas of material, water, and energy. Learning from nature not only drives sustainable technological innovation, but also reshapes the connection between man and nature. It turns it into a healthy and sustainable relationship, based on the perception of nature as a warehouse of knowledge and insights, and not just one of materials, as beautifully articulated by the Biomimicry Institute. Our interest in nature is shifting from the extraction of resources, which is more closely associated with the Industrial Revolution, to extraction of knowledge, which is more closely associated with the Biomimicry revolution.

• **Public domain**: One biomimicry publication I came across boasted a defiant headline: "Stealing ideas from nature." Who really owns nature's inventions? Is imitating them considered theft? Inventions found in nature are public domain. Each and every one of us can go outside right now, find an interesting mechanism, research it, and patent its application, assuming that no one has done it before. You don't need to pay royalties to nature. It is permissible and sensible to copy from nature and imitate it.

And what do intellectual property lawyers have to say on the subject?[31] Their claim is that in order to turn "Nature Property (NP)" into intellectual property (IP), certain principles must be followed. In general, patents can be registered for novel compositions, machines, and processes including those that describe new uses for compounds or materials and new production methods. Natural laws or natural phenomena cannot be patented. In other words, after discovering a solution in nature, one can register a patent for the application of the solution or method in the technological or engineering field. For example, a patent was registered for the attachment mechanism of Velcro but not for that of the seed attachment mechanisms which inspired it; and for an antibacterial nanostructure for cleaning surfaces but not for the durable shark skin on which it was based. Isolated proteins and peptides that were not changed from their natural state fall within the realm of "natural products," and are not patentable. However, applications inspired or based on mechanisms learned from natural proteins and peptides may be.

• **Escaping fixation:** Mental fixation often derives from the perception that something is unlikely or even impossible, but when we see a surprising example of it being done in nature, fixation dissipates. For example, the idea that bacteria can be treated without antibiotics, but by using a smart nanoscale structure may sound impossible, but this "science fiction" has been proven to work on shark skin; the idea that material can turn from white to transparent upon contact with water may sound unfeasible, but it exists in nature in the Diphylleia grayi flower. Its white petals turn translucent when exposed to water due to a structural change that occurs through water adsorption that affects light reflection. Nowadays, engineering systems inspired by nature are designed to maintain and repair themselves, and alter frequently according to changes in the environment. These concepts were initially perceived as impossible from an engineering viewpoint.

There are fields in which nature significantly outperforms today's technological capabilities and demonstrates superpowers that spark the imagination of engineers. These superpowers help engineers define goals to aspire to, make the impossible possible, or at least get closer to the high bar that they set. Observing nature and learning from it removes the block that many engineers have unconsciously or unintentionally imposed on their imagination, since the block is a product of certain design paradigms, manners of thinking, and habits.

Boston Dynamics is a company that develops incredible robots which mimic animal and human movement. Their humanoid robot called Atlas is capable of performing leaps and even backflips. When I was first exposed to these robots, my spontaneous reaction was admiration. I was particularly impressed by their human-like ability to emulate nature's machines. But a moment later, I couldn't help but think how nature's machines are several times superior in complexity and performance than the imitation. Observation of these complex mechanisms of movement set a high bar for Boston Dynamics engineers.

Another field in which there is a large gap between natural and technological abilities is that of sensory systems. Senses in nature are simply unbelievable and are not perceived as possible in the engineering world. Fire-chaser beetles are able to detect fire from a distance of 80 kilometers; foxes locate their prey under snow, pouncing directly at it using sound and, presumably, geomagnetic sensing;[32] the Striped Kribensis, which lives in shallow, murky, dark waters, is able to locate its favorite prey (shrimp) by visualizing near-infrared wavelengths of light, and shrimp reflect a unique near-infrared radiation that can be identified like fingerprints; sharks detect prey that is outside their visual field by sensing miniscule changes in the electrical fields surrounding their prey; and some animals surpass the most advanced seismic sensors available today in detecting earthquakes. Natural senses set high bars for artificial sensors, one that still exists beyond the limits of human imagination. "We can never see with the vision of a condor, or hear with the ears of a mosquito, but we can at least close our eyes for a moment and point our imaginations in roughly the right direction."[33] concluded Chris Baraniuk, a scientific journalist in the fields of nature and technology.

• **The innovation cascade effect:** Waterfalls in nature are associated with abundance – a source of constant flow and perceptible intensity that crashes in every direction. One of the characteristics of solutions in nature is their ability to generate a cascade of innovation. One generic solution found in nature can lead to a wide range of potential applications. Typically, these generic mechanisms are suffixed with "effect" or "principle," which implies the ability to apply them to a variety of uses.

For example, the shark skin effect – surfaces that repel bacteria and reduce turbulence – has already been applied in a variety of applications, including wall tiles; coatings for ships, aircraft, and medical equipment; and even antimicrobial fabric. The lotus effect – surfaces that repel water and dirt – has been translated into developments in the paint, glass, textile, aviation, and other industries. The pinecone effect – an opening and closing mechanism resulting from changes in humidity levels – has also been linked to a large number of applications in various fields and industries, such as the textile, architectural, and energy industries. One single principle identified in nature can lead to immense innovation.

INNOVATION

The mind is not a vessel to be filled but a fire to be kindled.

Plutarch

L egend has it that inventor Thomas Edison lived in a house that had a large garden with an iron gate at its entrance that barely opened. Friends who would come to visit him were consistently surprised to find that Edison, the great inventor, had not yet repaired the gate of his house, which creaked so much on its hinges that it took a lot of force to open. Edison repeatedly promised to lubricate the hinges and spare his visitors the effort, but never did. Only after his death in his old age was the secret revealed: the gate was attached to a pump, and with every opening of it, water got pumped into the inventor's bathroom.

This tale demonstrates a fundamental principle of fostering innovation: connections. In this case, the connection between the gate and the bathroom was hidden from view and buried as an underground pump. Connections are not always visible, but if we dig deep, we will unveil them. At the basis of all innovation are connections between ideas, thoughts, worldviews, and knowledge, that arrive from different fields. Something new occurs in the nexus. An idea is a new connection that never existed before, and the art of weaving ideas is actually the art of weaving networks.

Even in the brain, new knowledge is synthesized from new neural connections that did not exist before. Plutarch, a Greek philosopher who lived in the 1st century AD, long before the discovery of neurons, understood that the brain is much more than a vessel filled with information, and likened it to a fire that can be kindled, much like wood that can be set aflame. It is known that neurons have extensions called dendrites, whose name derives from the Greek word for 'tree' (dendron) due to its shape: a tree trunk-like structure that splits into sections, which continue to split like tree branches. It is also known that voltage changes in dendrites produce nerve impulses that cause neurons to "fire" and activate the process of transmitting information in the synapse that connects the neurons. Ultimately, this is nothing more than a description of a flame igniting and passing from branch to branch!

What's New?

My father owned a metal factory in Haifa Bay that manufactured aircraft parts. It was there, among the sparks of welding, scents of processed metal, and the sound of presses, that I was first exposed to the manufacturing world. Many years later, when I began engaging in creative and innovative processes, I realized that while production has to do with quantity, creativity is about quality and originality. The metal parts are the duplication of patterns, while creativity is the product of insights. But creativity, original as it may be, doesn't necessarily lead to commercial innovation. The innovation process also requires creating value.

"There's an important difference between being innovative and being an innovative enterprise: The former generates lots of ideas; the latter generates lots of cash."[34] This beautiful insight was mentioned once in one of the Harvard business reviews. Innovation is a key factor for economic growth. It drives productivity, spawns new industries, and transforms traditional ones.

It contributes to the formation of competitive advantage, efficiency, and reputation. Innovation is critical to the survival of the organization and even becomes vital when conditions are limited, such as increased competition or strict regulations. In economics, as in nature, organizations that manage to adapt to the changing environment survive. But unlike in nature, people and organizations don't have to wait for long-term processes of change to occur. The decision to change is theirs to make. Therefore, in order to adapt to the changing business or technological environment, companies and organizations devote considerable resources to driving innovation. In recent years, an official position has even been introduced: Director of Innovation, with the understanding that innovation, like any other process, requires management, direction, and promotion.

One of the fastest ways to create innovation is to form connections in general and to nature in particular. Connections are the core of biomimicry: connecting the biological world with the technological world. A good connection refreshes the way we think, provides knowledge for decoding, research, and discovery, and leads to practical ideas and valuable solutions.

The Raw Materials for Forming Connections – Curiosity and Courage

The world of biomimicry is replete with innovation stories that began as a result of different inventors' affection toward nature and their curiosity. For example, Dubi Benyamini worked for many years in the aerospace industry as an esteemed engineer, but was also a butterfly enthusiast since childhood. He followed them around the world and even coined Hebrew names for butterflies native to Israel. He was amazed by their ability to survive despite their small and vulnerable nature, and viewed them as sophisticated engineering machines capable of flying around for an hour fueled only by two sips of nectar. Benyamini's passion for butterflies also entered his engineering work, and after many years as an engineer, he decided to combine his work with his passion. He ran a development lab of crazy people, who set a high bar for bioinspired dreams. Among other things, he led the invention of a mechanical butterfly that mimics butterfly flight and can enter closed areas, photograph in real-time, and chase after targets.

Curiosity is the glue that binds disciplines together and generates innovation. In his book, *Originals: How Non-Conformists Move the World*,[35] Adam Grant shows how connections to non-scientific fields have contributed to scientific progress and success. A study he mentions in his book compared Nobel Prize-winning scientists from 1901 to 2005 with scientists of the same era who worked in the same fields but did not win the Nobel Prize. It was found that Nobel Prize winners tended to engage in artistic hobbies in their spare time. Similar results were found among entrepreneurs and inventors. It was discovered that people who started businesses and filed for patent applications were more likely than their peers to have leisure time hobbies. The variable that can explain the relationship between hobbies and success is curiosity. Interest in other areas reflects a quality of curiosity that leads to research and discovery.

As such, discoveries throughout history often involve converging different areas of content. Galileo Galilei was the first to recognize that there are mountains on the moon. It was Galileo's experience in painting and drawing and his use of a shading technique called chiaroscuro that helped him detect the mountains based on a zigzag pattern of light and dark areas observed through his telescope; Dmitri Mendeleev cracked the code of the periodic table thanks to his love of card games: In an attempt to match elements with their properties more easily, he created a deck of cards displaying their atomic weights. He would play solitaire-like games with these cards until he discovered the location of each element in the table.

Even in business organizations, innovation is formed via connections. Steve Jobs studied calligraphy as an elective course in college. A decade later, he utilized the knowledge he learned in the course to create the fonts for Apple's first Macintosh computer; Microsoft built a data center in an unusual location: submerged in the Northern Isles, thanks to one employee who was an amateur diver. When a data center is below sea level, the great cooling power of the water and heat-exchange processes can be leveraged quickly and easily.[36]

But curiosity alone is not enough. It also takes courage to connect seemingly unrelated concepts or issues. In one of his most bizarre experiments, Darwin, who not only engaged in biological research but also played the bassoon, decided to monitor the effects of his bassoon playing on plant growth. He did not succeed and later called the study a "fool's experiment" ... But we now know that plants actually do respond to music or, more accurately, to air vibrations that yield sound waves, so in retrospect, the study was not foolish at all.[37] It often takes courage to suggest connections that initially seem unrelated and even foolish, as Darwin put it, but in reality, these connections are the engines of invention. The more there is to connect, the greater chance there is of inventing.

Nature's Engine of Innovation

In order to realize nature's innovation potential, we need a cognitive engine to systematically and efficiently manage the connections between nature and technology. This engine is based on patterns of open, interdisciplinary, and analogical thinking.

• **Open thinking**: Connections are out there and we cannot find them without open thinking. Open thinking is about being receptive and seeking out external stimuli and information as part of the knowledge shaping process, similar to a living organism in constant dialogue with its environment as it grows and develops. Those who consider solutions that differ from what is known and familiar, demonstrate open thinking. Open thinking leads to open innovation—a concept coined by Henry Chesbrough of the University of California, Berkeley. In contrast to the closed innovation approach, according to which innovation is achieved through internal sources, open innovation encourages integrating knowledge from external sources, based on the assumption that no organization has all the answers for managing innovation. Biomimicry demands open thinking that looks at nature's reservoir of solutions even if they differ from what is known and familiar. This connection breaches the boundaries of the organization and generates open innovation.

• **Interdisciplinary thinking**: Openness is insufficient. One must also employ interdisciplinary thinking, merging different fields of knowledge to form a new concept. What are the chances that one person holds all the knowledge required for the innovation process? In most cases, we need to collaborate with experts from different fields of knowledge to create the necessary connections that will lead to something new and meaningful. Biomimicry is essentially an interdisciplinary innovation process that requires learning and merging complementary fields of knowledge, such as physics, chemistry, materials theory, or mechanics, depending on the nature of the biological phenomenon being studied. Each field offers its own explanation for the phenomenon, and then the question arises: How is the complete phenomenon formed? How, when studied together, does physics, chemistry, and structure, produce the unique property being studied in nature?

Sometimes people from one discipline come up with an idea and people from another put it into practice. For example, a team of a designer and a biologist developed WikiFoods, a plastic-free food and beverage packaging solution made from natural, edible, nutritious, and biodegradable ingredients. The concept was inspired by nature. The biologist noticed that the skin of a grape is an edible and protective package: it protects against the loss of fluids and entry of pollutants, and provides unique nutrients, while at the same time, the grape is eaten entirely with its skin. The designer translated this concept into a practical product by selecting appropriate ingredients – both edible and protective – and used them to design the packaging.

• **Analogical thinking**: Analogical thinking connects different fields for the purpose of transferring knowledge between a field defined as the source of knowledge and a field defined as the target. Connections between fields are found through their similarities – similarity in form, structure, process, or function. Every analogy has a dimension of comparison – two areas with knowledge gaps between them. The path from comparison to inspiration seeks to realize the potential identified between the source and target domains and to enable flow between them. For example, hospitals are similar to hotels in their functioning. A customer arrives, is admitted, receives a bed, food, cleaning and laundry services, and is eventually released. It is true that lying on a hotel bed is better than a hospital bed, but operationally, there are many similar processes and great potential for knowledge transfer.[38]

Biomimicry is essentially an analogical process, in which knowledge is transferred from the field of biology (the source) to the field of application (the target). The key question is where in nature a challenge exists that's similar to the challenge concerning us or, alternatively, where in technology a need exists that's for a solution similar to the solution we found in nature. For example, it is customary to add substances that break down lipids to laundry detergents, but their effectiveness decreases in cold water. Arctic fish, which live in temperatures approaching zero, also need to break down lipids from their prey. This analogy could lead to the discovery of enzymes that catalyze lipid breakdown in Arctic fish, and the incorporation of similar-functioning ingredients into laundry detergents. This solution will make it possible to launder at lower temperatures and preserve water-heating energy. It stands to reason that a chemical engineering expert looking for the solution in the field of chemistry would not have come up with this solution. The challenge of breaking down lipids in cold water shared between Arctic fish and laundry detergents led to the formation of an analogical bridge between the problem and the solution.[39]

Research supports the relationship between analogies and innovation, and the main recurrent finding is that the farther apart the disciplines, the greater the innovation.[40] The analogies used in biomimetic innovation are far removed from one another and interdisciplinary analogies that form a connection between biological solutions and technological challenges, and therefore promise high potential for innovation.

The Medici Effect

Frans Johansson expanded on the idea of analogies, positing that the effect of innovation is created at the intersection of disciplines, which he describes in his book called *The Medici Effect: Breakthrough Insights at the Intersection of Ideas, Concepts, and Cultures*.[41] The effect is named after the House of Medici, a dynasty of influential Italian merchants who lived and operated between the 13th and 17th centuries in Florence. This dynasty of merchants supported the work of people from a variety of disciplines, including da Vinci, Galileo, Michelangelo, and Raphael. Thanks to their support and that of similar families, a large group of sculptors, scientists, poets, philosophers, painters, architects, and others gathered in Florence, met with and learned from one another, and began dissolving the boundaries between disciplines in preparation for new mergers. These mergers formed a new world based on novel ideas that are associated with the Renaissance: The era of rebirth.

Interdisciplinary connections are now being formed at an accelerated pace. People traverse the globe with ease and at low cost. Looking at the worldwide flight map teaches us about the scope of global traffic. Each person is a "host" of knowledge, culture, ideas, and thoughts, and can easily meet other "hosts." As time goes by, more and more separately discovered scientific phenomena unite and emerge as different expressions and manifestations of the same phenomenon. These points of union are nexuses joining various phenomena. Understanding one can shed light on another, and their convergence can evoke insight of a different order.

Computational development today is also forming virtual nexuses. The network of global information is now in the palm of our hands, and with the click of a button, we can access nearly any computer in the world and the information it contains. Social networks also enable rapid connectivity between people from around the world, like never before. There is an endless opportunity here for branching knowledge and for tremendous acceleration of development for humanity. The years of waiting in line with phone cards to use payphones and being enthralled by chatbots now seem to belong to a different era.

Johansson provides some real-world examples of biomimicry in his book, which details a world of connections, and even claims that it is possible to consciously produce the Medici effect and manage interdisciplinary relationships. In everyday life, every movement – physical or mental – moves in the direction of connecting. In the old days, junctions occurred at ports. Sailors returning from travels around the world would sit down and enjoy some beers together, tell stories, exchange thoughts, and forge relationships. Today, you no longer have to go to the port, since the port is any place where people meet people. The pint of beer could be the cup of coffee you drink with a co-worker you just met in the break room, and perhaps that first conversation will open up new worlds and surprising connections.

In the world of biomimicry, every act toward receiving biological information – spending time in nature, coming across a biological text, and noticing incredible phenomena – forms a nexus between nature and the fields of application. If there is one force that can unite so many disciplines, it's nature. Anyone involved in creating, designing, or building processes or systems can point out many connections in nature, sources of sustainable ethos, design principles, and innovative solutions.

A Different Design Paradigm

*We cannot solve our problems with the same thinking
we used when we created them.*

Albert Einstein

I often present the connection between nature and technology using two images: a picture of Albert Einstein and one of an owl. When I ask what they have in common, I get a surprising response: They look physically similar. Both have large eyes, slightly prominent noses, and pulled back hair or feathers. Einstein would walk around with unkempt hair and joke about his appearance. I once heard that he said his hairstyle was designed by neglect. But beyond their physical similarities, which can be argued against, both are symbols of wisdom. Einstein symbolizes human intelligence and the owl symbolizes nature's intelligence. By the way, even though owls are cast as wise characters in children's fairy tales, upon examining their intelligence against that of other birds, we don't find a discrepancy in their favor... Hence, considering the symbolism alone, biomimicry is in fact a connection between natural and human intelligence, a connection that yields innovation.

Continuing Einstein's sentiment on how "we cannot solve our problems with the same thinking we used when we created them," alternative ways of solving problems can be found in nature, since it is based on a different design paradigm. Unlike technological systems, which are designed through conscious cognitive action, natural systems simply come into being, and we can only investigate the forces, patterns, and principles that shaped them. The word 'paradigm' in ancient Greek means pattern or example. Nature's design paradigm embodies, expresses, and demonstrates principles that lead specifically to one design and not another. Changing the pattern changes its products, and this is the great opportunity inherent in adopting nature's design paradigm.

One day, a veteran engineer asked me, "So what exactly am I looking for in nature? If I am already familiar with the solution that appears in nature, then it hasn't taught me anything new." This engineer helped hone the realization for me that what we are looking for in nature are solutions that do not follow the path of technological development, but are based on a different design paradigm. We are looking for a real opportunity to innovate, to seek out a solution that is neither from the branch of engineering, nor from the realm of imagination.

Similar Challenges – Different Solutions

A study conducted at the University of Bath analyzed some 2,500 design challenges and examined their resolutions in biology and technology.[42] The study found that although design challenges in biology and technology are similar, the principles behind their solutions are different. In fact, the study shows that there is only a 12% similarity between the principles behind the solutions in biology and technology.

The study shows that design challenges in the field of technology are primarily resolved by manipulating energy (switching the energy source, adding energy) and material (altering properties, adding material). In contrast, solving these challenges in the field of biology is done extensively through the use of information (regulation, synchronization, feedback cycles) and structures (surface, shape, form). Here are two examples:

• **Electrical load management:** When the demand for energy from various consumers increases, engineers typically respond by increasing the total energy supplied to the system to meet the peak demand. In nature, the preferred solution is to synchronize the demands in order to flatten the demand curve at any given moment. This solution was implemented by the company Encycle. They developed a solution for optimized energy management inspired by bees. Bees communicate with each other without centralized management, based on simple rules, and demonstrate optimal performance at swarm level. Energy guzzlers such as air conditioners, pumps, and compressors often operate in cycles. When their activities are not coordinated and they are activated at the same time, peak demand ensues. The bioinspired solution is called Swarm Logic®, a data-driven energy management technology that synchronizes activity of the building's energy guzzlers to adjust their operation based on the overall needs of the building. The moment several machines act simultaneously, a protocol is activated to determine their optimal order of operation. The result: reduced demand during rush hour and savings in energy.

• **Mechanical load management:** Engineers tend to add material to reinforce systems. Nature's solution works the opposite way: it subtracts material and creates hive- or sponge-like structures based on supports and air cavities, similar to bone structure, which excels in energy absorption. Most of these structures in nature have hexagonal patterns. The German company Dr. Mirtsch applied this solution and developed metal-reinforcing technology using hexagonal vault structures. The technology was developed after discovering that a self-rigidizing effect was activated when applying exterior pressure on a thin-walled cylinder which is supported by internal rings. At a critical value of

pressure (instability point), the material between the supporting rings is spontaneously self-organized into hexagonal structures. Following the discovery, a patented metal-processing
technology was developed, currently marketed by Dr. Mirtsch,
that gives metal a hexagonal pattern. The company supplies
thin and lightweight metals to be used wherever system reinforcement is required while maintaining reduced weight, in automotive, construction, and other industries.

Shaping Forces and Design Principles

The fact that nature solves challenges through structures and
information rather than material and energy is the result of a
different design paradigm, stemming from other shaping forces.
The force that shapes living organisms is that of sustainability.
Organisms are designed and act in a way that promotes continued existence. In contrast, technological systems are not necessarily designed for continued existence. Sometimes the opposite
is even true: they are designed for short life cycles. The force of
sustainability is expressed in nature in dynamic, holistic, and
efficient design. Technological systems, on the other hand, are
characterized by static, reductionist, and sometimes inefficient
design. As a result, it is possible to identify different design principles in nature and technology.

• **Dynamic versus static design**: Living organisms are dynamic,
growing, and emerging systems. Flowers, for example, change
in color, shape, and size, and respond to changes in the environment. The ability to respond to changes and identify opportunities and threats is key to continued existence. Organisms can
also repair injuries such as fissures, sometimes regrow severed
body parts, and even disappear from view. In this sense, their
design process never ends, but develops continuously. In contrast, technological systems are static, and their formation

usually comes to fruition when the design process is complete. They change less in real time and in response to large-scale variations.

One example of dynamic design in nature are cuttlefish, which can alter their color, shape, and texture to camouflage in different environments. It can resemble a lump of stone in one moment and coral in another. In an amazing experiment, cuttlefish were exposed to an environment with differing decor: a yellow and purple striped wall, chessboard-like flooring, and a colorfully spotted chair.[43] Within a few seconds, the cuttlefish's skin took on the design of the background surface, even in areas outside its line of sight. It turns out that its body is covered with light-sensitive cells that respond to different wavelengths (*see 5).

Another example are sea sapphires, which belong to the group of animals classified as crustaceans.[44] Not only can they camouflage but they can literally disappear. Their hues are generated by an array of hexagonal crystal reflectors located beneath the chitin plates that comprise their outer skeleton. The thickness of the spacing between these plates vary from 50 to 200 nm, a variable which determines the reflective color. When wavelengths are reflected in a range invisible to the human eye and probably also to predators, the sea sapphire simply "disappears" (*see 6).

• **Holistic versus reductionist design:** Systems in nature are holistic in design and view the ecosystem as a whole, while addressing the complexity of the connections among the parts. Systems in technology are reductionist in design, targeting decomposition and abstraction, reducing complexity. All components of living organisms are connected and merge together. There is no material in nature that is not related and adapted to structure. There is no structure or form in nature that is not related and adapted to function. The material is the structure, form, and function. On the other hand, the leading way to design technological systems is to break the system down into its components in a way that relates to each component separately, perhaps due to the mental challenge of including all the components. As a rule, with each separation into parts during observation, reflection or design processes, something of the quality of the whole system gets lost.

Living organisms are part of a rich web of life and are connected to other organisms and their environment. Flowers don't pollute their environment but support and enrich it. They host insects and microorganisms, and their beauty embodies the efficiency and elegance of design. Designs of technological systems are more focused on the system itself and less on how it interfaces with the environment.

Natural systems use environmental factors as system parts to solve challenges. System parts can be, for example, energy sources for performing operations: birds use thermals (rising currents of warm air) for flight; beavers gnaw halfway through a trunk and let the wind do the rest, knocking the tree down; wheat seeds contain bristles that bend and straighten in response to changes in humidity, thus dispersing the seeds on the ground. Comparing this to an engineering system, the bristles can represent the engine, and the source of energy is the change of humidity throughout the day. Sometimes environmental factors are used as actual working parts and play a role in the operation of the entire system. Lotus leaves use drops of water to clean dirt from their surfaces. The drops roll along the leaves and remove the dirt themselves. Peregrine falcons use sun rays to dazzle their prey. During an attack, they position themselves in front of the sun at an angle that temporarily blinds the prey. The principle of integrating environmental factors as system parts in solving challenges is not always considered in the design processes of technological systems, due to a reductionist approach that focuses on the system itself and less on its connections with the environment. But if this principle is tested, it will lead to innovation.

Natural systems also give parts back to the environment by breaking them down and returning them to the material cycle. Natural ecosystems contain decomposers: bacteria, fungi, and worms that help break down organic matter and return the nutritious elements to the material cycle. A substance in nature that cannot be broken down, that gradually piles up and never disintegrates, is inconceivable. Even at the level of the individual organism, there are design solutions for decomposition. Seeds are attached to branches by a type of connective tissue that gradually dries out and weakens – preparing the seeds for detachment when the time comes.

What makes decomposition possible is the fact that nature makes do with a limited number of basic building blocks. Proteins and polysaccharides, for example, are used to create a wide range of substances whose performance often exceeds that of synthetic materials. For example, the giant squid, a marine mollusk that can reach 13 meters in length, was considered a creature of legend until it was spotted in real life in 2004. The giant squid has a beak that is more resistant to deformation than nearly all recognized metals and polymers. The beak serves as a tool for killing and tearing down its prey. Examination of its structure reveals that it is composed of protein and sugar, the last two materials one would choose to build an incredibly hard, stiff, and tough tool.[45] Even elements that are most essential in nature for sustaining life are few: simple compounds of carbon, oxygen, hydrogen, and nitrogen. The advantage is obvious. The fewer building blocks used, the higher the efficiency of construction and disassembly. It is much simpler to dismantle a system made up of a few repetitive building blocks. The technological world, on the other hand, is producing more and more polymers with various properties that are used to manufacture different types of materials. Polymer-based plastics are one of the most common materials in the world, but they take about 500 years to break down. When we transform the industry building blocks from petroleum-based products, whose functionality and ability to decompose are limited, to a substance like chitin, which provides a wide range of functions but also breaks down after use, the world will undergo a significant change.

• **Efficient versus inefficient design**: Organisms are designed and operate in a way that efficiently enables their continued existence while striving to maximize resources. The pursuit of efficiency is a shaping force in nature expressed in the clever use of shapes and structures:

1. **Straight lines** – Raise your head for a moment from the book and look at the room you are sitting in. Look at the leading lines and angles in the space. Technological structures and systems are characterized by straight lines and right angles, but these are very rare in nature. Instead, in nature, we find curves and spirals. The fact that there are no straight lines in nature is no coincidence. Curved lines have an advantage of flow and load alleviation, which translates directly into energy savings. For example, shells are shaped in spirals adapted to the flow regime (water movement) of their habitat.

    Spanish structural engineer and architect Santiago Calatrava applied this principle to the design of skyscrapers, which are better adapted to wind regimes at high altitudes. In the skyline of Malmö, Sweden, stands its famous skyscraper, its design based on the form of a human torso (in a twisted form), where each floor is rotated relative to the previous one by about 1.6 degrees, and as a result, the building makes a complete 90-degree rotation. The design of a different building, the Chicago spire, which was never fully built, resembles a helical seashell.

2. **Surfaces** – While we strive to manufacture smooth surfaces in the engineering and technological world, surfaces in nature are not smooth even if they appear to be. The lens of a microscope will always reveal protrusions, tiny denticles, cavities, hair, and more. The reason for this is simple. Surfaces in nature are functional, matter is connected to structure and function, and there is no structure that is useless. In nature, you can find surfaces that clean themselves, repel dirt, deter bacteria, repel water (hydrophobic), or attract water (hydrophilic), repair cracks, increase light absorption, and more. For example, the Nepenthes pitcher plant, a carnivorous plant that grows urn-shaped structures from the tips of its leaves. Ants that venture near the plant's rim fall in and get trapped inside with practically no chance of escaping since the walls are especially slippery. Engineers at the Wyss Institute at Harvard University studied the plant to understand what makes the leaf's walls so slippery. They found that the slick coating is caused by microscopic ridges on the surface

that lock in moisture, creating a thin water layer on the surface. Researchers adopted the idea and created a synthetic coating by infusing a micro-structured porous material with a lubricating fluid. The surface is so smooth that it even repels crude oil and liquid asphalt. The research has matured into the development of a technology that creates ultra-smooth surfaces, a technology with extensive potential for applications, such as surfaces that are antiseptic, remove chemicals and liquids, prevent corrosion, get rid of pests, and more. The trade name of this development is SLIPS technology.

3. **Multifunctionality** – Structures in nature have several functions, because this is more efficient than producing several separate structures, each of which provides a different function. An architect once told me about a design exercise he used to give his students: the students were asked to design a system that included a long list of functional mechanisms found in trees, without mentioning the word 'tree' or implying any connection to it. The overwhelmed students didn't know how to cope with the complexity required for this design. After experiencing mild frustration, he revealed that this system exists and is very common in our world. It's difficult to think about an engineering system that performs so many functions – and here it is in nature.

Benyus provided a beautiful example of multifunctionality in her TED talk, *Biomimicry in Action*.[46] A chip bag is composed of several layers, each made from a different material and each with a different function: one for keeping out moisture, one for sealing in oxygen, one to provide mechanical strength, and one as a surface for printing ink. In contrast, a "package" in nature, such as an insect's cuticle (i.e., exoskeleton), is composed of one substance – chitin – which is common in nature and has many functions. It provides exoskeletal strength; it is light, flexible, and perforated; it allows penetration of air but not water; it is colorful, changes hues, and ultimately bio-degrades.

Materials in nature have a number of functions. For example, hippos secrete a viscous, rust-colored, fatty substance called 'hippo sweat,' even though it's neither sweat nor water-based. This secretion not only cools the hippopotamus but also serves as a sunscreen, an antiseptic, and insect repellent! The fluid allows hippos to spend hours in water, protected from the sun and from airborne pests. And if injured, due to being territorial and aggressive animals, it also protects them from potential infection.

I heard a beautiful example of the multifunctionality of materials in nature from Boaz Mizrahi, a biomaterials researcher at the Technion. There are about 20 different ingredients in a paracetamol pill which has one functional purpose: to reduce fever. Nature doesn't use so many materials to produce one function. On the contrary, one substance in nature can provide 20 functions.

The concept of a multifunctional structure or material points to nature's economical and efficient design paradigm, while engineering thinking is more oriented toward breaking down the system into required functions and designing each function separately with assigned components.

From Living Organism to Machine

In the past, people built structures that resembled living organisms. These structures were developed in response to climate or topography, and they could change their shape when necessary and regulate temperature and humidity. As is the way of nature, different forms of structures developed in different places, just as plants and animals vary from region to region: for example, an igloo built from snow bricks in the frigid north or cooling towers in the desert heat. In the 20th century, when technology was considered a symbol of progress, the metaphor that dictated the design paradigm changed – from structures that resemble living organisms to structures that resemble machines.[47] The metaphor of a machine implies exploitation of nature and solving problems through force and energy, and is conceptually linked to a system that affects the environment rather than lives in harmony with it.

For example, modern buildings are similar to each other even though they are built in different countries, climates, and cultures. Technology makes it possible to detach buildings from their surroundings and provide climatic comfort. Technological systems, just like buildings, are also associated with the metaphor of a static machine, which strives to provide functions even at the expense of the environment through considerable use of material and energy resources.

With the growing awareness of nature's solutions, humans are starting to return to the old metaphor, which represents nature's design qualities: systems that resemble living, emerging, and dynamic organisms, that function as part of their environments and are efficient in extracting material and energy resources. It is nature, in fact, that is being identified with progress and leading us toward a new future.

PRODUCTION PROCESSES IN NATURE

Animals produce biominerals under natural conditions,
without furnaces and pressure devices used in laboratories.

Boaz Pokroy

As a child who grew up in Haifa and the daughter of an indus-
trialist who founded a metal factory in the same city, the
pungent smell that wafted through the air during the descent
from Mount Carmel to the industrial zone in the bay is forever
burned in my mind. This scent signaled to passersby that they
had arrived at an industrial zone. For me, the factory experience
was a sensory one: the sounds of the giant presses and CNC machines producing metal parts – bending, crushing, and processing, the smells wafting from the coating tanks, the sight of paint
splashing every which way in the paint booth, and the heat I felt
as I approached the furnaces used for thermal treatments.

The term 'plant,' which is synonymous with factory, supposedly stems from its biological connotation. This dissonance between a polluted reality and pastoral nature may evoke a sense
of contradiction. On the other hand, nature's factories certainly
deserve the title 'plant.' For example, the process of photosynthesis. This is one of the most sustainable production processes.
It is executed at ambient temperature, without the need to apply
heat or pressure. The process uses clean energy from sunlight
and water – both renewable resources. The process also uses carbon dioxide, which, being a greenhouse gas, would have caused

damage had it remained free in the atmosphere. The product is energy stored in bonds of carbohydrates: the primary energy source that serves all life systems. No pollutants are emitted in the process, on the contrary – the byproduct is oxygen which is necessary for life. Production processes in nature are different than those in the industrial world and invite us to look at the cleanest, shiniest production floor in the world.

Production in Living Environments

Industrial zones are usually located far from population-dense areas in order to distance civilians from any negative repercussions. Sometimes they are sent to the ends of the world, to underdeveloped countries where environmental awareness and regulations are low. Out of sight, out of mind. Unlike industrial production, which takes place in areas that are isolated and removed from residents and the living environment, production in nature takes place in the living environment. Organisms live inside their own production plant. They can't operate polluting and aggressive production processes that harm the environment for the simple reason that if they do, they will not survive. They themselves produce the materials necessary for their own existence – in their bodies, in their environment. These materials often surpass fabricated materials in their abilities and functional qualities, even though they were produced in a living environment.

Organisms also produce structures from elements in their environment. For example, chalk is a common material in nature used in construction. In its raw form, chalk is a weak, soft substance that is easy to crack and break, and it seems that engineers wouldn't choose it as a building material. But "nature's manufacturing plants" work with the materials available, combining different strategies to strengthen them. These strategies are very different from the production paradigm in the industrial world since they occur in living environments. This means giving up three harmful and polluting, energy-intensive means of production: heat, beat, and treat – as coined by Janine Benyus – referring to heating up materials, beating them with high pressure, and treating them with chemicals.[48]

How does nature produce without heating up materials?
I have already mentioned spider silk as a strong and flexible material that arouses great interest among scientists and researchers around the globe. The strongest fiber of the web is dragline silk, which is primarily used as frame threads and web radii, and it may also be used for evading predators. The "production plant" for web spinning is located within the spider's body. The raw material is a liquid protein produced in specialized silk glands located in the spider's abdomen. From there, the liquid passes through narrowing tubes and extrudes through six spinnerets located on the spider's underbelly. The protein liquid turns viscous upon air contact. With the claws on their feet and the help of tiny hairs, spiders turn the fibers into a web with a resulting thickness that doesn't exceed a few microns. This web is created in a living environment and doesn't involve a heating process. By comparison, steel, which has less tensile strength than a spider web of the same thickness, is manufactured in a process that requires heating to a temperature of about 1,200 degrees Celsius. If the spider had to heat its protein to a high temperature, it simply wouldn't survive.

Glass, like steel, is also industrially produced through a polluting process that involves heating to high temperatures. But glass structures in nature are synthesized sans heating. For example, sea sponges – ancient multicellular organisms that dwell mostly in saltwater – produce glass needles called spicules that range from a few microns to a few meters in length. The spicules provide the sponge with structural support, mechanical strength, and protection against hostile elements. Spicules are made out of silicon dioxide, a raw material used in industrial glass production, but while it is mixed with other materials and heated to 1,000 degrees Celsius in the industrial world, spicules in nature are formed at ambient temperature along organic filaments composed primarily of silicates – enzymes that catalyze the growth of silicon dioxide.

Emil Zolotoyabko from the Technion, a member of the research team studying the formation of spicules in sea sponges, used a key insight to summarize the process: "Using the crystalline axial filament, nature has mastered the fabrication of extremely complex glass structures at low temperature – a capacity that is far beyond the reach of current human technology."[49]

Brittles stars, also known as serpent stars, are marine organisms resembling starfish that also demonstrate production of strong material without using heat. Brittle stars have hundreds of micro-lenses on each arm that focus light on specific nerve bundles. These are essentially the eyes of the organism, according to Boaz Pokroy of the Technion. In a study he conducted with his team, they discovered that these lenses are actually uniquely tempered at room temperature without heating or cooling processes. Industrial tempering is carried out by heating the material to a high temperature, keeping it at that temperature for a while, and then rapidly cooling or 'quenching' it. In this process, the outer section of the material cools faster than the inside, thus compressing and hardening it. In a study on brittle stars, it was discovered that the critical phase in this process of lens formation is the crystallization stage, that is, the transition from the amorphous state (the phase between liquid and solid) to organized crystalline solids. At this stage, the difference in concentration of magnesium in the calcite particles (building mineral for the lenses) causes varying degrees of rigidity, density, and pressure in different areas of the material. These magnesium-rich zones press on the inside of the lenses as they crystallize, thus "tempering" it into a strong crystalline material. This is essentially the strategy for strengthening brittle material and increasing its resistance under natural conditions.

How does nature produce without high-pressure beating?
Abalones are marine mollusks whose shells are made from calcium carbonate, the same material that forms limestone. Despite the softness of this biomineral, shells become effective armor, due to a sophisticated structure that increases its fracture resistance 3,000 times more than other structures made from the same material. The shell consists of alternating layers of hard material (calcium carbonate) and soft material (protein), such that the pressure is absorbed by the soft layers and does not get passed on to the hard layers. In this way, the tendency to develop cracks decreases significantly, and the structure of the alternating layers gives the shell its strength. The result is armor whose strength approaches that of a layer of Kevlar, the material used by security forces to make bulletproof vests. This shell is also twice as strong as any ceramic material. Instead of breaking like ceramics, it warps under pressure like metal. If I drive my car over an abalone shell, it most likely won't be damaged, but if I drive over a piece of ceramics, it will likely break.

Ceramics are inorganic, nonmetallic solid materials that are used to produce a wide variety of products. Ceramic production involves applying pressure of 400–4,000 tons and burning it in furnaces at a temperature of at least 1,000 degrees Celsius, a process that consumes a lot of energy and pollutes the environment. Beyond the environmental issues involved in the ceramic manufacturing process, the product is usually brittle and of low strength, so its range of use is limited and unsuitable for structural applications. But while ceramics are produced through energy-intensive efforts of pressing and compression, in nature the shell's toughness is achieved through an elegant structural strategy, without the use of high pressure or destructive temperature. In order to improve the strength and reliability of ceramics, we must improve the toughness of its structure while reducing its sensitivity to cracks. Researchers at the University of California, Berkeley, developed shatterproof ceramics by adding a layered structure of aluminum oxide bricks, which mimic the tough calcium carbonate, and a polymer to fill in the spaces between the layers of aluminum oxide, which mimics the soft protein. This material can be used in any application that requires resistance to mechanical loads.[50]

How does nature produce without chemical treatment?

Blue mussels attach to rocks in coastal areas exposed to currents and waves, using a bioadhesive it produces that has a strength comparable to that of synthetic glue. The adhesive is produced in the living environment, without toxic chemicals, and forms the connecting threads that glue the mussel to the rock surface. If you have ever tried gluing a wet page to something, you have probably noticed that it is not an easy task, but mussels even stick to aquatic surfaces successfully. The secret behind mussel adhesion is an amino acid that causes the surface to overcome its preference for water molecules. Regular synthetic adhesives which lack this feature fail as wet-setting adhesives. Mussels are not attached to rocks forever. At some point the connective tissue decomposes easily, and then another organism can come and eat this connective tissue, which of course is not toxic.

Adhesives are essential and fundamental tools in many industries. During their manufacturing process, pollutants are emitted into the environment. Sometimes, toxins continue to be excreted from the product even after using the glue. For example, wooden furniture may contain adhesives that excrete toxins. Inspired by blue mussels, Purebond adhesive is nontoxic and water-resistant. Synthesis of the adhesive is based on modification of the amino acid composition in soy to match the structure identified in mussels. This adhesive has the potential to revolutionize the paint and coatings market. It can replace surgical sutures. Today, the solution is primarily being implemented in the timber industry and is used in the production of plywood for furniture.

Morpho butterflies flaunt colorful wings that look blue one moment and brown the next. Their ability to produce dynamic color is related to the multi-layered microscopic scales scattered on their wings. These scales diffract the light beams that hit them, reflecting only certain wavelengths. As the wings' angles shift, the reflected color does as well. Unlike ordinary color pigments that fade over time due to influence by solar radiation or dust hovering in the air, these tiny scales maintain their luminosity for many years and allow the butterfly to swap colors as a means of communication.

Like butterflies, peacocks and other iridescent animals synthesize physical color using nanostructures and demonstrate effective strategies for producing color without toxins. The paint industry is now considered one of the most polluting industries. Until about 150 years ago, all dyes (pigments), which affect the color of light through selective transmission and absorption, were made of natural materials such as clay, soil, plants, insects, and slug extract. Today, the use of natural pigments has come to an almost complete halt, and most pigments are produced from artificial materials in laboratories. Some pigments are formed by grinding various minerals, but most are made of metals ground into powder, some of which are toxic. The pigment production process also involves activities that consume energy and emit pollution, such as heating, grinding, refining, and exposure to acids. In addition to the fact that most pigments are toxic and polluting, pigment-based paints fade when exposed to the sun and cannot be dynamic like the wings of morpho butterflies and produce different colors at different points in time.

Using nanostructures that mimic the butterfly's wings, various companies have been able to produce dyes, fabrics, and even cosmetics free of toxic metals. For example, the Japanese textile company, Teijin, developed the world's first structural chromogenic fabric called Morphotex, which consists of different nanoscale layers and creates the same color illusion as morpho butterflies. The fabric was designed to produce a physical color and it appeared blue, though no paint was applied at all. The structural effect obviates the need for the chemical effect. L'Oreal developed cosmetic hues that are also based on physical colors and has achieved various effects such as shining and mirror effects. Perhaps in the future, we will be able to enter a house and change the color of its walls if we look at them from different angles, depending on our mood.

Production in Closed or Open Systems

Manufacturing processes in nature are characterized by production, consumption, and decomposition, which allow the structure of the material to be repeatedly recycled. In a natural ecosystem, the primary producers are plants, which take raw materials from the air, water, or soil and operate as a production plant for carbohydrates – the primary energy source. The primary consumers are herbivores, secondary consumers are predators, and finally come the decomposers, which break down energy remaining in the dead animals and plants and return the ingredients to the soil. The material flows through this production carousel-like system over and over again.

For comparison, the decomposition component is missing in

industrial production systems. These are open production systems that take resources from nature or industrial resources, use them, and release waste that does not return to the natural or industrial material cycles. What is buried underground as waste may go unnoticed, but it occupies valuable land space and can also be a source of hazardous noise or odor, and even pollution of air, soil, or water. Products which require a lot of energy and investment in resources are casually buried along with the value they could still provide. The "cradle to cradle" model offers a different design approach, which "closes" the circle and returns waste to the production system at the end of the process (for more details, see chapter "From Cradle to Cradle" on page 283).

Systems of industrial production that harness waste for manufacturing processes are more similar to production processes in nature. For example, cement is the second most consumed product on the planet after water. It is a product of heating limestone and clay to extremely high temperatures. In recent years, we have witnessed new methods for creating biomimetic building materials that are both more beneficial to the environment and stronger. These methods use the waste product carbon dioxide to create limestone or reinforce concrete, thereby reducing carbon dioxide emissions.

The biological process used as a model is the formation of calcareous sediment in a marine environment. The formation of limestone, which is also referred to as calcium carbonate (calcite), involves calcium ions and carbonate ions, the conjugation of which in a marine environment creates a sediment that does not dissolve in water. For example, this sedimentation reaction is how coral skeletons are formed. Carbonate ions produced by coral, using carbon dioxide and water, bond with calcium ions that naturally dissolve in seawater. This interaction takes place on the exterior of the polyp – the coral's living body – so that over time, a thick sediment of limestone forms around it.

Examples of solutions offered by various companies: Fortera uses the excess carbon dioxide emitted during the regular cement production process from cement factory kilns to create limestone. Blue Planet developed mineralization technology that extracts excess carbon dioxide from any source in any concentration to produce building materials. Carbon Cure injects excess carbon dioxide directly into concrete during its production process, strengthening the concrete and removing the carbon dioxide from the atmosphere.

Even if these are still small amounts, the trend demonstrates industrial treatment processes of carbon dioxide waste and waste in general. This trend is based on emulating the functionality of ecosystems, which operate efficiently and in a balanced way. Attempting to follow the path of nature and use waste as a resource leads to innovation in the world of production.

Natural Capital – Nature's Free Services

Nature provides many services such as air and water purification, waste decomposition, wildflower pollination, climate regulation, sanitation, soil creation and conservation of its fertility, nutrient recycling, conversion of solar energy to organic compounds, and more. The value of these services is significant and they have no technological substitute. They are considered free services, but clearly have economic value, even if often complex and impossible to quantify.

Production processes in nature, that are based on optimal use of energy and material resources, preserve the value of natural capital. Industrial production, on the other hand, exploits abundant natural resources while not taking their true value into account. In the book *Natural Capitalism: Creating the Next Industrial Revolution*,[51] the authors posit that there is a misconception surrounding market-based principles of natural capital.

The global economy depends on natural resources, but industrial capitalism doesn't recognize their capital value. Labor is considered valuable while natural resources are considered cheap. According to the authors, the actual costs of natural resources should be included in the cost equation of production processes, and the value of natural capital – which has great economic value, some of which is irreplaceable – should be recognized.

Bottom-Up vs. Top-Down Production

Nature creates from the bottom up, from building blocks that join together. Just like a game of Lego, you can construct different combinations from them, and assemble or disassemble them quickly and efficiently. Construction here is modular, so there is no wasted material and surplus. For example, termite nests – impressive structures relative to the size of the organism building them – are built from grains of soil attached to more grains of soil through intensive, collaborative work. In contrast, the manufacturing world has top-down production processes that yield products from blocks of material and leave waste and surplus. Metalworking and electronic cutting are examples of such manufacturing processes.

New manufacturing technologies such as 3D printing enable bottom-up production, similar to systems in nature that grow according to the requirements and characteristics of the environment. For example, the generative design studio co-founded by Jessica Rosenkrantz, an MIT lecturer with a double major in biology and architecture and a master's degree in design.[52] Work in the studio does not include conventional processes such as drawing, sculpting, or modeling, but rather developing software for developing objects from building blocks, similar to nature's production process. One of the studio's projects, in collaboration with the sportswear brand New Balance, is the development of a running shoe midsole, which allows variable density cushioning as a function of the pressure level. Like wood or bone, which grow according to strain maps to build reinforcement using minimal material, the 3D-printed midsole resembles a spongy structure with varying cavities. The distribution of material is adapted to the load data of different runners' feet. When biology and architecture meet, design principles from nature, such as generative design, are realized in the field of design.

Just-in-Time Production vs. Production for Inventory

Biological systems produce when there is demand. The spraying mechanism of the aforementioned bombardier beetle, which sprays liquid at a temperature of 100 degrees Celsius when attacked, is an example of a production process that occurs on demand. The production plant of the sprayed substance is a tiny organelle in the beetle's abdomen that is only about a millimeter in size. The organelle functions as a combustion chamber in which an exothermic (heat-producing) chemical reaction takes place, controlled by muscles and a unique valve. The beetle controls the time of production, and in fact the material is only produced when an attack occurs. Sea cucumbers also respond in real time to threats by emitting long tubules that, upon contact with water, immediately turn into a sticky fibrous mass that immobilize predators and makes it difficult for them to attack the cucumber. The tubules are discharged only when necessary, in response to a threat.

The concept of on-demand production has also been adopted in the industrial world as a method for lowering operation costs and reducing inventory. The method is called just-in-time inventory and aligns the timing of raw-material orders with the production phase, and the timing of production with the supply phase. Each item reaches the customer as soon as they need it – leaving no need for storing high-cost inventory. The method was developed and perfected at Toyota as part of its manufacturing philosophy. The opposite approach, just-in-case inventory, advocates storing sufficient inventory to meet maximum market demands. However, it is complicated to apply the just-in-time inventory method in any production environment, especially when the environment is diverse and replete with different types of products.

Pure or Impure? That is the Question

Are we obsessed with pure materials? "Our manufacturing processes are based on the idea that our materials need to be 100% pure. But in nature, everything is a mixture of materials," argues John Warner, CEO of the Warner-Babcock Institute for Green Chemistry.[53] Not only are materials impure in nature, but every natural environment is characterized by a multitude of species, and it is precisely this diversity that produces resilience and strength.

Viktor Schauberger, an Austrian forester and philosopher, described this insight in simple terms: "A healthy forest, untouched by forestry technology, is made up of a strange mixture of vegetation... A great deal of sensitive concern and observation is necessary to begin to understand why nature depends on an apparently chaotic disorder."[54] It is actually the mixtures in nature, the combinations and fusions that create a stronger whole.

A New York materials company called Ecovative adopted the idea of mixing existing with natural materials, and inspired by this natural model, proposed using mycelium as a substitute for plastics and polystyrene foams for packaging, building materials, and other applications. Mycelium is actually the body of fungi, resembling thread-like branches growing in organic matter or soil. It has a very large surface area relative to its volume, which allows it to absorb food efficiently. The fungus, nicknamed "nature's glue" by Ecovative co-founder Eben Bayer, naturally binds ingredients and can grow and fill any shape.

In a manufacturing process developed by the company, mycelium is added to wood waste, and the fungus begins consuming and binding the fibers together. This piece is later compressed and turned into a board that can be used as a substitute for chipboards. The process eliminates the need to use formaldehyde – a dangerous chemical component found in industrial adhesives to bind wood fibers in the manufacturing process of chipboards. Another use of mycelium is combining it with crop waste, such as corn stalks or husks, in a cast mold which suits the required packaging form. As the mycelium grows, it binds to the waste fibers and becomes a solid mass that fills the mold. Following heat treatment that arrests the growth process, the material is removed from the mold and the designed packaging is ready for use. Today, packaging for bottles is produced using this method. Although mycelial fiber production takes longer than conventional fiber, the process can reduce the total cost of packaging production by about 30%. In 2018, IKEA announced that it would replace its polystyrene packaging with Ecovative's biodegradable mycelium packaging as part of the company's efforts to reduce waste and increase recyclability.[55]

Nature's production paradigm is based on the fact that production is part of the living environment, thus it must sustain life without heating, beating, or treating with chemicals. Such production respects natural resources, is based on a mixture of materials that create resilience, and is executed in a timely manner without leaving excess and material waste. The paradigm expresses a sustainable ethos that leads to sustainable innovation – yet another reason to learn from nature.

Sustainable Innovation

*We need to learn how to work with nature
rather than against it.*

David Attenborough

I recall being a young couple without children moving into a large, empty house. We still had nothing to fill the rooms with. In one room, we put a mop, in the other a broom... but soon the voids filled up pretty quickly. The birth of our children also brought materials, primarily for the children's bedrooms. Korean photographer, JeongMee Yoon, began photographing American and South Korean children in their rooms with their toys in a project dubbed 'The Pink & Blue Project,'[56] which featured a gender preference for colors. But beyond the color differences, when the son in the photo sits in a pile of blue toys and the daughter in a pile of pink toys, they are so swallowed up by the mass of toys that it takes time to recognize them... The reality is that the majority of toys have an average lifespan of six months. And not just toys. Apparently, 99% of the products we buy get trashed within six months.[57]

If we let nature design our children's playrooms, they would most certainly look different: more varied in color, since diversity is a value in nature, more harmonious, and much less cluttered. The toys that nature would choose to put in our children's playrooms would be durable and offer long-lasting pleasure, would evolve along with the child's maturity, and adapt to their needs.

Why Learn about Sustainability from Nature?

At the top of the list of humanity's 21st-century challenges is the demand for sustainable development. There needs to be a fundamental change in the way we think, plan, manufacture, consume, and end the life of our products. Nature is an excellent source of knowledge and inspiration for innovation in general and sustainable innovation in particular. Many of the challenges concerning humanity have actually already been resolved in nature: how to find, store, and transport food and water; how to protect against pests; how to cope with changes in weather and diseases; how to move efficiently from place to place; how to communicate in groups; and more. Species in nature do so in a way that does not harm their natural environment nor the chances of future generations to exist. Structures and shapes in nature provide a wide range of features with minimal use of material and energy resources. Production processes in nature take place in living environments, and all this is done within the limitations of life on Earth.

An Updated Snapshot

In order to capture an image of sustainability today, we need to collect a lot of pixels to understand the overall picture. These pixels are warning signs that are seemingly unrelated to each other, when in fact, they indicate a trend of unsustainable design and management among human society.

Modern society is still completely dependent on oil and fossil fuels, which cause greenhouse gas emissions. These emissions are considered the cause of the average rise in temperature of about 0.7 degrees Celsius in the world since 1980[58] (it should be noted that there is also a minority opinion claiming that global warming is unrelated to emissions); today's extinction rate is much higher than the natural baseline rate; air pollution is the greatest threat to public health and causes "silent deaths;" and global waste is constantly on the rise.

United Nation (UN) reports published in 2019 indicate human activities causing direct damage to land and water resources, such as construction, deforestation, agriculture, and over-exploitation of animals for food and raw materials. Alongside population growth, which has currently reached eight billion people, there is also a rapid increase in per capita consumption, such that resources and ecosystems are in decline, while the demand for them is growing. Inefficient and wasteful use of resources, along with damage to ecosystems that maintain these resources, may leave future generations and even ourselves with insufficient resources. Although nature has self-repairing mechanisms, such as plants and bacteria that can break down pollutants in water, when the water is over-polluted, the ecosystem gets overloaded, and the pollution stays put or is cleared at too slow a rate to reuse the water.

The combination of all these pixels – the extinction rate, emission levels, habitat destruction, air pollution, increased waste generation, ecosystem damage, and more – indicates that we are currently on an unsustainable trajectory. These pixels have also been documented by the camera lens of nature photographer David Attenborough for many years. In his latest film, *A Life on Our Planet*,[59] he delivers a personal testimony on the ongoing damage to ecosystems, which he witnessed during his 70 years as a naturalist and filmmaker. But this film is also an optimistic will, indicating the possibility of change. Just as humans possess the power to destroy, they also possess the power to repair. UN reports also estimate that it is not too late.

Humanity stands at a crossroad, in a window of time that requires correction. "We need to learn how to work with nature rather than against it," said Attenborough. We need to learn from nature how to design, build, and exist in a way that fosters resilience and prosperity. Then the pixels that make up the picture of sustainability will shift.

Design Failure

The fact that there is an island of garbage in the Pacific Ocean twice the size of the State of Texas containing plastic debris and other waste is indicative of poor design. The fact that a significant amount of all garbage in landfills is disposable diapers, which take up to 500 years to decompose, is a design failure. Someone calculated that if we spread all these diapers over an area half the size of the State of Israel, we would be stepping on a diaper with every stride.

In many apartment buildings, residents suffer from a myriad of physical symptoms including headaches, eye irritation, dry cough, itchy skin, difficulty concentrating, fatigue, and exhaustion. This problem is known as "sick building syndrome." It is believed that around 30% of the buildings in the world are the focus of tenant complaints. But it's not the building that is sick, it's the design that is lacking. These buildings may feature design failures in air flow, access to natural light, proximity to radiation, exposure to toxins, or formation of bacterial colonies.

Following the journey of a can of Coca Cola takes us on a trip spanning many months and countries, where in each one, a different stage of the production process takes place: quarrying the bauxite; transporting it to an aluminum oxide refinery; processing the oxide into ingots; pressing and preparing them for production; perforating the cans; washing, painting, coating, and filling them with Coca Cola liquid; and packaging them in cartons. Ultimately, it takes three days on average for one can of Coca Cola to get sold, a few minutes to drink, and one second to throw away. We use raw materials that took millions of years (iron, coal, and oil) or decades (wood) to form, process them over several months, distribute and consume them within days, and post consumption, it takes them anywhere between a few days to hundreds of thousands of years to decompose.

In nature, we won't find massive islands of harmful and non-biodegradable waste, "sick" buildings, or continent-wide manufacturing processes that use matter and energy in excessive and illogical ways. "Design is the first signal of human intention," said William McDonough, one of the founders of the cradle-to-cradle design strategy. The failures described above are indicative of an industry that is short-term, resource-focused, and operates on the erroneous assumption that they have no limitations.

• **Short-term**: Focusing on a narrow window of a product's chain of impact on its environment leads to a narrow view, one that does not take the product's long-term health and environmental implications into account. In nature, we won't see structures or processes that produce long-term damage to their environments. I came upon a cartoon once that explained the folly of short-term thinking quite simply: It depicted a man stuck in a deep pit. There is a wooden ladder in the pit that can save him, but he decides to dismantle the rungs of the ladder instead and use it as material to light a fire and keep himself warm. A Native American proverb expresses a similar idea: "The frog does not drink up the pond in which it lives." It will reserve its living space for tomorrow, for others.

• **Resources and growth**: Economic growth today is based on resource consumption. In order to grow, more and more resources are needed. This notion is presented in simple and elegant terms with the analogy of the Impossible Hamster.[60] From birth to puberty, hamsters double their weight every week. If they didn't stop growing at some point and continued doubling in size each week, they would reach monstrous proportions within a year and would be able to eat an entire year's worth of corn in a single day while still remaining hungry. There is a reason why things in nature grow to a certain size. Is resource consumption the only way to grow?

• **The cylinder illusion versus the funnel reality**: The Natural Step organization points to a false perception of reality: On the one hand, the population is growing and the demand for natural resources is growing with it, and on the other hand, available resources are being depleted. In practice, this is the reality of the funnel closing in on us – as demand increases, supply decreases – but we live under the illusion that reality is more like a cylinder in which the amount of resources remains forever constant. This illusion prevents us from operating like a sustainable society, one that exists over time in balance with the limitations of the natural system.

The design failures described above are associated with an industry that is a product of the industrial and technological revolution and not a product of the sustainability revolution. Though the situation today is improving and industrial changes are evident due to awareness and regulations, the road to redesigning the industry is still long. The path to change lies in the ethos. When the intention changes, the signal expressed in the design will also change. When the ethos is the ethos of nature, design will be sustainable.

Riding the Waves of Innovation

Innovation waves occur when a connection forms between a clear human need and a critical mass of technologies that can address that need. The Natural Edge Project has thus far researched and identified six waves of innovation that began with the Industrial Revolution.[61] Today we are in the midst of the sixth wave of innovation, driven by an urgent need for sustainability. The existence of this wave is also reflected in the Investment Map. Investments in technologies that address sustainability and climate challenges are on the rise, reaching an all-time high. At the political and social level, this need is met by environmental regulations and social movements aimed at reducing environmental damage and consumption. At the technological level, a critical mass of technologies related to life and environmental sciences have emerged which can address our sustainability challenges. Alongside green chemistry, nanotechnology, renewable energy, and industrial ecology, biomimicry is also regarded as a knowledge base leading the sixth wave of innovation: sustainable innovation.

Nature offers a wide range of solutions for various challenges in the core environmental fields: energy, matter, and water. Inspired by models and mechanisms found in nature, technologies for environmental challenges have been developed. For example, algae, which are not called "green gold" for nothing, have served as a source of inspiration and knowledge for developments of solutions in energy harvesting, smart material production, and wastewater treatment.

• **Energy – Nature as a model for energy efficiency**: Giant brown algae (Bull Kelp) can be found on ocean shores. Their impressive size is difficult to ignore. These algae reach lengths of about 30 meters, from the seafloor to near the water's surface. They produce energy through photosynthesis, like all plants, and thrive in spacious zones. Bull Kelp possess a unique structure that includes a strong and flexible stem-like organ called a stipe, and at its lower tip a holdfast, that allows the algae to anchor in soil; leaf-like organs or blades attached to the upper tip of the stipe whose shape allows currents to pass through them;

and gas bladders that function as floats that keep the algae upright and close to the water surface. The movement of algae in sea waves served as a source of inspiration for the development of a solution for harvesting wave energy. BioWAVE is a flexible, elongated system balanced by buoyant 'blades' attached to the end of a 'stem,' similar to algae. But unlike algae, under harsh wave conditions, the buoys balancing the extended stem in water are emptied, the mechanism sinks to the bottom, and as the storm passes, it reassembles again. A BioWAVE pilot project designed to produce 250 kilowatts was launched in 2016 off the coast of Australia, but technical difficulties ensued.[62] Perhaps one day, when the technology matures, wave-harvesting farms will be deployed in oceans.

• **Material – Nature as a model for producing smart materials:** Algae adhere to various surfaces, such as rocks and ships, and are capable of doing so in environments of strong forces such as tides or the drag force resulting from ship movement. Algae doesn't detach from these surfaces thanks to an adhesion mechanism based on the materials they secrete, which are resistant even under wet conditions. For years, Havazelet Bianco-Peled of the Technion studied the adhesion mechanism of algae. The Israeli start-up Sealantis was founded in 2007 following the accumulation of knowledge about this biological adhesion mechanism. The company developed a protein-free, biocompatible tissue adhesive that reduces the chance of infection or allergic reactions and does not require transportation or refrigerated storage. The adhesive is intended for a wide range of medical indications – for example, to prevent leakage of intestinal contents, as a surgical sealant in orthopedic surgeries, and to prevent blood leakage during reconstruction of large peripheral blood vessels. In the beginning of 2019, this technological achievement was translated into a business achievement, when the company was acquired by the British company Advance

Medical Solutions. The adhesive is currently based on Alginate, a natural polymer produced from algae, so the development is still considered biotechnological, while the inspiration behind the development came from nature, with the goal of imitating the attachment mechanism of algae.

• **Water – Nature as a model for balancing and purifying water sources**: Algae are known for their ability to assimilate nutrient pollutants such as nitrates, phosphates, and ammonia, the accumulation of which, when found in bodies of water intended for drinking, poses an environmental and health hazard. Algae ingest pollutants as food, grow as they consume them, and release oxygen into the water during photosynthesis. Can this ability be mimicked to purify bodies of water? Diverse purification technologies today are attempting this. For example, the Algal Turf Scrubber® (ATS) is an algae-based water purification system that absorbs excess pollutants from the water. After the algae grow, they are removed from the growth surfaces that were placed in bodies of water, and are used as raw protein-rich material. It turns out that assimilating nitrogen increases protein content in algae. The growing algae serve as food for fish and perhaps in the future for human consumption, as well. They are also used to fertilize agricultural fields, eliminating the need to produce new fertilizer phosphates. Here, too, a component from nature, algae, is still being used to realize the solution, while the inspiration came from natural processes of water purification.

Sustainability as an Engine of Innovation

Working toward sustainable practices is not only a necessity in our reality, but it is an engine of innovation. Corporations and nations practicing sustainable development will find themselves at the forefront of the innovation wave, while those that don't take part risk losing market share. The demand for sustainability is beginning to change the rules of the competition. Companies will need to shift their line of thought around products, technologies, processes, and business models. Studies have shown that despite concerns among corporations about environmental policy, competitive fitness has not been affected. A study that examined sustainability initiatives in 30 large organizations in the United States indicated that sustainability leads to technological innovation. Contrary to the concern of corporations that sustainability will be an economic burden that will harm their competitiveness, improved business performance has been recorded, including streamlining processes, cost savings, improved products, penetrating new business niches, and more.[63]

THE STORY OF ECONCRETE: FROM UGLY CONCRETE TO A THRIVING MARINE ENVIRONMENT

In nature, nothing exists alone.

Rachel Carson

One of the most special moments in nature I have experienced in my life was diving near the coral reefs of the Red Sea. The unbelievable kaleidoscope of color, variety, and abundance – an entire world in itself of intoxicating tones, shapes, and movement. I went back recently to visit the depths of the Red Sea, many years after those moments were etched into my memory. I was disappointed to find that the colors were much less vibrant and the variety less rich. Did my memory deceive me or is the marine population actually dwindling?

One of the dangers to marine wealth and diversity is marine development. Approximately half of the world's population reside along coastlines. As a result, various infrastructures such as ports, desalination plants, power plants, breakwaters, and promenades are replacing natural beaches. Today, the primary material used to build around 70% of marine infrastructure is concrete, which is considered hostile to marine environments. Concrete is restricted in its ability to encourage biological recruitment, that is, to attract different species and serve as a substrate for their living environment. Very few species attach to concrete: it displaces the natural population and inhabits invasive species.

ECOncrete is an Israeli company that has successfully overcome this challenge through inspiration by nature. It develops concrete-based ecological solutions for marine infrastructures in a way that meets the engineering requirements of concrete while also serving as a habitat that supports marine environment restoration. The company was founded in 2012 by entrepreneurs Ido Sella and the late Shimrit Perkol-Finkel, both marine biologists. They summed up their vision in simple terms: turning "something ugly into something healthy and enriching" – turning gray, desolate infrastructure into a thriving and robust ecosystem serving both nature and people. Their mission is 'to build a future where marine ecosystems and infrastructure work symbiotically for the benefit of the environment.'

Observation and Wonder

Perkol-Finkel and Sella began working as a team to harness their extensive knowledge of marine ecology to aid industrial consulting processes. In their joint work, they were exposed to the issue of concrete and realized that existing infrastructure does not meet ecosystemic needs. On one occasion, they went diving and came upon a seaside wall of a power plant in the city of Hadera. They noticed that the concrete in a certain area of the wall supported a wider variety of species and featured more animal settlement. They inquired about the difference between this and other areas and received the following response: the wall was cast by the same contractor but at a different time, and the material composition of the cast mixture was apparently slightly different. They started brainstorming and looking into what is different about concrete that better supports biology. Could it be that a certain material got mixed in with the concrete that improves species recruitment but doesn't harm the concrete's engineering properties? The two set out to find a comprehensive solution: concrete that meets all engineering requirements and can be used for construction, but is also ecological. They founded ECOncrete and initiated R&D projects, during which they observed and learned from nature.

Imitating Nature

Biogenic buildup processes occur in nature, during which cal- careous skeleton-building animals such as oysters and coral set- tle on rocks and cling to each other in such a way that produces calcareous sediment or rock cover. Concrete covered in layers of calcareous organisms would provide substantial advantages in protection, strength, and longevity, growing stronger and in- creasing in lifespan over time. The reason is that after they die, their shells remain attached to the substrate and then the next generation of oysters, mussels, and other invertebrates settle on their shells, repeating the same process, so over time, a biogenic rock is formed. This process would contribute both to reinforc- ing the concrete and nurturing the population of organisms. The developers investigated why natural rocks serve as a good basis for settling oysters and coral and what helps them become habi- tats for additional animals, applying the principles they learned in developing a new type of concrete.

• **Bio-enhancing compositions**: In nature, rocks do not con- tain toxic elements. This principle was applied to create chem- ically-balanced concrete. ECOncrete developed a unique and patented concrete technology based on an additive supplied as powder to concrete manufacturers. The mixture balances the concrete's chemistry and neutralizes toxic chemicals, making the concrete more organism-friendly. Using this mixture also reduces the carbon footprint and byproducts created by the concrete production process.

- **Complex surface textures:** Surfaces in marine environments are not smooth. Rocks are coarse, and coral and oysters feature bumps, depressions, and grooves. Observing nature shows that certain species, such as oysters and barnacles, prefer settling on specific surfaces, such as coral skeletons, oysters, and calcareous algae, and even cling to their own species. Meaning, the surface's structural complexity is a significant factor in its ability to recruit species. This principle was applied at the micro level when designing the concrete's surface. ECOncrete developed technology that modifies concrete casting molds to create complex surfaces that mimic oyster and coral textures, which encourages rich, diverse species settlement in marine environments.

- **Science-based molds:** Sea rocks contain natural cavities that supply fish and other organisms with protected hiding spots and encourage biological recruitment. This principle was applied at the macro level when designing the concrete's surface. ECOncrete added tiny alcoves to the concrete units that mimic natural niches in rocks. These nooks become habitats and places to hide, breed, and nest, expanding the range and variety of species that settle on the concrete.

- **Optimal structure:** Biological structures are characterized by geometric parameters that produce optimal living environments. ECOncrete attempts to implement the optimal ratios found in nature while designing their concrete units, within industry standard limitations. For example, rocks in coastal areas and above sea level form natural ponds that serve as protected habitats for fish and other organisms. ECOncrete studied the concentration, height, temperature, salinity, and flow characteristics of water optimal for sustaining life in these pools, and designed pooling ponds located in breakwaters that hold water in the desired quantities and qualities needed to constitute

microhabitats without compromising on engineering requirements. "We advance toward the solution in nature and are held
back by industry standards," Sella described the design process
simply, where nature sets an optimal bar and the industry dictates the constraints.

Results

The solutions developed provide long-lasting concrete infrastructure, but also provides benefits for the ecosystem, such
as increasing biodiversity and adding biological niches. Maintenance costs are reduced thanks to the biogenic buildup that
provides additional protection. "The products act like natural rocks in the sea. They get covered in rich marine flora and
fauna without incurring the expense of quality infrastructure,"
Percol-Finkel concluded. ECOncrete was the recipient of the
prestigious Anderson Foundation Ray of Hope Prize® in 2020
for $100,000.[64] The prize is awarded annually to a single start-
up developing a nature-inspired solution with an environmental impact. This was the first time an Israeli company won the
prize, an award recognizing and appreciating the design process of learning from and giving back to nature – an ecological
solution that enables humans and nature to live in balance and
thrive side by side.

PART III

HOW?

OBSERVATION

"How wonderful it is that one can observe one tree in a forest
for hours – one leaf on the tree, one vein of the leaf –
with wonderful hours flowing and passing through the soul."

Janusz Korczak

One day, I drove to Aviel Spring. It was deserted. A vehicle suddenly stopped. A man exited the car calmly and quietly, walked over to the spring, removed his shoes, and began doing all sorts of obscure actions that looked like raking and then cleaning with the water. At one point, he took a bucket, pumped water, and went over to a small bush and watered it. He repeated this action several times and then sat down to rest on a chair, enjoying the sun.

"May I ask what you're doing?" I asked curiously.

"I adopted this spring. I come here every day. I planted cherry tomatoes for visitors to enjoy," he said, handing me a juicy, reddish tomato. "I also planted some trees that will provide shade for visitors in the future," he added. "I grew up by the sea, and I miss the water, so I come here every day."

Wow, I thought to myself, what a deep connection with nature and other human beings, so much generosity and love. I couldn't help but imagine how all of humanity once behaved this way. Humans were part of nature. They would venture out to a corner of nature in the morning, really get to know it, nurture it, and create a thriving and nourishing connection with nature.

Having a deep connection with nature in ancient times was also a mode of survival. Since the dawn of time, nature's cycles and phenomena have determined the way of life. Hunter-gatherers needed to know when the fruit would ripen, when it would rain, and when it would be a dry year. The ability to predict the future was required to manage life and called for deep observation of nature and the stars. I have always been amazed by the ancient people's knowledge of astrology. On display at Berlin's Museum of Prehistory and Early History is a stunning gold hat covered in symbols, dating back to 1,000 BC. The symbols were used to predict the state of the sun and moon, and whoever wore the hat performed astronomical ceremonies.[65] Ancient Egyptian priests used what's called a nilometer to measure the Nile River's water level, which they used to compute the levy of taxes: during drought years, when the Nile was low, and during times of flood, when it was high, a lower tax would be imposed due to low expectations of agricultural yields. I can imagine how being one with nature in these ways, motivated by an intense yearning to be near it, leads us to observe and learn from nature.

Even today, in the modern and technological age, there are still delicate threads connecting us with nature. We yearn to be near it and sense its positive impact on our mental and physical well-being. Nature enhances the sense of connection. When we are in a relatively empty spot in nature, we are more likely to greet a hiker crossing our path on the trail. The chances of us greeting that person on a busy street are close to zero. This attraction to nature has even earned itself a name of its own: biophilia (bio = life; philia = love or affection), a concept describing the basic need to be part of nature and in contact with living systems. When near nature, humans feel a sense of well-being and elation.

Biologist Edward Wilson popularized the term 'biophilia,' which later encapsulated a number of practical recommendations: the Japanese recommend forest bathing, Israelis recommend sunbathing, and there are places in the world where doctors even prescribe their patients to go out into nature.

During the Corona period, many people rediscovered nature. The natural landscape near my home suddenly became a highway – I have never seen it so bustling with life. When the physical world closes in and shuts down, the soul remains open in nature. Aaron David Gordon, a Zionist thinker who promoted the agricultural movement in Israel, said that "nature renews the works of Genesis at every moment, and constantly acts on the human soul." Particularly during the days of COVID-19, which had many of us feeling stuck, there was great value in connecting to qualities of change and renewal.

The affinity we have for nature is a good start for learning and finding inspiration. If we want, a forest bath can also be a bath of wonder, a sun bath can also be a bath of inspiration, and we can self-prescribe going outside into nature as hunters and gatherers and view it as a model, measure, and mentor. Observation is the first stage that supports the process of unveiling biological models, the starting point of bioinspired innovation.

Where and When to Begin

When we first moved into our new home that is near a natural environment, we trimmed the tall vegetation that closed off the garden. I remember the excitement of seeing the natural space suddenly coming into view, like a beautiful face revealed after a haircut. But on this pretty face, directly in our line of sight, was a black telephone wire. Its presence was unpalatable, until one day a pair of kingfishers landed upon it. Since then, our beautiful and gentle neighbors have been returning each year, sitting atop their telephone cord and nesting in one of the holes in the nearby fence. Little by little, our acquaintance is deepening. Like any good neighbor, they invite us over occasionally to dine with them on a lizard or caterpillar they've managed to capture. They, or perhaps their descendants, have been coming back for over a decade, and when they do, I am happy about their presence and that of the black telephone wire – my means for communicating with nature.

In order to enjoy nature's inventions, one must look for a way to be in touch with them, to notice their existence. Just as we do not expect to find a patent without entering the patent database, we cannot expect to discover inventions without entering nature's database. Dr. Seuss's advice fits best here: "The places you'll go!... You'll be seeing great sights!" and you don't have to travel far. You can also look at small, nearby things. Look nature right in the eye. Once upon a time, I traveled to Central America. I got up in the middle of the night to go on a night hike with a group of trekkers in search of a giant sea turtle that was expected to lay eggs. We wandered around for a few hours, not knowing whether we would find her or not – and finally, we did manage to see her laying a huge egg in a large hole. Where I come from, everything is smaller – even our turtles are smaller. But it is no less exciting to meet them on their first journey to the sea and ask questions: How do they know where to go? (they detect the bright light reflected off the foam of the waves). What are their chances of successfully completing the journey and surviving to adulthood? Their chances are extremely low.

Most of us tend to wait for the right moment to connect with nature: to wait for a time when we can go on a "real" vacation in nature, travel far away, reach a popular nature reserve, fly to a safari that will bring us face to face with rare encounters we cannot see in everyday life. But the truth is that nature is everywhere: in our backyard, in the planter on the window, in the bird's nest on the tree in front of the house.

Henry David Thoreau, an American writer, poet, and philosopher who lived during the 19th century, was curious about nature's knowledge and engaged in the study of flora and fauna through observation. In a book he wrote titled *Walking*, he comes to the conclusion that it is possible to be a nomad without even leaving home: "He who sits still in a house all the time may be the greatest vagrant of all; but the saunterer, in the good sense, is no more vagrant than the meandering river, which is all the while sedulously seeking the shortest course to the sea."[66]

Reconnecting with nature can begin here and now, quietly, even without wandering afar. If you cannot reach nature, let nature reach you. Pay attention to information, articles, and nature films that reach you in abundance. Let them be the initial stimulus that ignites your curiosity and motivates you to continue learning and exploring.

The Art of Observation

In the past, humans dwelled in nature and lived off the natural environment. Today, observing nature can lead to a reconnection with the natural world, enabling us to learn from it and uncover its solutions. In general, observation is a state of mind which can be practiced. In order to observe nature in a way that connects us to its wonders, a number of basic insights and qualities are required.

• **The insight that we are all part of nature**: It is often easy to forget that we too are organisms – we are alive like animals, grow like plants. We are complex and sophisticated organisms that have developed technological capacities expanding our human abilities, and often use nature for our benefit – but we are first and foremost organisms, part of a diverse and natural network of individuals that nourish one another. Jane Goodall, who has been observing chimpanzees in nature for years, says that observing them has sharpened her understanding that man and the animal kingdom are one. In one of her lectures, she said: "There isn't a sharp line dividing humans from the rest of the animal kingdom. It's a very fuzzy line."[67] The more we observe nature, the more the dividing line between us will blur. A consequence of investigating nature is our connection to it.

• **Sensitivity**: An important quality for observation is sensitivity. When you observe with sensitivity, you see the ripening process of fruit, which looks a bit different today than it did yesterday, you notice fluctuations in a lake, and the differences between raindrops: there are drops that are large and heavy and there are those that are small and delicate. "Have you ever watched a raindrop?" asked the Indian philosopher Krishnamurti, "The raindrop contains the whole of the rain, the whole of the river, the whole of the ocean. That drop makes the river, makes the ravines, excavates the Grand Canyon, becomes a vibrant thundering waterfall."[68] And the nature photographer Doron Horowitz said: "In the subtleties of hue hides the soft part of things." To some extent, sensitive observation is meditative observation – it enhances awareness of small details and is a catalyst for creativity.

Reuben Margolin is a kinetic artist who creates sculptures that explore mechanisms of locomotion in nature. He focuses on flow and motion phenomena in nature, such as single water droplets or powerful vortices, creating elegant and mesmerizing kinetic sculptures. He doesn't try to copy nature, but instead relates to it and reflects its qualities: the intensity of whirlpools in nature, the delicacy and magic of a drop hitting water, or the scattering of waves formed when a pelican lands. Margolin reports that the most exciting stage of his work is just before the wave he designed and created is first activated. He is always curious to know if the wave he sculpted will be interesting, flowing, and beautiful... as in nature.

Sensitive observation allows us to identify subtleties and

differences, which can also allude to vital functional information. For example, this is exactly what is required in the field of zoopharmacognosy – the science of animal self-medication where humans observe animals to discover potential remedies.[69] As we are aware, plants possess high healing potential, but how do we know which plants to study in a medical context? By peering into nature's pharmacy with sensitive eyes. Animals use different plants to heal themselves. For example, studies on chimpanzees have shown that before chewing a medicinal plant, they roll the leaves, swallow them while grimacing, and tend to eat them on empty stomachs in the morning. In this way, we can identify plants with medicinal potential as opposed to plants used only as food sources.

• **Patience and perseverance**: two other qualities important for observation. The film *My Octopus Teacher* [70] depicts a rare relationship between a human and an octopus, documented daily by cameras. Every day, for about a year, Craig Foster, a film producer who grew up off the coast of South Africa, returned to the ocean to meet an octopus. He actually accompanied her for about 80% of her life, slowly and gently gaining her trust. Some of the film's most moving moments show the octopus reaching for Foster's hand, and later lying down on the producer's bare stomach. Foster explains that by returning to the same place in nature every day for a year, he was able to truly see nature, notice the subtleties, understand the language, feel as though he is a part of it and not just a guest. He behaved like a researcher and detective in nature, exploring the connections between different organisms, exposing them and gaining an understanding of the delicate balance in the marine ecosystem. Patience and perseverance paid off. Foster was able to gain knowledge and insights that no scientific-academic study has reached, and even documented dramatic moments in which the octopus intelligently and cunningly manages to subdue a shark attack. Life is happening in nature all the time and isn't waiting for a camera lens and our attention. Nature cannot be staged.

Foster, who became a permanent resident of the octopus's habitat, also managed to document some fascinating mechanisms related to biomimicry:

- Octopuses have a huge number of suckers that may even reach 2,000. Their complex nervous system can manipulate their suckers in a coordinated manner.
- They can regrow their tentacles if amputated. Apparently, they have the ability to grow organs.
- They can change the color of their skin rapidly, just like an actor undergoing a costume change.
- They use tools: Foster's first encounter with the octopus was when he noticed a puzzling clump of shells moving in front of him which turned out to be protective armor that the octopus had donned herself in.

At a certain point, Foster began to wonder what motivated the octopus to bond with him and concluded that their relationship offered her stimuli to develop her intelligence. A fine example of bioreciprocity. We all need kindness, and perhaps we have more in common with the animal kingdom than we think. In one of the most moving scenes at the end of the film, the octopus is even seen playing with a school of fish.

Goodall, who studied chimpanzees in Tanzania in the 1960s, led the longest continuous field study of any living creature. She said it took her around six months (!) to form a sense of security among the chimpanzees. She almost gave up when they began approaching her. The first was a curious adult male, and the rest followed. Her observations led to conclusions about chimpanzees' intelligence, "humanity," curiosity, and even cruelty, but she says that she not only learned *about* chimpanzees, but also *from* them. Goodall said that by observing and being near one of the chimpanzee mothers, she herself became a better mother to her son. Motherhood is yet another thing we can learn from nature.

• **Hushing our wisdom**: Another important quality of observation is "hushing our wisdom" so we can hear the "wisdom of nature." Goodall was chosen for the study specifically because she had no scientific background. In fact, she was the assistant and secretary of the scientist who received the research grant, and he chose her for the task because of her curiosity, tolerance, and love for animals. The fact that she arrived without scientific knowledge, without previous assumptions, gave her the opportunity to observe from a quiet and humble place.

The ability to be an empty vessel waiting to be filled and the understanding that we don't know – are basic conditions for learning in any field. Even Socrates confessed, saying, "I know that I know nothing."

Sushi masters in Japan must first observe for many years to acquire the precise traits required for preparing sushi. The trainee works as an apprentice for years, observing the work of the talented master and occasionally experimenting with elements of the art. In Japan, sushi preparation is considered an artistic practice. The person undergoing training is not regarded as a cook or chef but a master, an honorary title equal in social prominence to a lawyer or doctor. Even after their training period, masters continue observing, in order to ensure a sushi experience that is difficult to measure, similar to a sensory experience evoked by a work of art.

When it comes to learning from nature, the idea is to leave everything we know and have learned aside and to look on with modesty, attentiveness, and openness to what nature brings forth, from a deep understanding that we have much to learn from nature and out of appreciation for its wisdom. This type of observation will yield revelation and wonder.

"If you approach nature with a dismissive attitude, it will close its doors to you. If you show it respect, it will take you on a dreamy and riveting journey," said Roie Galitz, who practices nature observation as a photographer.[71] Nature photographers must also blur the line between themselves and nature, immerse in it, employ patience and perseverance, observe with sensitivity, modesty, and respect. The art of observation will lead photographers to capture the drama and exciting moments in nature through their camera lenses, and will lead us to capture the exciting inventions of nature through our technological lenses.

Practicing Observation

There are many different ways to practice observation:

• **Explore like children:** Pippi, the protagonist of the beloved children's book series, *Pippi Longstocking*, defines herself as a 'thing-finder' and naively describes a worldview usually adopted by children. She explains to her friends that a thing-finder is "someone who finds things! The world is full of things and there's a crying need for someone to find them,"[72] and the three of them go on a search. Children act in nature as though it's a playground or laboratory. They are intrigued, wander around, and go searching for things. Every find becomes a treasure. They stoop down to the ground, lie on top of it, peek about, approach things, climb trees to see what's going on at the top, and earnestly push their way into burrows and caves.

They pick up slugs to find out what's leaving those marks and disassemble pods to discover their insides. Children observe and ask questions just before everything becomes obvious, just before the curiosity dissipates.

• **Switch perspectives:** Trees look different from below. In dense forests, one can discern gaps between trees that allow light to penetrate to the lower levels of the forest floor. Looking up, these patterns of light trails form a striking spectacle. This phenomenon is named 'crown shyness,' perhaps after the modest yet noble act of bringing light to others as well, and perhaps because the paths of light adorn the treetops like a crown. We have a tendency to see what is in front of us. What is above or below our line of sight becomes invisible, but with every switch in perspective, more details are revealed.

• **Neutralize some of the senses**: Neutralizing one sense increases the sensitivity and range of information received by the other senses. Being blindfolded in nature inspires many insights: suddenly you pay attention to the direction of the wind, the angle of the sun, the textures of the trees. Trees that until now seemed identical suddenly feel different to the touch: one has an eye and a protrusion while the other does not, one is very rough and the other is smooth.

• **Go off the beaten path**: Life in nature occurs outside the main trails, outside the paths where everyone else walks. Main roads are noisy, replete with disturbances and threats, and animals avoid them. A good way to get closer to nature is to reach its beating heart. Get off the beaten paths and trek the small ones, those created by animal traffic. It is worth spending time there, patiently observing and noticing new and intriguing phenomena.

• **Notice patterns**: Patterns are found everywhere in nature and are expressed in repetitive motifs of shape, size, color, position, and more. If we ponder their existence, we will discover design adaptations to environmental conditions and challenges. This is how, for example, pebbles are formed in nature's "stream factory" – where they receive their rounded shape and slippery surface. Areas exposed to heavy wind feature trees with thicker trunks and more complex root systems to anchor them to the ground. In beautiful lupine fields, flowers that have already been pollinated have a different shade. The change in color communicates to pollinators which flowers have already been fertilized, so that they can reach flowers that still require their services.

One can observe a pattern of gradual growth among squill plants: the flowers woven along the flowering stem gradually open from the bottom up. Each day, a new group of flowers blossoms, and the previous one withers. This growth pattern indicates a strategy of dividing the blooms in time to maximize the chance of encountering a pollinator.

• **Let nature get close to you**: Yoina lives in the rainforest. Every day, she goes swimming in the nearby river with a tamarin monkey on her head. She was documented in an award-winning photo presented at an international nature photography exhibition held each year by the Natural History Museum in London and the BBC.[73] In her tribe, when monkeys carrying infants are killed, the tribespeople raise the infants as pets and later release them. The tamarin hated being bathed and spent most of the time on Yoina's head, away from the water. Little Yoina let the tamarin monkey approach her and sit on her head in the simplest way. Although the natural tendency of all of us is to shy away from being in close contact with animals we are unfamiliar with, there is value in this closeness, whenever it is possible and while maintaining precautionary measures (*see 7).

• **Flirt with uncertainty**: In one of the seminars I took, I had a supervisor who refused to tell us the names of the plants and trees we were studying. Natural phenomena were also left with a question mark and we were sent home without answers. I recall the discomfort, frustration, and even anger I initially felt with this teaching method. I understood the importance of the question, but for me, learning was a duo dance of questions and answers. I wasn't yet familiar with the solo dance of asking and answering questions myself. I had become accustomed to finding answers externally, in studies that had already been done, because what is the point of asking questions that have already been answered by well-established and tested research?

The crux lies in self-exploration, in the ability to glean knowledge from ourselves and by ourselves. Not knowing creates doubt, but what doubt closes, a question mark opens. It arouses vigilance, encourages an enquiring mindset and motivates us to investigate and uncover the answer. Going out into nature without knowing, with question marks instead of exclamation points, will allow you to discover what you didn't even know how to ask.

• **Use artistic or technological means**: Seeing images of wildlife in nature immediately makes me think of the effort that is required to memorialize the encounter. I can literally imagine the photographer lying for hours in a burrow, fusing into nature, attempting to eliminate their presence to allow the animals to get near. Perhaps they are silently praying for that perfect moment which they can freeze forever. But nowadays, we no longer have to stand for hours on end in uncomfortable and challenging positions to capture an awaited moment through a camera lens. The tools through which one observes today make it possible to draw nearer and move farther away, as well as document a passing moment and observe it later calmly, under zero pressure. Today, there are even portable microscopes that we can attach to our phone's camera and magnify objects and structures in nature. They make it possible to see what is not visible to the human eye.

As for painting or drawing nature, one need not be a professional artist. Freehand painting and drawing actually heighten attention to detail. Suddenly, as the hand moves on the paper, you feel the contours, pay attention to skin spots, a protruding bone, the shape of the joint. This type of observation averts the eye from looking at the whole to looking at the parts and zooms in like a camera lens. Using methods like photography, painting, or drawing can improve the experience and quality of observing nature.

• **An alternative handbook**: Another tool for observation that doesn't exist yet but that I dream of, is an alternative handbook for plants and later, an alternative handbook for insects, butterflies, and mammals, as well. In the new world of deep connection to nature, the traditional plant handbooks we all grew up on no longer satisfy. Although they are important since they organize the information in an orderly and accessible way, they address nature from a distance, leave us to struggle with unusual plant name pronunciations, and make nature seem distant and irrelevant to our lives. Naming a plant places an exclamation point and blocks us from getting further acquainted with it, often turning it into a some*thing* instead of a some*one*.

Viewing nature as a driver of innovation leads us to connect with nature in a new way: the question isn't what plant this is, but who is this organism we are looking at, which challenges exist in its life, and what strategies does it use to solve these challenges. The alternative handbook, which is actually a non-handbook, will answer these questions. Why classify? Let's get acquainted.

Observation as a Mindset for Innovation from Nature

While working on my doctoral dissertation, I was asked to mention the gecko's attachment mechanism. I approached Keller Autumn, a German researcher who studied this phenomenon, and requested permission to use the picture of a gecko's foot that appears in his works. His response surprised me. I expected to receive permission to publish the image, as is customary in the world of scientific writing, but was instead directed to a website with spectacular pictures of gecko feet. "Choose from here," he said, and for a moment, I was confused as to whether he was a gecko researcher or photographer? And then it hit me

– he is both. First and foremost, he is a gifted scientific researcher trying to understand the gecko's attachment mechanism, but
through many years of exploratory observation, he apparently
also developed a sensitivity to beauty and aesthetics, to nuanc-
es. Or perhaps he always possessed this sensitivity and it helped
him become a better researcher? Either way, I chose a spectacular image and thanked him for it and for his insight into the
connection between exploratory observation and sensitivity.

Exploratory observation is detective work where you search
for clues while aiming to understand the thing being observed.
The exploratory eye will notice the unusual, the repetitive pattern, the functions. Just as a writer gathers inspiration from
stolen words, from listening to conversations, from random encounters kept in storehouses of inspiration, and one day pulls
them out to weave together a tale – observing nature helps us
gather inspiration and functions that can one day be used for
innovation processes. Observation invites us to read the book
of nature and walk among its pages. During peak moments of
contemplation, we can momentarily pause on one of the pages
and feel the sense of wonder. In these moments, we will identify extraordinary phenomena in nature with great potential
for innovation.

WONDER

Never neglect an extraordinary appearance or happening.

Alexander Fleming

When I was young, I traveled to Africa, equipped with an old-fashioned camera and a huge curiosity for the expected animal encounters. One day, I saw a pair of colorful grasshoppers mating on a local boy's palm. The colors stunned me, as if extracted from a psychedelic trip – radiant, out of this world. They stood out even more vividly against the backdrop of the small hand that held them. I photographed the moment, documenting the awe and beauty, confident that this was a rare moment of a rare species on the palm of a rare child's hand. From that moment until the end of the trip, I never again encountered these grasshoppers.

When I arrived home, I excitedly handed over my film to be developed. I was waiting to see that picture in particular, to see if the magic of the moment had been preserved. The picture did not disappoint, and I thought that its place should be on the cover of one of those nature magazines, at least. Why should only I enjoy this beauty? I enlarged the picture and it hung in my office for many years. I tried to research and understand who it was that I met, who these beautiful grasshoppers were and whether they were actually rare. I asked everyone I could, since Dr. Google had not yet been born by then, and I was left alone with the mystery.

Later, with the help of the internet, the mystery was solved. I conducted an image search and found them. I discovered that they are the most common grasshopper species in Africa and that these colors are especially noticeable during courtship. I must say that I was not disappointed for even one moment. Until I met these colorful grasshoppers, the only fluorescent colors I had ever seen in my life were the highlighters I bought at the office supply store. For me, these grasshoppers will always be rare. They were the first to teach me what awe is, and how it produces an internal drive of research and discovery.

On Observation and Wonder

When we observe curiously, there comes a moment when we discover something rare, incomprehensible, and unexpected. A moment that focuses our attention ... a moment of wonder. Haim Shapira, a lecturer and multidisciplinary researcher, defined 'wonder' in one of his lectures as a peak of curiosity. "A curiosity that grows should eventually reach an emotion called awe."[74] The slope of curiosity rises to a peak of awe, much like our eyebrows raised in amazement as we marvel at something. Awe is actually the moment we leap from cognitive activity (exploratory observation) to emotional activity (awe).

Wonder is a feeling of amazement, astonishment, and awe. It is associated with enigma and magic, and often even miracles. Awe faces us with what seems impossible. Therefore, awe is associated with situations of uncertainty. We don't really know how to interpret what we just saw, what caused it, and what it means.

Moments of awe are primordial moments, moments of discovery. For example, the first time we saw what Earth looked like from space, the moment a new continent was discovered, the moment we laid eyes on an animal which humans had never seen before. I remember the awe I felt as a child the first time I saw squirrels roaming outside like stray cats. Until then, I perceived them as animals one would only encounter in fairy tales, or perhaps zoos. Years later, I met people who were surprised to see cats roaming free here in the streets of Israel. On the surface, it seems that everything has already been discovered, when in fact there are many more moments of genesis waiting to occur.

Moments of awe are also moments of identifying the extraordinary, when something we thought was impossible is happening before our eyes, such as the magic of a mentalist or juggling acrobats contorting their bodies in ways that make us hold our breath, or maybe even skip a heartbeat. At the base of all awe lies tension between what is known and familiar, and what exists in reality. We didn't think the mentalist would know what we were thinking about or biographical details about our past, and yet here it is, written in a locked box opened up before our astonished eyes.

As a child, I loved flipping through the *Guinness Book of World Records*, through people's highest achievements, and I couldn't believe my eyes. There were those with rare traits and skills, and there were also those who reached these achievements through immense effort. What was impossible even in my imagination became possible in reality. Nature's Book of Records is no less riveting than the *Guinness Book of World Records*, presenting features and mechanisms that are simply unbelievable. For example, some species of froghoppers can jump up to 70 cm in height, a noteworthy leap for such a tiny insect; rhinoceros beetles can carry 30 (and some species 100) times their body weight – impressive physical strength in relation to their body size; and polar bears can smell their prey from several kilometers away, exhibiting an excellent sense of smell over long distances. Like the *Guinness Book of World Records*, Nature's Book of Records is constantly being updated, as research and new discoveries progress.

The Role of Awe

Awe as an emotion has occupied emotion researchers around the world, who have tried to understand what happens in the brain as we experience it, what are its evolutionary and social roles, and what behavioral and psychological benefits it provides. " Awe is what moves us forward," said Joseph Campbell,[75] an American scholar and author whose work has tackled various aspects of the human experience. But how does awe advance us and to where?

Beau Lotto, a neurobiologist and author at the University of London, explains that the experience of awe actually rewires the brain and allows us to deal with situations of uncertainty that otherwise cause paralysis and fear.[76] It is awe that removes us from a place of stagnation and restores movement. Like a re-boot button on a computer, "holding our breath" in a moment of wonder also removes any fear in situations of uncertainty.

In order to explore awe as a profound perceptual experience, Lotto teamed up with the masterful creators of awe – the Las Vegas Cirque du Soleil – which puts on awe-inspiring shows. The study recorded the brain activity of people watching the performance and identified changes in the brain state that occurred during experiences of awe. For example, there was increased activity in brain areas associated with creative thinking, removing barriers to action and open-mindedness.

When we buy tickets to attend Cirque du Soleil or mentalist performances, we merit much more than two hours of pure pleasure. We pay for the experience of awe. But you don't have to go as far as Las Vegas to feel it. The experience of awe is everywhere. In works of art, in the objects around us, in the people we meet, and, of course, also in nature. We can also find awe in the small things and use it as an engine that creates movement in our lives, that extricates us from states of stagnation and fear, and that gives us the courage to dwell in the unknown until we do know or until the next moment of awe.

First Sense of Awe – Childhood

Awe is an innate force and important life skill, one that leads to discovery and invention. The childhood stories of the greatest inventors and researchers are filled with events of awe. Richard Feynman, winner of the Nobel Prize in Physics in 1965, wrote in his book, *What Do You Care What Other People Think?*[77] about the place awe had in his childhood. He describes an encounter with a bird who behaved in a puzzling manner. Feynman's father drew his attention to a bird facing backwards, pecking at its feathers. The young Feynman assumed that the feathers got messed up during flight and that the bird was pecking at them in order to straighten them out. The father suggested that they look at other birds that had just landed to see if the hypothesis was correct and that these birds would actually comb their feathers for longer. The father and son watched the birds as they were landing and came to the conclusion that there was no difference between the birds that had just landed and the other birds in how much time they took to peck at their feathers. Only after the father aroused awe in his son and gave him tools to test his own hypothesis did he agree to tell him the answer: the birds were suffering from lice which were eating flakes of protein from the birds' feathers and by pecking at them, the birds were trying to remove the lice. This is an example of being in awe of a behavior in nature that began with a small bird and ended with a Nobel Prize.

Suzanne Simard, a Canadian forest ecologist, also spoke about her roots of awe which are related to other roots she was exposed to as a child. In her TED talk, *How Trees Talk to Each Other*,[78] which has received millions of views so far, she recounts how her awe as a child sparked her scientific curiosity.

Simard grew up in the forests of British Columbia. She would lie on the forest floor and look up at the treetops, sharing her curiosity with her grandfather. The "aha" moment occurred one day in the outhouse by their lake. Her dog slipped and fell into the pit, and her grandfather hurried over with a shovel to rescue the dog. Simard watched her grandfather dig through the forest floor in an attempt to reach the dog, and was fascinated by the roots that later turned out to be mycelium—the fungal webs connecting the red and yellow mineral layers to the trees. The dog was rescued and a scientist was born that day. Simard realized that the exquisite palette that stood out with its colors was the true foundation of the forest. When she got older, she studied forestry and assumed that trees were connected to each other by an underground network of mycelium. She even proved it in a series of experiments: mycelium is a network connecting different players in the forest, as well as different species, and just like the internet's invisible web, it is used to transmit material and information.

Curiosity and awe even in childhood contribute to the maturation of researchers, scientists, and inventors. "Every child is an artist. The problem is how to remain an artist once we grow up," said Pablo Picasso, and I will add that every child is also a researcher, a scientist, and an inventor; every child is born with the tools of curiosity and awe. The question is how to preserve them as we age.

Awe within Reach

World explorers and naturalists have always exhilarated me. They journeyed for years on end, undergoing hardships and upheavals, being at the mercy of the sea, all to collect artifacts, understand and explore nature. Only deep wonder and a strong desire to explore the unknown can explain these journeys. I remember that as a child, whenever I received a homework assignment that required searching for information, I would visit the public library. It involved considerable effort. I rode the bus for about half an hour, scoured encyclopedias and books for information, used coins to operate the photocopier so I could have the material in my hands and process the research in the comfort of my home.

Today, information from all over the world, including latest research studies and incredible nature films which have been shot using unique photographic techniques, bring glimpses of nature that no naturalist had ever seen before, directly to our home screens. The process of observing, identifying patterns, and drawing conclusions becomes a much easier and quicker task. Naturally, there is no substitute for the stimulating and awesome experience of being in nature, but it is definitely a way to make information accessible and accelerate processes of innovation.

Researchers and inventors who explore nature's inventions often mention that one of the most exhilarating things about this type of research is that inspiration is all around us. We are surrounded by wonderful nature. Some animals possess qualities that arouse awe, that are perceived as impossible, and spur an intense desire to understand how they work. William Parker is a researcher of Thorny Devils,[79] a type of lizard that lives in the Australian deserts and resembles a walking thorn. Spiny bumps jut out from their bodies in every direction, between which are channels for absorbing dew drops that fall from the plants they dwell under. And then the miracle happens: the droplets climb up the channels against gravity via capillary action directly into the lizard's mouth – an unusual survival mechanism in arid deserts. Parker spoke about his experience spending time in nature as a biomimetic researcher: "I could look through here and find 50 biomimetic projects in half an hour [...] I try not to walk here in the evening, because I end up getting carried away and working until midnight..."

Formulating Awe Question:
BIO-WOW questions

"Philosophy begins in wonder," said Aristotle, who dealt extensively with imitation and representation of nature and understood the importance of awe or wonder as a driver of gaining
wisdom. At the beginning of my journey in the world of biomimicry, I coined the term 'BIO-WOW,' which describes the moment
when a miraculous feature in nature is identified: a phenomenon that contradicts our expectations of the world, our work
assumptions, and the way we think. Identifying the moment
of wonder and formulating the BIO-WOW question sparks the
process of bioinspired innovation. A barking dog probably won't
excite you. The fact that a dog can smell from a few kilometers
away is sure to pique your interest. But if you are told that a
dog can detect the presence of cancer cells in the air it breathes,
here you will surely reach a peak of awe and excitement at this
wonderful trait and the ability to harness it to benefit humans.
This is exactly what aroused the curiosity of Hossam Haick of
the Technion, who developed an "electronic nose" that identifies early-stage cancer biomarkers from a sample of the patient's
breath. Inspired by the incredible mechanism found in dogs, the
electronic nose detects patterns of volatile organic compounds
released by cancer cells.

Alexander Fleming, known for discovering penicillin in 1928,
was actually researching an infection that causes influenza at
the time when he noticed an unusual phenomenon. Mold developed in one of the petri dishes he was using to grow bacteria
in the laboratory, and a bacteria-free ring formed around it. His
awe at seeing the clean ring led him to investigate the properties
of mold as a bactericide and identified penicillin – the first antibiotic discovered. "Never neglect an extraordinary appearance
or happening," said Fleming, describing the importance of wonder in the face of the extraordinary in the process of invention.
Many bioinspired inventions began with a BIO-WOW moment

and the formulation of an awe question. Here are more examples of awe questions that led to research and innovation.

• **Bacterial resistance:** The BIO-WOW question – *How do insects contend with bacteria without antibiotics?*

Developers of the Jerusalem-based company Omnix Medical noticed an incredible phenomenon: insects exhibiting bacterial resistance – one of the greatest medical challenges of the 21st century – without antibiotics! It is well known that bacteria adapt quickly to antibiotics and that this resistance poses a serious threat to public health. Scientists Moshik Cohen-Kutner and Niv Bachnoff set out to investigate how insects contend with bacteria sans antibiotics. Apparently, insects are also susceptible to disease-causing bacteria, but their immune system manages to destroy them through a rapid release of antimicrobial peptides (proteins composed of a small number of amino acids) to the area of infection. These peptides cause physical damage to the bacterial cell membrane: they form pores in the membrane and kill the bacterium. It has been shown that bacteria do not develop resistance to this physical damage in the evolutionary arms race. Although these peptides are unstable in nature, Omnix Medical has developed a patented technology that enables the synthesis of stable, soluble, and safe antibacterial peptides. To date, a number of antibacterial compounds have been developed, and it will be possible to develop more according to therapeutic need in the future.

• **Anti-icing surfaces:** The BIO-WOW question – *How does ice not accumulate on penguin feathers?*

Temperatures in Antarctica can plunge to minus 90 degrees Celsius, and yet the penguins that live there don't freeze thanks to a number of traits that make them superhydrophobic. Pirouz Kavehpour of UCLA's Department of Mechanical and Aerospace

Engineering grew interested in penguin feathers after watching a nature documentary. He recounts the moment of awe he felt while watching it: "I noticed the penguins were coming out of very cold water and sitting in very cold temperatures, and it was curious that no ice formed on their feathers." This awe question led to a study in which penguin plumes were found to contain tiny pores that trap air and make the surface extremely water-repellent. When water gets on their feathers, the droplets roll down or are shaken off by the penguins, and ice formation is prevented. This feature can be used in future applications to prevent ice from accumulating on aircraft wings. "It's a little ironic that a bird that doesn't fly could one day help airplanes fly more safely" Kavehpour concluded.[80]

- **Skeleton construction:** The BIO-WOW question – *How do freshwater crabs build exoskeletons in a matter of days?*
Yossi Ben was a farmer who reared blue crayfish on a unique breeding farm in southern Israel. He noticed that the crayfish grow new exoskeletons in just a few days – a puzzling phenomenon given that there was no calcium abundant in their freshwater habitat. Marine crabs molt their skeletons at sea and take a month to build new ones. How is it possible that crayfish, which are exposed to low calcium levels, manage to build new exoskeletons so quickly? This strike of awe led to a study at Ben-Gurion University in which transient calcium deposits called gastroliths were discovered on both sides of the stomach walls of crayfish. Before they shed their exoskeletons, crayfish concentrate calcium in these deposits. As the molting process begins and they require more calcium, the gastroliths are dropped into the stomach acid where they quickly dissolve, and within just a few days, these large sources of calcium get absorbed through the intestine to the rest of the body and skeleton. The calcium is stored as amorphous calcium carbonate (ACC), a calcium salt

rarely found in nature due to its high instability. However, once successfully stabilized, this salt features unique chemical and physical properties that offer extremely high bioavailability and absorption of calcium compared to other calcium sources. Following the discovery, the Israeli company Amorphical was established, which imitates the production process of amorphous calcium and currently develops calcium supplements that have the advantage of being better absorbed in the human body.

The Story of Awe:
On Cobwebs and
One Wild Carrot

In every walk with nature,
one receives far more than he seeks.

John Muir

With every nature outing or encounter with texts, films, or data about nature, one can practice the art of awe. The following are two stories of innovation that began with wonderful interactions with nature – the first, in a scientific journal and the second, in a blossoming field.

Ornilux

In the late 1990s, Alfred Meyerhuber, a bird-loving German attorney, read in a scientific journal that spider webs reflect ultraviolet (UV) radiation to prevent bird collisions. That's when his camera caught an unusual feature in its lens of wonder. Spider webs blend into the natural environment and appear transparent from a distance, such that they are difficult to notice when moving quickly in their direction. Birds could easily fly into them thereby wasting the precious proteins and energy invested as they were spun, but they notice the ultraviolet radiation emitting from the webs since they can see in this range and therefore do not crash into them. A simple, smart, and sustainable solution.

Meyerhuber was an entrepreneur. He didn't just put the article down and go back to living his life. He realized the connection between the solution he identified in nature and a major challenge being faced by his good friend, Arnold Glas, the owner of a veteran glass manufacturing company in Germany. Hundreds of millions of birds collide with glass-covered structures every year. They see reflections of trees and the sky in the glass and crash into it. Glass manufacturers all over the world were searching for a solution to prevent these collisions without compromising the aesthetic appearance of glass.

Meyerhuber was also a fan of the value that guided his friend: "Doing things differently." Here was an opportunity to take a different approach, to solve the collision issue, and create a competitive advantage in the market. The initial strike of awe led to research aimed at applying the principle of collision prevention identified in nature to glass production. The human eye doesn't see in the ultraviolet range, so an ultraviolet coating can be imprinted on glass with no harm. Since people will not notice it, the appearance of the glass will not suffer any aesthetic damage.

The research team examined different types of coatings and patterns and found that a coating with a UV-reflective mesh pattern is more effective than coating the entire surface without this pattern. The contrast between the UV-reflective mesh screen and the background appears to be a significant factor. And then the question was asked, what would the screen look like? Printing a screen that directly resembles a spider web is extremely complex and difficult to implement. The team sought out to find the minimum number of lines on the screen that would be useful in reducing collisions. The first product, ORNI-

LUX, was released in 2006 and consisted of vertical lines only. Three years later, an improved version was released with lines reminiscent of randomly scattered sticks.

The development involved many experiments with wind tunnels showing that the window with protective coating indeed significantly reduces the number of collisions (birds were recaptured pre-collision). Effectiveness of the solution was also tested in the real world. Glass installed at a polar bear exhibit at a Munich zoo prevented bird collisions, and visitors could continue observing the bears undisturbed.

A major breakthrough in the solution's application occurred when the issue of bird collision entered the American Green Building Standard (LEED). Urban planners, municipalities, and architects are becoming more and more aware of the danger of birds colliding into buildings and are aiming to implement the requirement of bird-friendly glass facades during stages of design.

Carrota

One day, I was standing in front of a field of wild carrots, a plant identified primarily by a black dot in the center of its white inflorescence. Some of the flowers were closed, some were fully open, while others were at their halfway point, partially opened. I saw that the blossom was "placed" on a system of stiff stalks connected to the central stem, similar to the structure of umbrella ribs, only inverted, more flexible, more plentiful, and based on several flower clusters. I approached the plants and thought to myself that there was an interesting opening and closing mechanism here and that something had to be done about it. This moment of awe will be etched in my memory for many years to come, waiting patiently inside the idea drawer until the time comes to open it.

One day, I heard about the "Shade Aviv-Yafo" competition organized by the Tel Aviv-Yafo Municipality. Climate challenges and
global warming are increasing the need for shade, and the demand for shade in urban public spaces is on the rise, especially
in hot countries including Israel. The Tel Aviv-Yafo Municipality
announced a competition for shading solutions at three traffic
light intersections in Tel Aviv to provide shade for those waiting at crosswalks without endangering passing vehicles. I immediately recalled the wild carrot and already imagined people
entering under its wings and taking refuge under its shadow. I
approached two friends – an architect and a mechanical engineer – and suggested that we develop a shading system concept
inspired by wild carrots to be presented at the competition. We
named the system Carrota, after the wild carrot, and began researching. In the initial stage, we examined the wild carrot under a biomimetic lens in terms of an awning system that opens
and closes in a fascinating and dynamic way, and identified several analogies between the plant and the shading system.

- **Strength**: The central stem is hollow for strengthening purposes and to preserve material.
- **Dynamic system**: The inflorescence is connected to a system of stalks, each with a degree of freedom to move up and down on its own. The stalks are coordinated in such a way that they either spread out or fold up. A shading system that applies the principle of separate clusters – each connected to a beam with individual degrees of freedom – can produce dynamic shading: opening and closing parts of the awnings as needed. Using an appropriate algorithm, the system will be able to "lock" its shadow in the desired area, for example pedestrian waiting areas near crosswalks. Wild carrots, like any other plant, respond to seasons, light, and humidity. The shading system will also respond to changes in sunlight while offering a beam structure that will create optimal shading at any time of day.
- **Fractal structure**: The inflorescence which is analogous to the shading surface consists of small flowers separated by gaps organized in a fractal structure. Each inflorescence unit attached to the stalk resembles the flower as a whole and is itself composed of small flower clusters with exactly the same structure. A shading surface that will similarly consist of several separate units will allow air flow between the units and prevent the formation of heat pockets.
- **The art of shading**: When we looked at the shape cast by the shadow of a wild carrot, we saw a spectacular sight that reminded us of the art of shading. In our imagination, we saw a varied and dynamic game of shading taking place on the ground, a sort of different shadow "signature" for each position.
- **A source of energy**: The wild carrot, like any other plant, uses solar energy to survive. Our shading system will also operate using solar energy that will be used to move the beams, to provide lighting at night, and as an energy source to interact with passersby.

- **Point of attraction**: Wild carrots feature black dots in their center. The contrast between the black dot and white background attracts flies that pollinate the flower. In our vision, the shading system will attract passersby and will offer them technological "nectar" in the form of a charging station for cell phones, an information screen, and joy from viewing the shading art on the ground.

In the next stage, we contemplated how to apply these principles. We began with the skeleton, examining ways to create a similar structure of a central column with beams emerging from its circumference at different heights that can move independently. We quickly realized the complexity of such an engineering system and looked for a simpler and cheaper solution. We decided to consult with an origami expert, assuming that there are simpler ways of producing a folding and extendable system that does not exactly mimic the mechanism of wild carrots but can provide an alternative solution for dynamic shading. The origami expert introduced us to the work of John Edmark, a professor of design at Stanford University and origami artist. One of his works is Helicone, a kinetic sculpture consisting of rotating arms resting on top of each other.[81] Compared to the carrot model, where the arms move up and down, Helicone arms rotate around a central pillar. This seems simpler to implement while still being able to provide dynamic shading due to the ability of the rotating arms to alter their positions relative to each other. We set out with this design concept and were assisted by a group of architecture students to model the system and calculate its shading effectiveness.

The final design submitted to the competition included a central pillar crowned with a solar panel and floating lighting, with a number of rotating awnings similar to the Helicone. The height of the column and length of the rotating wings varied according to the required shading area. The degree of rotation for

each shading plane could vary, thus creating different shading shapes in different areas alongside a spectacular design façade. Control of the awning position and movement was supposed to be carried out using an algorithm to lock the shadow in selected areas. The system was equipped with technological nectar in the form of a touch screen with charging stations and a Wi-Fi connection, which can attract users and interface with them, and even serve as advertising space.

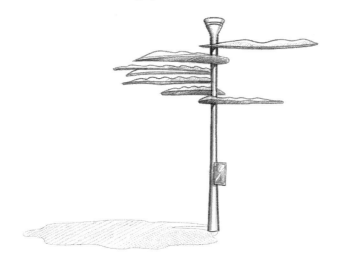

The process itself was a celebration of interdisciplinarity. We hopped between disciplines. We began with nature, devised a preliminary design inspired by it, met a production barrier, and visited the world of origami, where we found a simpler design solution. Just like in nature, we chose the simplest solution that still provides the benefit. Sometimes a structure in nature is too complex to implement. In this case, we can search for ways to design a different, simpler design that still upholds the principles gleaned from nature. The project was presented in the competition and won third place. So far, it hasn't actually been built, but since then, each time I meet with my project partners, we drink carrot juice together, just like we did during all the meetings in which we worked on the project.

HUNTER-GATHERER TOOLS
OF THE 21ST CENTURY

It is not enough to be busy; so are the ants.
The question is: What are we busy about?

Henry David Thoreau

In recent years, I have begun defining myself as a 21st-century hunter-gatherer. If the hunter-gatherers of ancient times went out into the wild to hunt for food and gather fruit, then hunter-gatherers of the 21st century go out into the wild to hunt for inventions and gather inspiration. Ancient hunter-gatherer tools must have been sharp stones, sticks, and hides for gathering fruit. Today's tools are thinking tools that enable focus and exploration.

We begin by identifying the starting point and continue by assembling the lenses of function and strategy, noting the biological hierarchy, and focusing on the level of imitation. Ever since I began exploring nature's reservoir of inventions with these tools, I have never stopped noticing inventions around me. Every organism is a walking function, every vegetative region is a field of strategies. This habit enriches my experience of being in nature and connects me to its reservoir of solutions.

The Starting Point

One can start the innovation process in biology, the reservoir of solutions, and in technology, the reservoir of challenges. Which one is easier – to pair a challenge with a solution or find a solution to a challenge?

Today, most reported innovation case studies begin with biologists identifying an interesting biological phenomenon and succeeding in recruiting engineers to aid in its research and imitation. To some extent, development of the field rests on these biologists having good luck in finding these "inventions" in nature and understanding their potential. But as time passes, the field becomes more methodological, the path from challenge to solution becomes more illuminated and straightforward, and we witness more cases of innovation that begin with the challenge. Below are examples of different starting points.

• **From technology to biology – challenge to solution:** A few years ago, a worker in the field of water technology approached me after he noticed that a lot of water gets lost during industrial cooling processes. He dreamed of returning this precious resource to the industry. He was searching for an elegant and efficient solution that could be integrated into existing manufacturing systems without interfering with operations. In this case, identification of the challenge by this worker was the starting point of the innovation process. After recognizing the issue, we set out to investigate condensation and water harvesting mechanisms in nature and came across natural design principles based on these models that were eventually incorporated into the proposed concept for solving the challenge.

• **From biology to technology – solution to challenge:** One day, a senior engineer at a leading defense contractor called me. He told me that he saw an amazing nature film that he couldn't get out of his head. The film shows a barn owl flying over a snowy area that manages to locate and hunt a mouse which was buried under the snow thanks to its well-developed sense of hearing. "That's what I want," he told me, "the barn owl's ability to detect an object from a distance, even when it's out of view." Identifying the barn owl's solution for object detection was the starting point of the innovation process. After recognizing the solution, we set out to investigate sensory mechanisms in nature that enable identification of hidden objects. We discovered miraculous and surprising systems, including the object localization mechanism of the barn owl, which we explored in depth.

Function and Strategy

After locating the starting point, we assemble the lenses of function and strategy, whose purpose is to identify the invention and help us understand it. In the world of engineering technology, functions are regarded as design targets. Engineers design systems to perform various functions. In biological systems, due to conceptions of evolution and religion, it is difficult to claim that a mechanism was designed or determined in advance, but we can determine what the biological system actually does and observe its functioning. Hence, use of the term 'function' in the context of biological systems refers to the actual behavior of the system and the action it performs.

Functions answer the **'what'** question. What does the system do? It refers to the benefit the system provides, to the function (action) of the biological system that one aspires to emulate. Strategy, on the other hand, answers the **'how'** question. How does the system perform what it does? What mechanism explains the observed action? In other words, strategy is the story that explains the observed behavior.

Function and strategy complement and nurture one another. Clearly, a function is meaningless if there is no strategy to execute it, and a strategy is meaningless if it doesn't strive to realize a specific function. As Thoreau once said, "It is not enough to be busy; so are the ants. The question is: what are we busy about?" Thoreau linked behavior to function, strategy to function. It is a link that creates meaning, and is explored in processes of bio-innovation. The function is the design challenge that concerns designers, while the strategy is the solution to this challenge found in nature. Take pine cones, for example.

• **Function (observed action):** the opening and closing of pine cone scales. During dry transition-season heatwaves in Israel, from May to June, you can hear the popping sound of pine cones opening. The dryness triggers the scales to open, giving the pine nuts a good chance to get far away from the mother plant with the help of wind. The farther the seed from the mother plant, the greater its chance of germination. If it rains, the scales will close back up and wait for their next opportunity with the next sirocco (hot dust-laden wind). We can observe this function by placing a dry pine cone into a glass of water. The pine cone will close up in about half an hour. After removing it from the glass, it will dry out and open up again (*see 8).

• **Strategy (mechanism of the action):** Pine cone scales consist of two layers, external and internal, which differ in their hygroscopic coefficient, that is, the amount of water adsorbed by the cells, and in the directionality of the cell layers. When humidity levels rise, cells in the outer layer, with the higher hygroscopic coefficient, swell more than those in the inner layer, creating pressure to close the scale. When the scales dry, the opposite process occurs: cells in the outer layer lose moisture and shrink more than those in the inner layer, pulling the scales out until they open. This strategy explains how scales open and close using a unique structure that responds to humidity gradients in the environment. Humidity is the source of energy for the opening and closing operations. It is essentially a hydrostatic engine activated by changes in humidity levels.

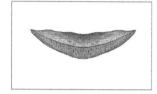

- **Application:** This strategy has been dubbed the "pine cone effect" and is already being implemented in a number of developments. For example, MMT Textiles applied this strategy to design a smart fabric called INOTEK™ that responds to humidity levels in the micro-climate. Conventional fibers tend to swell as they absorb moisture. This causes a reduction in air permeability of the textile structure, hence the fabric's poor ability to wick away sweat. INOTEK™ textiles respond in the exact opposite manner. When the fabric absorbs moisture, the fibers close up and tighten, forming microscopic pockets of air in the textile structure that increase air permeability. Under dry weather conditions, the fibers open up like a pine cone, air permeability decreases, and insulation properties of the fabric increase. This is an example of a bio-responsive fabric that responds to changes in the environment and brings us a little closer to nature's dynamic design paradigm, a design that responds and changes like a living organism.

Other developments specifically focus on aspects of hydrostatic engines, demonstrating how energy can be harvested from changes in humidity levels. A team of researchers at Columbia University designed spore sample units that contract and expand with changes in humidity, similar to pine cone scales. [82] The units were integrated into a wheel and as soon as half of the wheel was exposed to moisture, magic happened: a small toy car attached to the wheel began moving with an invisible force, the force of moisture. The contraction and expansion effect of the units was achieved by placing bacterial spores on plastic strips of tape. Spores are reproductive units common among plants, fungi, and bacteria that expand and contract, like muscles, in response to changes in humidity.

At the moment, the car is a toy car and spores are still being used for the solution, but we may soon find a different substance to replace the spores, one that can contract and expand over many cycles without getting tired. So we might be driving an actual hydrostatically-powered vehicle along the coast, looking out the window and seeing systems spread out over the ocean that harvest moisture from evaporation. The natural water cycle offers infinite energy potential.

Biological Hierarchy

Systems in nature are generally organized in a biological hierarchy model. Each level is encompassed in the next level: molecules → cells → tissues → organs → organism → populations or ecosystems, and so on. As you move up the scale, the orders of magnitude also rise from nano to micro to macro. Each level has functions and strategies that can be explored and emulated, and all of them bear the potential for innovation, but each level is associated with different applications.

• **The level of molecules and cells:** Observed functions in molecules and cells are implemented in areas of biomimetic chemistry and biomimetic materials. For example, Galia Maayan from the Technion studied molecule selectivity. Different molecules in the body or in nature bind exclusively to specific metal ions in order to function. In her lab, they emulated the selectivity mechanism of metalloproteins and created a highly selective molecule that only binds to copper ions from among a "sea" of metal ions. Future applications in the medical world may be possible: diseases related to improper brain function in old age, such as dementia, are associated with excess accumulation of metal ions such as copper, zinc, iron, or aluminum. Future developments of biomimetic selectivity may enable selective binding of these ions and their removal from the body.

• **The level of tissues:** Observed functions in tissues – groups of cells that function together as a unit and share similar structures – are implemented in functional surface applications. For example, the Namib Desert beetle, or fogstand beetle, lives in the Namib Desert, one of the most arid areas of the world, where only about 40 mm of rain falls annually. Like other creatures, these beetles must survive despite the lack of water. During some early mornings, when their bodies are still cool from the night but their surroundings begin to warm up, and when the temperature still allows for condensation, they spread their wings, raise their hind legs, and then the magic ensues: Namib Desert beetles have tiny hydrophilic bumps on their wings that collect minute droplets of water from the fog. The droplets coalesce and fall into grooves between the bumps. The grooves, on the other hand, are hydrophobic. The droplets are pushed off the grooves and slide down the slope formed by the lifted hind legs, falling straight into the beetle's mouth. And just like that, the beetles drink water from the air. This wonder takes place on the cuticle – the outer shell of the wings.

Many researchers are working on imitating this strategy of harvesting water from air. The World Health Organization estimates that billions of people worldwide still don't have access to clean water.[83] Many people live in remote, undeveloped areas that lack water infrastructure. But the humidity in the air is available, and if we know how to harvest it using large-scale wa-ter-harvesting facilities, we will solve one of humanity's chal-lenges. The road to realizing the vision of "water for all" is still fraught with challenges. The quantities collected by Namib Des-ert beetles are miniscule, and similar wings designed on a large scale will be exposed to winds that impair efficiency of the pro-cess. According to estimates, the morphology of a surface with bumps and grooves collects two to three times more water than a smooth surface without this morphology.[84] Time will tell if this structural effect will be enough to realize the vision.

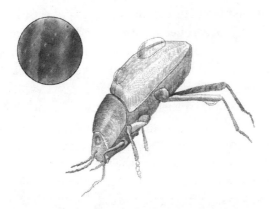

• **The level of organs or the organism:** Observed functions in organs are used in a slew of applications in various fields and for developments in engineering, mechanics, robotics, med-icine, and more. Usually, only one organ's functions are ob-served. For example, when looking at a pomegranate tree, we can focus on the pomegranate fruit and discover its structural wisdom. The seeds are packed very closely to each other, and as the fruit ripens, the seeds grow with it, filling up with liquid and exerting pressure on each other. The seeds are distributed in a way that allows them to swell without producing pressure that will split the rind. The rind remains intact and beautiful even as the pomegranate grows into a juicy fruit. The spatial structure of pomegranate seed distribution was studied at Stanford University and helped solve an issue related to silicon batteries: silicon batteries have a much greater storage capacity than other batteries, but silicon anodes tend to swell and cause cracking. At Stanford, they designed silicon nanoparticles and mimicked the geometric structure of pomegranate particles, ensuring pressure-free swelling – and as a result, they solved the swelling problem of the silicon anode.

• **The level of the population and ecosystem:** Observed functions at the level of populations or ecosystems are used in applications related to efficient and energetic group conduct, communication and transfer of information, and developments in organizational, social, or environmental fields. Take a school of fish, for example. Fish schools move as one body in efficient structures. Observations at the California Institute of Technology led to the discovery that not only does the location of each schooling fish not produce interference with nearby fish, but, on the contrary, they help accelerate their peers by moving a certain way. The physical explanation is that constructive hydrodynamic interference is formed between the wakes of neighboring fish. These physical principles, learned from observing schools of fish, were applied in the design of a field of wind turbines rotating side by side. The turbines were positioned according to the spatial geometric structure of the school of fish. Field studies have proven the effectiveness of this structure.[85]

Levels of Mimicry

Many of the phenomena observed on a macro scale in nature are results of unique designs on nano and micro scales, so it is important to understand where to invest research efforts. For example, the fact that no bacteria accumulates on shark skin (macro level) is explained at the nano level – in the structure of skin tissues. The fog droplet rolling down the cuticle of a Namib Desert beetle is also observed at the macro level, but its roots lie in the micro-structure of its wings. Once we define the level of biological hierarchy, we can study the strategy and identify the critical elements related to the function. "There are three types of biomimicry – one is copying form and shape, another is copying a process, like photosynthesis in a leaf, and the third is mimicking at an ecosystem's level, like building a nature-inspired city," said Janine Benyus. The function can be related to each one of these levels. Identifying the level of mimicry will direct and focus research efforts.

• **Levels of mimicry – Form and Shape:** This level focuses on forms, shapes, contours, surfaces, and structures identified with the function being studied. Forms and structures in nature are elegant, efficient, and provide the required solution, and there is no need to maintain them with external energy. The structure is formed once and the function is achieved over time. It is not for nothing that the first trend as biomimicry developed was the morphological trend. It seems easier to identify a major form or structure, and examine and mimic it, rather than pore over complex processes and algorithms.

An example of innovation based on this level of mimicry is the story of how the winglet was developed:[86] winglets are vertical extensions added to the end of aircraft wings. All things or bodies that fly, whether they be birds or planes, suffers from wingtip vortices. Due to the asymmetrical wing shape, the pressure generated under the wing is higher. Although this asymmetric structure is what creates the lift, it also produces wingtip vortices, where air currents of varying pressures meet. These vortices impair flight efficiency and incur higher fuel costs. If we take a moment to look at the world of soaring birds of prey, we will discover how nature solved this problem: when birds soar, they bend their wingtip feathers upward. This lift deflects the high-pressure air coming from beneath the wing and prevents it from mixing with the low-pressure air above the wing.

The concept of wingtip lift was well known in aviation, but the person who promoted its applied research was Richard Whitcomb, an aeronautical engineer who worked with NASA and was also a bird enthusiast. He noticed the raised wingtip feathers of soaring birds' wings during flight. With the outbreak of the global oil crisis in the 1970s and the growing need to find ways to save fuel, Whitcomb conducted a series of wind tunnel experiments, in which he tested different types of curved wingtips, and recorded an average fuel saving potential of 5%. The solution was first adopted by airlines that manufacture light aircraft, and later also by large passenger planes, where the savings are even more significant. When fuel consumption is reduced, there is also less strain on engines, which significantly lowers their maintenance and need for repair and spare parts. All in all, wingtips save billions of dollars in the aviation industry, savings which, of course, also translate into a major environmental impact.

• **Levels of mimicry – Process**: This level focuses on the process or algorithm, that is, a series of actions leading to the function being studied. The process is a result of an interaction between system parts according to scientific and natural laws. Emulating processes in nature is most often associated with dynamic functions of movement or change within a system. At the molecular level, we are talking about biochemical processes. In this context, Yuval Noah Harari said in a lecture at the World Economic Forum in Davos in 2018 that 150 years of biological research since Charles Darwin can be summarized in three words: "Organisms are algorithms." According to him, "This is the big insight of modern life sciences, that organisms, whether viruses or bananas or humans, are really just biochemical algorithms and we are learning how to decipher these algorithms."[87] And as we decipher these algorithms and processes, we identify strategies on the way that can be implemented.

For example, swarm intelligence is a fascinating field related to this level of mimicry. Intelligent conduct at the swarm level is the result of interactions between individuals demonstrating self-organized collective behavior without central leadership, while following simple rules. Ants, for example, use two rules to find the shortest path to food: secreting pheromones (odor signals) and turning toward the path where the smell is stronger. Ants moving along the shorter path return faster and thus their pheromone density is higher on shorter paths than longer ones. These two rules form the basis of the algorithm for identifying the shortest path. Algorithms learned from ants are called 'ant optimization algorithms,' and they have been implemented in various companies that route and transport information, goods, or people, such as Google, Fedex, or Waze.

Swarm intelligence is also seen in flocks of starlings, or murmurations, which consist of tens of thousands of birds moving relatively close to one another without colliding. Every few seconds, the murmuration unexpectedly changes shape, like a shape-shifting cloud. The sharp turns made in perfect unison by tens of thousands of individual starlings begin with the motions of just one starling, responding to an occurrence in the environment. Each bird reacts to the motions of neighboring birds using a few simple rules which have been identified and translated into a collision avoidance algorithm known as the Craig Reynolds model,[88] which can help route swarms of drones or vehicles, for example.

• **Levels of mimicry – Ecosystem:** This level focuses on design principles used to build or manage ecosystems that are related to the function being studied. For example, in the context of extraction and recycling of material resources, we encounter the principle of "waste=food." In nature, "waste" doesn't exist as a concept. Any waste or garbage is used by other organisms in the system that find value in it – or they break down, return to soil, and nourish the land. For example, cleaner fish feed on parasites and dead cells found on other fish. They feed on waste while providing a cleaning service in return.

The principle of waste=food has been successfully implemented in various places in the world and demonstrates how waste is worth not only food, but also a lot of money. How do you turn cardboard into caviar?[89] An environmental group in England designed a series of simple processes that do just that. First, they collect cardboard boxes from local businesses and restaurants, then they shred them, and sell them to equestrian centers as horse bedding. The spent horse bedding is then collected and transferred to a compost pit to feed worms. The worms are fed to Siberian sturgeon, which produce caviar, and the caviar is sold back to the restaurants. Sounds fictional and perhaps even strange, but that's how nature works. Circles open and close in nature all the time, material spirals, and the benefits flow.

The principle of symbiosis, which is characteristic of natural systems, has been translated into the principle of industrial symbiosis. Today, we see industrial parks that are designed and built according to the principle of symbiosis: waste from one plant is used as raw material for another. This saves a lot of material as well as energy since raw material doesn't need to be transported to the industrial park nor waste to landfills. One of these famous parks was built in the city of Kalundborg, Denmark. Excess gypsum generated from an electric power station in Kalundborg is transferred to a nearby gypsum production plant. Excess heat generated by the same electric power station is used to heat the homes of residents living nearby; gas produced at a nearby oil refinery is used to drive the turbines of the electric power station, while steam generated by the power station is used by the refinery. The steam is also used by the nearby biopharmaceutical factory, which in turn transfers excess yeast from its production processes to a nearby pig farm, as well as nutrient-rich fermented sludge to the local farmers, and it goes on. There are many symbiotic processes, as in nature, that reinforce the resilience of the entire system.

• **Multiple levels of mimicry:** Analysis often shows that the function you wish to mimic is related to several levels of mimicry, such as both structure and process. Pangolins, for example – mammals with distinctive armor that resemble walking artichokes – demonstrate intriguing behavior. When they feel threatened, they roll up into a perfect sphere, inside which their heads are fully protected. Predators attempting to bite them encounter hermetically closed balls. Documented attempts by people to "open" a closed pangolin with a stick or other means have been unsuccessful. They just remain closed. Their armor is rigid and strong, but also flexible, and can change shape. This unique combination of strength and flexibility is related to the fact that their armor consists of many separate, small scales, each able to move on their own and thus slide over each other, allowing pangolins to curl into balls or open up. This protective function is related to both structure and process. At the level of structure, there are rigid scales that make up the armor; At the level of process, there is a series of actions that allow the relative motion of the scales on top of each other.

• **Transitioning between levels of mimicry:** Even when the desired function is achieved at the level of structure, there is added value in mimicking aspects at the levels of the process and system. For example, the winglet, built to emulate the shape of wings of birds of prey, achieved the desired result: breaking the wingtip vortex and increasing the aircraft's energy efficiency. But looking at additional levels of mimicry will lead to setting additional goals, the achievement of which will bring us closer to nature's design paradigm. For example, the material used to build winglets is aluminum or similar metals. The attempt to mimic manufacturing processes in nature can lead to the identification of alternative materials that are produced in a more environmentally beneficial way, such as material that mimics spider webs.

Taking a look at the ecosystem level shows that just as the bird of prey is part of an ecosystem, the winglet is also part of a broader economy. This insight will lead to additional questions: Is the winglet transported far and wide? Is welfare provided for employees? Thus, from a holistic perspective, a design dialogue with nature will take place, which can sculpt our perception as designers, illuminate questions we didn't think to ask, and provide answers we never imagined existed.

STAGES OF THE PROCESS

Luck is what happens when preparation meets opportunity.

Seneca

Japanese Legend

The world of nature's inventions is replete with legends and tales that all share a common element: a chance and precise encounter between a solution in nature and an engineering or technological challenge. One of the well-known tales presents the solution to the noise issue on Japanese trains.

The Japanese Shinkansen train is one of the fastest trains in the world, reaching a speed of 320 kilometers per hour. High speed trains cause significant noise pollution during travel, especially when exiting a tunnel when the air pressure changes dramatically. This situation generates a loud sound wave – a supersonic boom – defined as noise pollution that spreads over a long distance. The noise was harming the quality of life of residents living in the area, and of course did not meet the delineated noise standards. The Shinkansen noise dilemma preoccupied engineers. They searched for a solution to reduce the noise without affecting the railway speed.

The railway's general manager of the technical development department, engineer Eiji Nakatsu, an avid bird enthusiast, was walking through the wilderness one day and came upon a kingfisher diving into the water. He noticed that the kingfisher's entry into the water was smooth, causing no sound waves, ripples, or splashes. Kingfishers feed on the fish they catch and their smooth entry into the water likely gives them an advantage in capturing their prey, since the noise would scare the fish away.

The engineer identified the connection between the kingfisher's quiet diving and the train's noise problem. Both kingfishers and trains have to switch from a medium characterized by a certain density to a medium characterized by a different density, and to do so without emitting noise. This insight led researchers to study kingfishers. The solution was found in the beak, the first organ to enter the water when diving. The beak passes from air to water, from low pressure to high pressure, respectively, with minimal energy loss. Using the beak's aerodynamic structure, kingfishers manage to overcome the sudden change in resistance and barely splash the water.

The train engine was redesigned based on the parameters of the kingfisher's beak, which served as the model for the solution. The shape of the train was redesigned using computer modeling techniques and now resembles the kingfisher's beak. The noise issue was solved and the train is even more energy efficient and runs even faster. The beak is an example of an optimal model, a product of the Natural Design Lab, proposed as a substitute for complex mathematical calculations in the field of flow dynamics.

One of the exciting parts of this story, beyond the happy ending of course, is the element of chance. The engineer got up in the morning, went out into nature, and happened to observe the solution. And what would have happened if the kingfisher had not passed by before his eyes at that very moment, if another bird had passed by? Would the locomotive noise problem not have been solved by now? We all love stories of good luck, but it seems there may have been a bit more than luck going on here. That engineer was probably very troubled by the problem – it must have been present in the forefront of his mind. As a lover of nature and birds, he must have been accustomed to observing, and when the solution and problem were in front of him at the same time – the connection occurred.

Today, there is no need to rely on luck anymore. We can replicate the kingfisher story systematically. Preparation introduces us to opportunity, as suggested by Seneca, a Roman philosopher who lived in the first century AD. As the years go by, there are more and more methodologies for managing processes of connecting nature's inventions to technological challenges. Invention is something worth finding. You just have to figure out what, how, and where to look. Today, more than ever, nature's inventions are accessible to everyone.

A Good Start

The Japanese railway engineers must have gone through all the basic design steps every engineer goes through when trying to solve a problem. Once the noise problem was identified, they must have begun searching for conceptual solutions. I can imagine them sitting in a room sketching, arguing, brainstorming, falling into despair, and becoming hopeful at times. One morning, the same bird-loving engineer must have joined the discussion, sharing with them the kingfisher solution he had come across. After discussing the feasibility of the solution, they proceeded to create the preliminary design, until they were satisfied. From there, they moved on to the detailed design stage, until they finished remodeling the train according to the spatial parameters taken from the beak. Biomimicry was incorporated into the initial stages of the design process; nature served as the generator of design concepts.

Examining design concepts for a solution is a critical stage for achieving success, but the human tendency to rush forward often leads to omitting this stage and sticking to the first idea that seems appropriate. At the beginning of my professional career, I joined a medical start-up company. The company began operating after they acquired a patent for sealing arteries post-catheterization. The patent actually dictated the manner in which the artery is sealed, but of course, there are other ways of getting this done. The company continued operating on the path of this patent, invested a lot of money in research and development, and reached the stage of animal testing without examining other sealing methods. At this point, a serious life-threatening problem was discovered, and this avenue actually failed. The company was financially sound and started over with a different solution, completely different from the one delineated in the patent, and operated on this path for several more years.

In-depth thought during the initial stages, while examining various solutions, saves time and resources later on. The first stages of any project, in which conceptual solutions are examined, are stages of low cost relative to the cost of the whole project, but their contribution to the final quality of the project is very high. This is what nature's innovation engine knows how to do: generate conceptual ideas using the biomimicry methodology during the early design stages.

Stages of the Innovation Process

When I began investigating the stages of biomimetic innovation, I came across many rather colorful charts. They all more or less described the same steps. In all these diagrams, three main steps were always repeated, arising from the analogous nature of the process. Biomimicry is an analogous innovation engine driven by the fuel of biological knowledge. This engine is a virtual "machine," that is, a method by which one can access the biological arena, identify solutions within it and simplify them,

so they are ready to be transferred to the application space. The three main steps are:
1. *Search* – discovering biological models for the solution
2. *Analysis* – abstracting and refining the biological solution
3. *Transfer* – emulating the solution for its use in the application.

Whatever the starting point of the innovation process, if you begin with biology (the solution) and move on to technology (the application) or vice versa, you will find these three core steps.

I chose to present the stages of the process as defined by the Biomimicry Institute.[1] The steps are described on a spiral diagram to portray the evolving and repetitive nature of the process. Spirals are one of the most beautiful, noble, and common shapes found in nature. They are identified with processes of construction, development, and growth. Spirals allow for gradual growth while developing. With every turn of the spiral, it seems we return to the same point, but are looking at it from a more distant, more experienced, and more understanding place. The bridge connecting biology and engineering is neither unitemporal nor unidirectional, or in other words not confined to just a single period of time or direction. The process involves many repetitions: moving between nature and technology, accumulating knowledge, examining feasibility in the technological world, and returning to discern and clarify things.

---

1. This chapter describes the stages of the biomimicry design process. The graphics and stages names are adapted with permission from the biomimicry institute. I explain the stages in a way I understand them and based on my personal design experience. This explanation has not been validated by the biomimicry institute.

From Biology to Technology

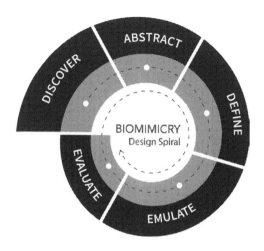

The biomimetic process of moving from biology to technology begins with **discovering** a model for a solution in nature (biological strategy) and continues with **abstracting** the solution in order to understand the functional mechanism and design principles. After understanding it to a sufficient degree and having "something to work with," we move on to **defining** an analogical design challenge and possible application. At this stage, we usually return to abstraction and to delving into the mechanism, this time with the application in mind. We continue on to **emulating** the mechanism in the selected application and then to **evaluating** the product. If necessary, we go back to the previous stages and improve the design.

Take the lotus effect, for example. The innovation process began with the **discovery** of a biological model, the lotus leaf, demonstrating a self-cleaning ability. As early as 2,000 years ago, people noticed that lotus leaves were clean. Although lotus grow in muddy environments, they always look clean, and are therefore considered a symbol of purity and beauty. The fact that the leaves are always free of mud allows photosynthesis to be performed efficiently and supports the plant's survival.

In the 1980s, Wilhelm Barthlott, a German botanist, noticed this with wonder. He left the little dwarves who come to clean the lotus at night for the fairy tales, and used the scientific research tools at his disposal. With the development of electron microscope technology in the mid-20th century, for the first time, he was able to understand the mechanism and move on to the **abstraction** stage. Barthlott revealed the design principles that enable the self-cleaning mechanism and called it 'the lotus effect,' which later became a trademark.

Intuitively, one might think that smooth surfaces are cleaner since cracks and grooves trap dirt. But the surface of the lotus leaf is not smooth, it is covered with microscopic bumps wrapped in nanoparticles. The distance between the nanoparticles is less than the diameter of a drop of water, so water cannot enter between them. This structure reduces the contact area of water droplets falling on the surface and forms contact angles of over 150 degrees between the drop and the surface, a characteristic of extremely effective water-repellent surfaces (superhydrophobic). Water droplets that fall on the surface take on a spherical shape, roll off the sloping leaf surface, and wash everything away in their path, including dust and dirt particles.

When the surface gets worn or damaged, it rebuilds itself via self-repair processes typically found in growing systems in nature. The result: the dirt and dust particles are constantly being removed by water droplets, thus utilizing an available resource in the leaf's environment that doesn't require any energy investment, but instead utilizes adhesion and gravitational forces. An elegant mechanism: create a structure once and get a lifetime of cleaning services. The self-cleaning effect is also seen in other plants, such as nasturtium and water lettuce. If we pour a little water on them, we can immediately notice small droplets rolling off the leaf like slippery beads. It's a mesmerizing spectacle (*see 9).

Excited by the effect he discovered, Barthlott teamed up with engineers to think about possible applications. He was able to convince large companies of the process's viability, and they continued to find more ways to apply it. In practice, you don't have to be an engineer to brainstorm applications. It's enough just to imagine and dream: a surface that cleans itself without energy investment, without detergents, using water droplets from the environment. Where would you dream of implementing it?

The publishing of scientific articles about this effect also spurred the imaginations of inventors and engineers worldwide, who began brainstorming to **define** possible applications. Anyone who identified a possible application could patent it. Searching the term 'lotus effect' in the patent database now yields thousands of results. This innocent mechanism is, without a doubt, responsible for innovation in many areas. Some patent holders even continued on to the stage of **emulation** and application of the lotus effect. Notable applications include:

House paint: Homes in most urban areas turn black after years of absorbing dust and soot. A company in Germany developed lotus-effect paint, Lotusan®, which is used as exterior paint for houses. The paint's surface contains bumps similar to those of lotus leaves. When it rains, water droplets roll down the walls and clean them, so houses painted in this color look clean for a long time, as though they had just been painted.

Glass: Self-cleaning windows can obviate the need for cleaning, at least on the outside. Today, the construction and automotive industries have integrated lotus-effect glass. Will there be no jobs left for window cleaners, who slip down buildings with buckets and brushes, cleaning windows? Self-cleaning houses are still a distant dream, but at least its exterior walls and windows have taken a step toward realizing this dream.

Smart fabrics: Smart fabrics that radically repel water and dirt have been developed that demonstrate the lotus effect. During my lectures, I ask a brave volunteer to step forward, someone who trusts nature. After they put on the lotus-effect shirt, I pour water into the chest pocket, and to the class's amazement, the shirt remains utterly dry. The pocket behaves like a sealed plastic bag. Then I pour some water on the shirt itself, and the water immediately turns into small balls that roll down the shirt and leave it dry. You can also throw mud, ketchup, and coffee on the shirt and it will remain immaculate.

Anti-icing surfaces: At the Shenkar College of Engineering, Design and Art, a team led by Hannah Dodiuk developed a technology that prevents ice accumulation on surfaces that is based on emulating the nano-structure of lotus leaves using hydrophobic silica particles. It reduces ice accumulation on surfaces by a factor of 18 to 20. The surface doesn't actually repel ice but reduces its adhesive strength, such that the droplets don't remain on the surface. One of the applications in demand is to prevent ice accumulation on aircraft wings, a phenomenon that constitutes a safety hazard. Another application could be protecting power cables from ice accumulation.

The **emulation** phase also includes research and development. These research processes can involve, for example, constructing several prototypes that differ in a number of parameters, and examining their performance in different situations. For example, in testing the efficacy of the lotus effect, we can produce several surfaces that differ in three parameters: the size, shape, and distribution of bumps on the surface. Research aims to define the parameters' values that optimize the self-cleaning performance. Lastly, we **evaluate** the performance. In practice, not every model that works in nature works equally effectively in its technological emulation. For example, unlike lotus leaves, which demonstrate self-repairing capabilities, biomimetic imitations currently lack this ability and suffer from wear and tear that impairs performance over time.

From Technology to Biology

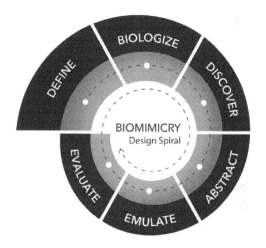

Biomimetic processes from technology to biology begin with **defining** the design challenge and continue on to **biologizing** the challenge, i.e., interpreting the challenge in biological terms that allow us to search biological databases. In the transition from technology to biology, the challenge must be formulated in biological language. Interpretation is done by crosslinking the challenge to a meaningful function in the biological world. After formulating the function, we begin the stage of searching and **discovering** models for solutions in nature (biological strategies). Following the discovery of biological models, comes the phase of **abstracting** the functional mechanisms and identifying design principles, followed by **emulating** the mechanism in the selected application to address the defined challenge, and finally, **evaluating** the product. If necessary, we return to the previous stages and improve the design.

For example, the development of an isolated, lightweight, and flexible wetsuit. Development began by **defining** a design challenge. MIT researchers visited a wetsuit manufacturing company and became aware of the need to develop materials that would allow surfers to maintain their body temperature while out in the water without compromising their agility or encumbering their movement. Surfers are constantly moving between air and water. A warm and dry wetsuit is the dream of many surfers (apart from catching the perfect wave), but wetsuits today are made from thick neoprene rubber that doesn't offer a satisfying solution in providing thermal protection while allowing the surfer to remain dry and agile.

The researchers **biologized** (interpreted) this challenge into the required functions: isolation + flexibility. They then tried to **discover** biological models for the solution in nature. Their approach led them to search extreme conditions in living environments where the challenges of isolation and agility are particularly profound. The researchers assumed that animals in Arctic environments that divide their time on land and underwater require insulation solutions. They focused on small, agile animals. This search led them to find beavers and otters: even though they don't have blubber, thick layers of insulating fat, like whales, they are still able to keep their bodies warm and even dry while diving underwater.

The researchers delved deeper in the next stage and began **abstracting** and refining the variables of the fur of these organisms, which is related to their insulating abilities. Following the study, they discovered that beavers trap air in their fur while diving, and sought to understand this air-trapping process. To do this, they created fur-like surfaces of different sizes using rubber castings. These surfaces were then plunged into liquids of varying viscosities and at different speeds. Using video imaging, the researchers were able to measure the amount of air trapped in the fur of each trial. They found that the spacing of individual hairs and the speed at which they were plunged played a big role in determining the amount of air a surface can trap. Based on these findings, the team developed a simple mathematical model to describe fur's air-trapping effect. Using this model, we can control the length of the hairs, the spacing between them, and their arrangement, and design textures for different diving speeds to maximize dry zones in the wetsuits.

Equipped with the mathematical model, the researchers continued to the **emulation** phase and created a fur-like rubber surface that mimics the insulating capabilities of beaver fur. Similar to the biological model, the surface is covered with a hairy texture. Suits made from this surface can give surfers the advantages of beaver fur: lightweight suits that keep the body warm in cold water and dry quickly – fulfilling the dream.

A Winning Direction?

As mentioned, innovation can begin from both directions – with a challenge or with a solution. While consumers are a good source for identifying needs and challenges, there are needs that consumers are not even aware of. Therefore, it is also worth listening to the voice of the "products" in the language of nature, a voice that describes how nature solves challenges. This direction can help discover solutions to challenges that have not even been defined as challenges yet by consumers. For example, someone in a focus group engaged in window design innovation is likely to think about easy-to-clean windows that leave no fingerprints or that filter out solar radiation. On the other hand, it's hard to imagine this person thinking about windows that are cleaned by rain alone.

The Mercedes-Benz Chicken – It's not all Biomimicry

One day, an acquaintance asked me if I knew the biomimicry story of Mercedes-Benz and the chicken.[90] I was surprised that I hadn't heard of it, since I am usually aware of classic examples of bioinspired innovation. He sent me a video of a chicken. The video shows the chicken's body moving up and down, side to side, turning left and right against the background of rhythmic music. While the chicken's body moved in all directions, its head remained perpendicular to the ground and was not affected at all by its body movements.

I realized that this was an excellent advertisement, one that gets etched into memory. The chicken was chosen to demonstrate an innovative suspension system integrated into Mercedes-Benz vehicles that allows the body of the vehicle to remain stable despite changing road conditions. Sensors detect bumps and dips in the road and adjustments are made to prevent jumps and vibrations. The message is full control of the vehicle's body, leading to uncompromising comfort and stability while driving.

The vehicle itself is not shown at all, but captions run on the screen with the following messages: Stability at all times, Magic Body Control, Intelligent Drive. They leave viewers with the image of dancing chickens and let the imagination run.

So what came first? The chicken or the car? Here, it seems as though the vehicle predates the chicken, and that this is not a process of bioinspired innovation. The chicken was merely chosen as an analogy to demonstrate the vehicle's capabilities, but, to my understanding, there was no systematic design process that involved researching the mechanism that allows the chicken's head to stay in place in an effort to apply principles from nature to design. The three core stages of the biomimetic innovation process – discover a biological model, abstract its mechanism, and emulate it in an application – were apparently not used here. It appears that the chicken wasn't a teacher, but a presenter or face of the company.

Sometimes companies associate a product they developed with nature even if it wasn't inspired by it, as a marketing tool or as a gimmick to draw attention to the product and make it stand out from competitors. Connecting a product to nature is connecting it to nature's magic, magic that acts upon us all. I call such a process "biomimicry in retrospect." It usually occurs when designers note similarities between their design and aspects of nature and declare that the design process is biomimetic only at a late stage, when the design is already complete. That being said, in the absence of a systematic design process following the described stages, the development is not considered biomimetic.

AN INTERDISCIPLINARY BRIDGE

Nature does nothing in vain.

Aristotle

Bridges excite me. The bigger, wider, and deeper the chasm beneath them, the greater the exhilaration. One's heart rate increases as you approach the center and slows down as you approach the other side. There are swinging bridges that are safe and there are rickety bridges that seem to be on the brink of collapsing at any moment. There are bridges that lead to isolated islands and others that connect bustling areas. There are transparent glass bridges that leave no room for the imagination and there are sealed and blocked up bridges that discourage any desire to imagine.

The Gap between Fields

The meeting of disciplines is a fruitful one that promotes innovation, but it is undoubtedly also challenging. Connecting people and knowledge from different fields raises hardships that stem from gaps in knowledge, terminology, and ways of thinking, and these gaps require bridging.

There is an old debate in the field of biomimicry: who is more essential for the field – engineers or biologists? Engineers argue that it's better to be engineers, since the engineering, systematic way of thinking that is necessary for emulating nature's inventions lies at the heart of innovation and cannot be forfeited. Biologists, on the other hand, argue that it's better to be biologists, since they possess the biological knowledge regarding the solution in nature, and that cannot be forfeited. Of course, both are important, but there is a fundamental difference in how they think, the way they look at nature, and even in their terminology. A basic concept like 'function' is defined differently in each discipline. Even scientists, who often take part in the biomimicry process, think differently than engineers and biologists.

The Weizmann Institute of Science studied the characteristics of practitioners in each of these fields.[91] The outcome revealed that biologists notice the details and complexity of systems. They deal with observable reality and identify many exceptions and few rules. They are less concerned with abstraction and formulating laws and perceive physical and engineering models as too simplistic. On the other hand, scientists, especially physicists, get lost in the details, excel in abstraction and mathematical thinking, express complex ideas by finding simple rules, and have difficulty grasping the biological knowledge in an organized way. They focus on the problem and try to understand it systematically and solve it through analysis. In contrast, designers (inventors, architects, and engineers) focus on the solution and solve problems through synthesis. They conduct preliminary investigations and then propose potential solutions until a good or satisfactory one is found. During the investigation process, they develop an understanding of the problem and use diagrams to structure thinking around possible solutions.

I observed these findings in real life. As a rule of thumb, each thought and idea can be expressed graphically, with the help of formulas or in descriptive verbal form, by going into detail. When I worked with groups of engineers, they immediately began writing formulas. Formulas for them are tools which direct their thinking and help them solve problems. Conversely, when I worked with industrial designers, they tended to immediately turn toward drawing and sketching and expressed their ideas graphically.

I also felt the tension between the two fields on a personal level. While working on my doctorate, the academic committee met to approve my research proposal. The committee included my principal supervisor – an engineer by trade who specializes in engineering design, and a biology professor – a veteran and experienced researcher in the fields of biology. My research sought to extract structural patterns in nature and model biological systems using engineering modeling methods, a process that involves a lot of abstraction at the expense of details. I recall the biology professor's discomfort with the concept of abstraction. He argued that nature is composed of many details and that trying to fit them into patterns means losing the wealth of information. Ever since, I have been much more sensitive to the abundance of details in nature, to the exceptions, the subtleties that are the core of life. However, I also appreciate the value of modeling and abstraction.

The chasm between biology and technology therefore stems from gaps in terminology, language, and manner of thinking. A key stage in the biomimetic innovation process is bridge building, which will allow moving safely between biology and technology. If you begin with the challenge, that is, technology, you need to **biologize** it, or interpret it in biological language, so that a solution can be sought in the biological arena. If you begin with the solution, that is, biology, you need to **define** possible applications that already exist on the other side, in technology.

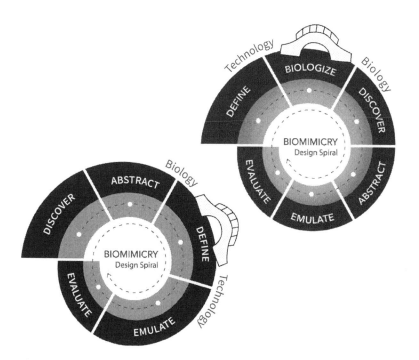

What is Used to Build the Bridge between the Disciplines?

For the bridge to be stable, it must be made from solid materials and elements on both sides, both in biology and technology. There needs to be a connection link that means something to both sides of the chasm.

A first clue to identifying this link can be found in one of Aristotle's famous quotes according to which, "nature does nothing in vain." Already in the early period in which he lived, before the Industrial and Technological Revolutions, Aristotle understood the immense value inherent in nature's creations, and with precise simplicity articulated our yearning for their utility. NASA released a spectacular video that provides another clue as to the identity of the connecting link, called the "*Travel with NASA from the biggest to the smallest distance of the universe.*"[92] The journey begins at a distance that is difficult for humans to comprehend, 10 million light-years from Earth, and ends at a distance that is also difficult to comprehend, 10-16 meters from a quark. A journey to Earth passes through galaxies (the Milky Way) and the solar system, and a journey on Earth passes through ecosystems, organisms (a plant), organs (a leaf), cells, molecules, and atoms. It turns out that there are systems at every level. The universe is made up of systems. Nature's creations are systems (*see 10).

A system is not just a collection of parts that span a common area, but a collection of **parts** that **interact** with each other to **function** as a whole unit. These parts can be tangible or abstract, but they are related to each other in a way that produces a needed function that provides a benefit. A pile of Lego building bricks scattered on the floor is not a system and has no value. But if the Lego building bricks are placed on top of each in a way that produces the structure and function of a house, for example, the pile becomes a system of value. In this sense, **the value of a system is its function**.

But value is not that narrow and doesn't end at one function or another. Each system is itself a part of a larger system, so from a holistic perspective that is in coordination with nature, systems provide different types of value. Natural systems, for example, being part of their environment, provide efficiency, diversity, resilience, and harmony beyond the initial narrow role they may be identified with.

In 1969, biologist Ludwig von Bertalanffy published the *General Systems Theory*.[93] Interestingly, it was a biologist who came up with the theory. Perhaps it was his sensitivity to nature's different life forms and to the delicate dependency that exists between individuals in ecosystems that led him to define what a system is and what its characteristics are. Von Bertalanffy argued that regardless of whether we are looking at biological, chemical, engineering, industrial, social, or ecological systems, they all share common characteristics. The same components, concepts, principles, and laws are common to systems in varying disciplines. A fundamental concept common to all systems is function. Both biology and technology have systems that provide functions (value). The connecting link between these disciplines is the function, and what bridges them is function.

Rules of Thumb for Building the 'Function Bridge'

The bridge is formed through systemic-functional-analogical thinking that defines a valuable biological function in the technological field. How can we build a good, solid bridge?

The basic functions in nature are survival functions related to obtaining food, shelter, security, communication, and reproduction. But defining functions at this level will form a very narrow bridge, since engineering interests in nature are much wider. Defining a survival function will make it difficult to find a connecting link between biology and technology. To build a solid bridge, the function must be formulated on a physical level that considers the changing parameters of the system after operation of the function. According to the engineering perspective, a function is an operator of a system. It acts on the system and leads to a valuable result through modification of system parameters.

Take the lotus effect, for example. The biological function is survival: covering the leaf in mud impairs the efficiency of photosynthesis processes. This can be linked to industrial processes where dirt interferes with energy harvesting, such as removing dirt from solar panels. But such a view of the mechanism is narrow, because the innovation potential of the mechanism is much greater. At the generic level, we have a system that knows how to remove dirt. The changing parameter in the system is the amount of dirt. Before the function operated, there were dirt particles of a certain amount, and afterwards their quantity decreased. If we look at the system this way, the range of engineering applications we can link to it is much wider: any surface can be self-cleaned using this mechanism.

Another example is the pine cone effect. At the survival level, we're talking about a seed distribution mechanism. Pine cone scales pop open in extreme dry weather to allow the seeds to travel as far away from the mother tree as possible, and this can be associated with movement and transportation in windy environments. But this mechanism actually has much broader application potential since at the generic level, we have a system that knows how to open and close in response to changes in humidity. The system's changing parameter is the position of the scales (open-closed). Defining the function at the physical level, that is, at the level of the system's changing parameters, will allow formation of a wide and solid bridge, which will safely lead us to vast prospects in the engineering sphere.

The function should be formulated as a verb. Adherence to this wording will help implement functional thinking and also look for solutions in biomimetic databases built on functional taxonomy. Functional thinking is at the heart of the process of bioinspired innovation. It develops over time and can be practiced. The required ability is bidirectional: both to scan biological literature and identify functional mechanisms within it, and to refine the relevant engineering challenge and draft it as a function.

Identifying the Functional Story in the Biological Literature

Biological information comes in various forms: texts, articles, films, or observation posts, and is replete with descriptions of organisms. Behind some of the descriptions hides a function. The more you practice the skill, the more you see the functions "jump out" from the biological stories and understand how to build the bridge to technology. The functional sensor is quickly activated within a mechanism with functional value, but remains dormant when trapped in a descriptive story that has no inventive value.

Here is an example of a description from the biological literature: Woodpeckers have an amazing ability of knocking on solid tree trunks and hammering out holes in them to look for insects. They peck at a rate of 25 knocks per second without getting concussions. By the time you read that last paragraph, a woodpecker has already made several hundred pecks. This narrative description can be extrapolated into a function: "shock absorption." Once the mechanism is identified as a shock-absorbing system, the range of applications we can link it to is huge.

The description you just read alludes to the function demonstrated by woodpeckers, but doesn't specify the strategy. Further reading about woodpeckers will lead us to the answer. It turns out that the woodpecker, which weighs less than half a kilogram, uses its entire body during impact. By contracting its leg muscles, it accelerates its head toward the tree. The mystery of shock absorption has always fascinated scientists. Leading theories suggest that the foamy layer that exists between the bird's beak and its skull play a major part in absorbing the impact, thus protecting their brains. However, a new study has revealed that since their heads and beaks act like one unit, similar to a sturdy, uniform hammer, woodpeckers actually minimize the need for shock absorption.[94] Their head is not designed to absorb shock but to deliver a harder and more efficient hit, while the brain is protected from concussions by its small size.

Woodpeckers inspired a new design by an Italian sporting firm that has been manufacturing ice axes for decades. Ice climbing is an extreme sport common in various parts of the world. Meeting an ice climber is exciting. The effort involved in gripping solid ice is astonishing. For years, the company produced axes designed like hammers with the axes poised at a 90-degree angle relative to the shaft. The designer who worked for the company asked: "What is the best example of a hammer in nature?" The question led them to woodpeckers. Inspired by woodpeckers, the ice axe was redesigned, and now the angle of the ax relative to the shaft corresponds to the angle between the woodpecker's beak and its body. They also designed a bend in the shaft that imitates the positioning of the stabilizing tail. The result: a more effective strike, less shock absorbed by the body, and better sales.[95]

Defining the Design Challenge as a Function

On the other side of the bridge, engineers and designers need to learn to formulate their challenge as a function in order to build a bridge to biology. The challenges are often expressed as "challenge stories" that need to be refined into a verb + noun. For example, a person lives in an insect-infested area but doesn't want to use insecticides. He is sensitive to the chemicals found in insecticides and fears for his health but also doesn't want to live in an insect-infested environment. This is a simple story about an everyday issue that surely bothers many people. Behind the story of the problem is the function to "deter insects." At this point, we can formulate a generic research question and ask: How does nature keep insects away? Searching through the appropriate databases will yield a variety of nature's strategies for repelling insects, including the use of colors, secretions, smells, and vibrations. Perhaps one of them can outline an innovative way to repel insects, without chemicals and in a way that supports health and the environment.

Bridge Interchange

Sometimes the problem story can be linked to several different functions, each of which leads to a different potential route to a solution. For example, I worked with a company whose challenge was to prevent blood clots from reaching the brain during cardiovascular activity. During transcatheter heart procedures, blood clots can be released in the circulatory system, reach cerebral vessels and cause brain injury. The basic function we can think of is to "trap the clot" or "stop the clot." This function will lead to one bridge, which will lead to searching for gripping or trapping strategies in nature. But we can also consider other functions, for example, "redirecting the clot" to a nonhazardous location, "changing the clot" so that it no longer poses a threat (i.e., crushing or dissolving it). The initial stage in the innovation process is to decode the function that bridges the challenge to biology. Sometimes it is one bridge and sometimes several.

The 'Function Bridge': Passersby

In the transition from biology to engineering, there is an exchange of functional knowledge, and several possibilities may occur:

• **One function – different strategies:** Most bioinspired innovation processes begin with a focused review of different strategies in nature while looking at one of the specific functions required for the process. These strategies are found among different organisms exposed to different environmental challenges. Several strategies are examined in the process, one or a combination of which will eventually be implemented into a single technological system. Sometimes we can identify recurring principles, which may indicate their importance in being implemented into the solution. And sometimes we find that interesting connections from different strategies produce innovative solutions, even if their connection to the organism hasn't been played out in nature.

Remember the entrepreneur who was looking for water harvesting solutions, to restore the water that had evaporated during cooling processes? The core function leading the search process was "harvesting water." During the innovation process, we asked: How does nature harvest water? We found various strategies related to structure, quality of material, and behavior: cacti covered with clusters of spines and hairs that collect water droplets; the wings of Namib Desert beetles adorned with hydrophilic bumps and hydrophobic grooves that collect condensed water and channel it directly into their mouths; the grooves on the body of horned lizards that condense water and pump it to their mouths by capillary force; water is retained in hygroscopic surfaces in the camel's nasal canals during exhalation. At this stage, we can identify recurring patterns in these strategies, such as anchoring condensation with bumpy surfaces, making a transport system from grooves between bumps, creating material asymmetry of hydrophilicity alongside hydrophobicity, utilizing gravity-based energy fields, and more. These principles were eventually incorporated into the proposed solution.

• **Different functions – different organisms:** Sometimes different functions are required in a single technological system. In this case, it pays to examine different strategies in nature for the different functions, and finally combine them into one technological system. For example, the development of Festo's Bionic Handling Assistant, which is based on two different organisms – elephants and fish, and combines two functions – transport and grip.

The elephant trunk, from an engineering perspective, is a transport handle and has impressive gripping capabilities. It can grab small items like a piece of straw or a peanut as well as big items like a log or watermelon. It can be moved accurately and efficiently from point to point in the shortest way possible. The trunk contains about 40,000 non-compressible hydrostatic muscles. This muscular system moves without skeletal support. When pressure is applied to a muscle unit, it doesn't contract and the pressure simply passes on to the next unit. This is how the movement is created.

Development of Festo's Bionic Handling Assistant included a system of pneumatic components filled with compressed air that move similarly to the trunk model. But that's not all. At the end of the handle, there is a unique gripper tool inspired by the fin ray effect. A Norwegian bionics expert noticed an interesting mechanical feature in the tailfins of the fish he caught on his fishing rod: when he pressed his finger against the tailfin, it didn't bend in the direction of the applied force as expected, moving away from the point of the applied force, but did the opposite and folded back in the direction from which the pressure was being applied. This unexpected displacement opposing the direction of the applied force is called the "fin ray effect."[96] The effect is detected in bony fish and is related to the structure of the tailfin: tailfins consist of several rigid units called rays. Each ray is composed of a pair of long, bony spines connected by soft, elastic collagen tissue, so they move toward each other when pressure is applied to the fin. The effect was translated into a triangular ladder-like structure, consisting of two flexible units separated by rungs. When pressure is applied to one side, the "ladder rungs" absorb the pressure and move sideways in a folding motion, causing the units to approach each other. The effect was patented and implemented in the design of a gripper tool consisting of three soft and flexible "ladder rungs." The gripper picks things up without applying pressure on them; it can be used for grabbing apples in packing houses, eggs, and even chocolate-covered marshmallow treats (*see 11).

- **One organism – different functions:** Every organism is a system made up of many functions. Each function can lead to innovation for a different technological system, depending on the design challenge. For example, dolphins are **a model for underwater communication** at long distances, based on chirping and singing across a broad frequency bandwidth. They excel at transmitting communication even in noisy environments and mask unnecessary echoes and background noises emanating from the expanses of the sea. It's actually quite sophisticated sonar with impressive performance. Dolphins are known for their excellent echolocation abilities, which allow them to track objects underwater. Some even claim that a dolphin can spot a tennis ball 30 meters away! The German company Evo-Logics investigated the communication mechanism of dolphins and subsequently developed underwater acoustic transmission technology called S2C (Sweep-Spread Carrier), which works successfully even under turbulent conditions and neutralizes communication interference. The primary uses of these devices are in oil and gas exploration, ocean research, collecting and transmitting seismic information such as earthquakes and tsunamis, as well as centralizing underwater data and transmitting them to information centers.

Dolphins are also a **model for energy efficiency in motion.** In the past, I assisted a doctoral student whose research dealt with increasing energy efficiency and reducing drag in submarines. Apparently, dolphin skin, like shark skin, is made up of microscales with grooves between them that transfer pressure fluctuations to the lower skin layer which is made of softer material. This layer produces waves on the dolphin skin and changes the pattern of friction. A coating based on the dolphin skin structure was developed in the 1950s and demonstrated the effect, but manufacturing limitations prevented its accurate imitation. 3D printing technologies may be a solution today, enabling the printing of coatings with similar functions.

Dolphins are also **models for anti-fouling surfaces.** Researchers are using nanotechnology to create synthetic, chemical-free, antibacterial surfaces. I am sure that if we delve deeper into the professional literature, we will find more inspiring functions and models in dolphins.

THE SEARCH

Errors, like straws, upon the surface flow;
He who would search for pearls must dive below.

John Dryden

Imagine opening your computer, and instead of the colorful Google letters above the search window which everyone is familiar with, it says 'Nature' in any color you choose. You can enter any question into the small search window and nature will answer you. The search will be carried out in nature's solution database and the search methods will be adapted to the natural search track.

One of the most significant challenges in imitating nature's inventions is finding them. There are millions of species and varieties in nature. Each one is a source of many potential inventions. So how do we know where to start looking? Based on personal experience and reports from others involved in the field, the search for nature's solutions is a time-intensive phase. Using search methods can shorten the duration of the search and improve the quality of results.

At the beginning of this section, I spoke about stepping into nature with an observational awareness and with the lens of awe, which helps identify solutions and later match them with problems, thus walking the path of innovation from biology to technology. I will now address the art of finding solutions to a specific challenge on the path of innovation from technology to biology. An entrepreneur is someone who knows how to ask questions, understands where answers may be found, and is able to reach them. Search methods support the biomimetic entrepreneur and connect the question that was asked (the challenge) to the answers given by nature.

We know that not every trip to the safari will show us animals, but if we go with a skilled guide who knows how to read animal footprints, the chances of encountering animals increase. Biomimetic search tools are a private safari guide, helping even designers lacking in biological knowledge access the reservoir of nature's solutions.

Enquiring Mindset

I once drove on a highway on a dark night. Suddenly, I ran out of gas. I pulled over in the breakdown lane behind a pickup truck and contemplated what to do. The road service center wasn't responding and I realized that my position on the side of the highway was a safety hazard. A few minutes later, the driver in front of me got out of his truck and told me that his car was stuck, but that he had a container full of gas. He, too, was looking for a way off the road. We improvised a funnel and filled the fuel tank during the short intervals between passing traffic. As I was extricating the two of us out of our predicaments, I thought to myself how lucky it was that I had stopped right behind a driver with a container full of gas. Sometimes a problem meets a solution thanks to luck, but an "enquiring mindset" will increase the chances of such an encounter. An enquiring mindset is the ability to "walk around" with the problem in mind and continuously scan for possible solutions like radar.

NSO Group's success story beautifully demonstrates what an enquiring mindset is. The company sought to develop a solution for gathering intelligence by controlling phones remotely.

Raising investment for the venture was conditioned on the recruitment of a technological partner who would confirm that the technological problem was solvable. The company turned every stone to find the right technologist: many meetings were held with people from academia, cellular networks, and high-tech companies who claimed that "the solution is impossible." Just before giving up on the venture, another meeting was held with an investor in a Ramat Aviv cafe. Entrepreneur Shalev Hulio, who was standing in line to order coffee, overheard a conversation between two people standing behind him discussing the technology of remotely controlling computers and phones for intelligence gathering purposes. "A very generic conversation, but there was enough there to catch my ear," Hulio later recalled. He turned to them and asked if they could speak for a few minutes. The fate of the company was decided in those minutes, after the name of a third person who knew how to solve the problem was mentioned. That same man was later recruited to become the top employee at NSO, which became a success story and rose to the top of the global cyber industry.

Sometimes luck is even involved when searching for solutions in nature, but an enquiring mindset is also required. Sometimes the solution appears before our eyes from nature's reservoir of patents, but one can easily miss a small straw floating on the water without awareness of its existence. The Japanese railway engineer was lucky when he watched the solution plunge into the water before his eyes, but he was constantly aware of the issue of noise pollution. In this case, the "straw" was not an error but a lead to the solution. However, in most cases, we have to make an effort, to dive into the depths of the reservoir and retrieve the pearls. Today, there are search methods designed to bring us to the kingfisher in a deliberate and systematic way.

During one of my trips in Central America, we came across a cornfield. We started walking through it, and pretty soon the area turned into a maze. The corn was surprisingly high and it wasn't clear where to turn. We walked for a long time without there being any sign as to which way we should go. After a long while, without a field of vision, we saw a power line high above us. It was clear that the path ran underneath it. We walked toward the power line and indeed reached the path. The search methods I will shortly describe will locate the power line at the edge of the cornfield and illuminate the North Star, which will at the very least point you in the right direction of the solution.

When I am faced with a new challenge and I want to look for solutions in nature, I start from the light to the heavy. First, I turn to the obvious – to my own knowledge base or that of those close to me. Later, I move on to the designated databases and finally turn to a general search on the web.

Starting with the Obvious

Sometimes the solution already exists in our field of knowledge and is even familiar to all. We're not talking about a rare animal, but of nature's invaluable assets, which we all grew up with and know about even without studying biology. For example, seeking a solution for a strong but lightweight structure in nature will most likely lead to turtle shells. Searching for camouflage solutions will lead to chameleons and searching for navigation mechanisms will lead to migrating birds.

The classics that everyone knows about are a door to a world of in-depth research and innovative mechanisms. For example, in 2020, a novel study on the navigation mechanism of migratory birds was published. [97] The fact that migratory birds sense and use the Earth's magnetic field has been known for years, but their sensors' identity had remained an enigma. The study identified magnetotactic bacteria, which actually serve as compasses and navigate birds during flight.

It's always a good idea to start looking for the obvious: to ask if a solution to the challenge at hand has already been identified in nature. Entering nature through a familiar door doesn't mean that innovative and inspiring mechanisms can't be found behind it. Innovation may be expressed in the actual realization of the inspiration and in the application itself. However, most often the solution is not found among the obvious, and then we must turn and look elsewhere.

Designate Databases

These databases were specifically developed to make nature's inventions accessible to engineers and designers. The information is entered manually and is therefore of high quality, precise, and accessible in a language adapted to the users – with a technological-engineering orientation. The search time is also shorter. The main disadvantage is the relatively limited scope of information in these databases – a mere drop in the ocean relative to nature's enormous potential. Another disadvantage is the fact that these designers are looking at a closed world of several hundred or thousands of solutions and are exposed to the same sources of inspiration as well as the same sources of solutions. The search tool used in these designated databases is taxonomy, i.e., familiarity with the method of classification and sorting of database information and searching according to it.

• **The AskNature database:** If nature could answer you, what would it say? The AskNature database[98] is a development of the Biomimicry Institute and is currently considered the largest database of nature's inventions in the world, containing several thousand records. The database invites us to consult with nature and ask how nature would solve various challenges. We can search via free text, but the most accurate and recommended way is to search according to the functional taxonomy used to classify and catalog records on the site. The taxonomy is detailed on the website itself which we can see and use to navigate.

Above each entry on the site is a "golden triangle": **organism–function–strategy**. This represents: which organism served as a source of knowledge; what function was being studied; and what strategy was described for realizing the function. For example, one of the database entries will display the Namib Desert beetle (organism); capture, absorb, or filter fluids (function); and an explanation of the wings that are covered in hydrophilic bumps and hydrophobic grooves, and positioned in a certain way (strategy).

In the database, we can find biological strategies, that is, solutions to various functional challenges. Each such entry includes at the top the function and an explanation of the strategy (biological mechanism) along with pictures and links to researchers and articles. Since nature has different strategies for realizing the same function, several records exist when searching one function. For example, if we focus on the function of maximizing sun exposure, several different strategies will be found for achieving the same goal: optimal leaf dispersion, movement toward the sun (heliotropism), getting to a higher altitude, increasing light absorption through structures that absorb more light, etc. The database also displays solutions that have already been implemented, in other words, products or technologies that have already been developed that were inspired by strategies from nature. For every entry of this type, we can read about the product, find the name of the company that developed it, and be exposed to the invention's biomimetic story.

The AskNature database is not only a nature search engine, but also a respectable database in the field of biomimicry. We can find case studies, curricula, films, and collections of nature's strategies for solving key challenges, such as strategies for climate change, transportation, and energy. I always tell my students to put aside extra time when they enter this database because it's like surfing social media, replete with temptations. The attractive visual design and beautiful images make exiting the database especially difficult...

• **The FindStructure database:** If nature's structures could speak, what would their language be? The FindStructure database[99] lets us search for solutions by both function and structure. Structures are the heart of innovation in nature; they are visual and not subject to interpretation. A layered structure is a layered structure. It's hard to argue with that. While on the other hand, there may be different ways to define the same function, so searching by structure may be more accurate. The database is based on my doctoral thesis, which dealt with the structural language of nature that produces functional solutions. The database contains several hundred records categorized according to structure and their functional context. Each entry contains a detailed explanation of the functional mechanism, a link to articles, explanations, and biomimetic products and technologies, if they exist. The database also helps with the abstraction phase. Not only does it find solutions in nature, but it also provides a complete description of the functional mechanism with reference to structures. The database has many examples that are not found in AskNature, thereby expanding the search field.

•**'Innovation from Nature' database** (in Hebrew): Between 2010–2018, this newsletter was published by the Israeli Biomimicry Organization. Every month, the newsletter covered a number of news items about bioinspired innovation from around the world in various fields, including materials, engineering, energy, design, architecture, and medicine. The newsletter is written in scientific language but in an understandable way and currently serves as a rich internet database available to all those wishing to find information in Hebrew in the fields of bioinspired innovation. The database allows you to search using any keyword, including functions.

- **BioM:** An innovation database called BioM[100] was developed at the University of Guelph in Canada, a collection of biomimetic developments at various levels – from concept to commercial availability – to support research and enable development. The database currently contains around 400 case studies and is an open source repository, where users can make contributions.
- **Academic biomimetic databases:** There are a few academic journals that publish research in the fields of biomimetics and bioinspiration. For example, *Bioinspiration & Biomimetics*, publishes articles on the study of principles inherent in nature with the aim of creating physical models or applications in engineering and technology. *Design and Nature*, delivers aspects of design that can be gleaned from nature, related to structure, dynamic systems, material, architecture, sustainability, and more. You can often find core review papers on particular topics. For example, when I was working on an innovation project related to the development of a biomimetic sensor, I found an excellent overview of different types of biomimetic sensors, which helped map out the field and jumpstart the process.

General Databases

General databases, which include biological information not necessarily intended for biomimetic research, are also an excellent gateway to nature's solutions. The advantage of these databases is the wealth and variety of information which yields great innovation potential. Nature's inventions will usually be integrated into general, descriptive, and less relevant text, but the function sensor and lens of awe you have already developed will help the biomimetic information "jump out" from the text and reach your eyes. Here are some examples of general databases:

- **Databases of zoological centers, zoos, and botanical gardens:** Large centers like these carry databases about the zoological or botanical collections they have on display. If you find something interesting, you have someone to turn to. You can always contact the curator of the establishment and request elaboration or clarification on the information that interests you.

- **Popular science literature about interesting facts and record breaking in nature:** Even though it's not scientific literature, popular science provides kernels of truth that can lead us to finding nature's inventions and dive deeper into research. For example, you can read in popular non-fiction that fleas jump 100 times their size. This is akin to a child a meter in height being able to jump to the top of the Big Ben and land back down safely. It is likely that the awe you sense from this fact will send you on a hunt to find more scientific information about the jumping mechanism of fleas.

- **Scientific literature in fields such as biology, zoology, botany, and ecology:** These databases, led by the journals, *Nature* and *Science*, are an excellent place to find traces of nature's inventions. I once heard a sweet and accurate sentence related to this: "Nature can always publish in *Nature*." The most famous and well-known biomimetic mechanisms, such as the pine cone effect, were first published in Nature, the journal every researcher dreams of getting published in. Another good source of information is the academic periodical, the *Journal of Morphology*, which publishes studies on the relationship between structure and function in nature, and since this is identified with the core of biomimicry, I often find interesting and applicable mechanisms there.

The Lucky Jar

Searching generic repositories can be time consuming and can lead to poor quality results. To obtain optimized and accurate search results, use keywords. A keyword is like a power line in a cornfield – it points to the right area. But keywords also need to be searched. I have a method for creating keywords that arose from a need to make my searches more precise and shorter in duration. Searching this way has often led me to find exact solutions right on the first page of Google results. The method begins with an "empty jar" that gradually gets filled with keywords formed from questions. Each question in turn adds more queries to the jar. By the end of the process, the jar will be full of intelligent keywords. And then we can pull words out from the jar at random and use them to search. Here are the relevant questions for filling the jar:

• **What is the 'challenge' environment?** Organisms in nature operate in the same physical space as the technological challenge. Physical phenomena and characteristics related to the challenge can be used as keywords. These terms likely appear in the explanation of some of the natural mechanisms that have been studied in the context of the desired solution. For example, the challenge of harvesting water. Relevant keywords related to the physical environment of this challenge would be fog, humidity, condensation, adsorption, super-hydrophobicity, temperature gradient, etc.

• **What are the extreme conditions?** Innovative solutions in nature can be found under extreme conditions, in habitats with limitations and constraints. The harsher the environmental conditions of the challenge, the more likely it is to find an innovative solution. For example, the challenge of maximizing light exposure. Innovative mechanisms can be found in habitats where there is little light, since in this extreme condition, strategies to increase exposure to light are likely to be found. Relevant keywords here are habitats with little access to light: the depths of the oceans, caves, the depths of earth, the forest floor, and the poles.

Ada Yonath, a Nobel Prize winning professor of chemical and structural biology at the Weizmann Institute of Science, shared that she found the solution for stabilizing ribosomes in extreme conditions in nature. Yonath studied ribosomes, which are intracellular particles responsible for protein synthesis. Ribosomes are comprised of a multitude of components. For many years, scientists have not been able to crystallize ribosomes due to their tendency to disintegrate upon exposure to the radiation required for determining their structure.

Yonat's ultimate success in crystallizing ribosomes was inspired by an article she read about polar bears, which described how ribosomes are arranged in a dense structure before hibernation. Yonat assumed that the ribosomes pack themselves densely to prevent their disintegration during hibernation – a time when they are almost completely inactive – describing this phenomenon as a mechanism for preventing disintegration under stressful conditions. This prompted her to investigate the ribosomal structures of organisms which inhabit the more extreme conditions found on the planet, for example, bacteria in the Dead Sea or hot springs, taking into account the assumption that their ribosomes would be more resilient in such harsh conditions.

Using a method developed by a German colleague, she was able to obtain large amounts of ribosomes from such bacteria. This marked the beginning of the successful mapping of ribosomal structure (in collaboration with other researchers).[101]

• **What is the analogical part of the system?** A biological system is a system like any other, and its structural and functional characteristics meet the definition of any system. Every part of the biological system has a function, and it interacts with various factors in its environment. The part of the biological system that's related to the design challenge makes a good keyword. The following table presents the analogies between the parts of the biological system and the parts of the engineering system.

	Biology	Engineering
1	Body	System
2	Skin, cuticle	Insulation of system
3	Bones, skeleton	Structure, reinforcements, struts and supports
4	Brain	Computer
5	Nervous system	Electrical system and communication network
6	Sensory system	Sensors
7	Muscles	Propulsion factors, Actuators

For example, the drag reduction challenge. Drag is formed at the interface between the organism's body and its environment and is related to skin or body shape and surface. Keywords which we can add to the jar are skin, surface, body shape (contours). Indeed, many drag reduction mechanisms in nature are identified with the contour of the body and the surface patterns of the skin, such as the contours of boxfish and the skin surface of sharks.

• **What is the functional terminology?** Naturally, the most essential and central keyword is the function – the bridge between biology and engineering – but as mentioned, the functional terminology in the biological and engineering literature is different. For example, using the function term *connect* is very common in engineering literature. The equivalent meaning in the biological literature is *adhere* or *bond*. Therefore, using the word *connect* to find biological connection mechanisms is unlikely to produce accurate information for the simple reason that the term *connect* is less prevalent in biological literature concerning connections. So, how can we know which functional terminology to use? For this purpose, a thesaurus, a functional glossary, was developed, linking engineering functions with their counterparts in the biological literature.[102] This thesaurus allows us to find the corresponding functional term in the biological literature. The function relevant to the challenge must be inserted into the jar using biological terminology.

• **What are the general and specific functions?** A function can be defined in general or specific terms. Changing the level of the function's hierarchy allows for a specific or a general search, as needed. An example of a specific search – instead of asking: *how does nature move air?* we might specify and ask: *how does nature regulate temperature?* We can also continue specifying and ask: *how does nature cool things down?* An example of a general search – Instead of asking: *how does nature pick up an object?* We might broaden the question and ask: *how does nature move an object?* We can insert functions of different hierarchy levels as keywords into the jar.

• **What are the qualities of the function?** Each function has a wide range of qualities. For example, the visual function. In his book, *Journey into the Consciousness of Nature (in Hebrew)*[103], Zvi Yanai demonstrates how enormous the variety of visual mechanisms are in nature. Each mechanism provides a different quality, depending on the need and the environment. Worms' primitive eyes can only distinguish between light and dark, while eagles' eyes can view hyraxes from 2,000 meters away. Dragonflies have eyes that allow them to see behind their heads, spiders have panoramic vision; insects can see ultraviolet light and snakes can see in infrared. One should first define the qualities of the function in question and add them as keywords. For example, if you're dealing with a vision challenge, you can add keywords like dark/light, near/far, panoramic, ultraviolet, and more.

AI Revolution

We are currently in the midst of an AI revolution. This revolution has fundamentally changed the ways people collect and process data. As a result, we can now experience a leap forward in the search of biomimetic information. AI tools are able to quickly scan and retrieve vital and relevant information. The dream is to have a search engine into which designers can insert free text describing the problem, and the results will yield nature's strategies for solving that problem. I believe that the future is leading us in this direction, and the more precise these tools will be, the higher the quality of our access to nature's inventions will be.

ABSTRACTION:
REACHING THE ESSENCE

*I'm not trying to imitate nature, I'm trying
to find the principles she's using.*

Buckminster Fuller

Buckminster Fuller, nicknamed Bucky, was an architect, inventor, and visionary who drew inspiration and knowledge from nature. The structure that he is perhaps most known for is the geodesic dome, a dome formed by small rigid struts joined together in triangles.

In his vision, Fuller saw entire cities covered in geodesic domes, which were designed to create insulated and protected living environments. One of his well-known quotes relates to the process of bioinspiration: "I'm not trying to imitate nature, I'm trying to find the principles she's using." In this sentence, Fuller describes his attempt to extrapolate nature's solutions into several design principles.

Once the biological information is identified through observation and awe or a systematic search in databases, it is time to refine the information and turn it into knowledge that will be used to solve the challenge. "Data is the new oil," the British mathematician and entrepreneur Clive Humby said back in 2006, but as we know, to derive value from crude oil, it must be refined.

There is a common yet erroneous romantic assumption that once an invention is identified in nature, it can simply be plucked like a flower from a field of flowers and planted in the field of application. Of course, reality is not that simple, and abstraction is required. In the abstraction phase, the functional mechanism is derived and described in simple terms, using a pattern or model, in order to turn the complex biological information into simple and clear information that explains how the function is achieved. This understanding will make it possible to "transfer" the function to technological systems as well.

By the end of the abstraction phase, we can figure out how the function is achieved, how the mechanism works, and what knowledge is transferred to the application space. Only after this stage, is it possible to disconnect from the biological system and use the knowledge learned from it for imitation and practical application, much like borrowing a book from the library, where we acquire the knowledge and then return it to its place on the shelf, alongside other sources of inspiration.

Reaching the Essence

Abstraction is a mental operation that makes it possible to relate to an object or topic in the desired context, while ignoring features and specifications irrelevant to the context being examined. During this stage, everything that conceals the essence is removed, the chaff is distinguished from the wheat, the most important aspect is observed and understood.

The act of abstraction is like glimpsing at a model of the human body that lets you "peel off the skin" and see what's underneath. You can view all the systems of the body, their locations, and how they relate to the other systems, and better understand their function. When it comes to emulating nature's inventions, the essence is the function. During the abstraction process, we focus on the function being studied (the challenge) and identify the factors in the biological system that are related to this function. The factors are identified via the three levels of imitation defined in the previous chapters:

• **Form and shape:** Geometric aspects, such as structures, forms, surfaces, and contours.

• **Processes:** Series of actions, an algorithm.

• **Ecosystems:** Operating principles; design, physical, inventive, or sustainable principles that dictate the system's functional mechanism.

The abstraction phase has us moving between the details and the overall picture in a process involving both divergent and convergent thinking. In this stage, we read and expand upon the knowledge, while at the same time, refine and focus our hypotheses until we form a clear model of the functional biological mechanism. We begin the abstraction process by defining the function we want to focus on and continue by researching the functional mechanism through various means: studying the literature to understand what knowledge has been accumulated about the mechanism so far; observing the functional behavior in different situations; and conducting field experiments or laboratory research. Research can be conducted in simple or advanced ways. Following the study, we identify the system parts that relate to the function being studied and the interaction between them, and translate this knowledge into a functional model that explains how the biological system operates.

Studying Mechanisms by Simple Means

Samaras are winged, dry fruit containing seeds, those same helicopter seeds we loved to play with as children, throwing them up in the air and watching them spin as they fall to the ground. The fruit consists of a seed wrapped in a hard, fibrous coat that expands into a wing-like structure. The fruit dries out as it ripens and changes its color from green to brown. It falls from the tree in a downward rotational spiral and gets carried by horizontal winds. The rotation actually decelerates the fall allowing the seed to remain longer in the air so the winds can carry it farther away and increase its chances of germination. This dispersal strategy is also seen in other trees, where the seeds are called 'helicopter seeds' because their rotational movement resembles a helicopter's rotor both in form and function.

What causes this rotational motion function? In a series of simple experiments using scissors and a lump of plasticine, we can identify the parameters that govern the rotation. If we cut the curved part of the wing and straighten it out, the seed will continue rotating but at a much faster rate. If we separate the spherical seed from the wing, the seed will fall straight down and quickly to the floor and the wing will move more slowly but stop rotating. If we change the seed's center of gravity by adding a lump of plasticine to the wing at the far end from the seed, the seed will immediately stop spinning.

In these experiments, we can see that the asymmetrical component of the seed is critical for rotation. The geometric asymmetry of the wing – where one side is curved and one is straight – and the asymmetrical center of gravity that is focused on one side of the winged seed are the parameters that generate the rotation function. If we turn to the literature, we can learn about additional parameters that are related to the rotation. It turns out that the rough surface formed by the wing's arteries also contributes to improved aerodynamics and rotation. This texture also provides a mechanical advantage: resistance to bending and torsion forces. There is also a precise balance between the weight of the seed and the length of the wing, which results in optimal rotation and stable movement, such that any deviation from this ratio will impair performance. Studies have shown that the autorotation mechanism has an advantage over the parachute mechanism in slowing the fall of a given seed size. It's an optimal solution for carrying seeds over a distance at "low cost."

This was a demonstration of studying a mechanism with a simple experiment, observing the seeds fall and examining the literature. In fact, the experiment is so simple that you can do it yourself or even with your children – a guaranteed few minutes of joy along with excellent practice in inquiry. At the Science

Museum in Barcelona, helicopter seeds were turned into a kinetic sculpture: the seeds are dropped from the fifth floor, falling slowly as they twirl past the visitors climbing the stairs beside them, collected on the first floor, and lifted up again to the fifth floor. Simple, intriguing, and beautiful. Among the developments inspired by helicopter seeds are tiny robots[104] and even a ceiling fan designed like a samara: with one blade as long as a wing and the other short like a seed. According to the designers, the asymmetry produces more efficient airflow.

Study Mechanisms by Advanced Means

Everybody has scissors and plasticine, but we often require more advanced research tools. In such cases, studies take place in appropriate research laboratories, usually in academic research institutions. Laboratories around the world are equipped with imaging equipment, state-of-the-art cameras, wind tunnels, acoustic rooms, 3D printers, mechanical equipment, and more, depending on the research topics. In these laboratories, we can examine various parameters related to the functional model being investigated and assist in the abstraction and refining of the functional mechanism.

For example, researchers at Harvard University wanted to deepen their understanding of shark skin, which is covered in dermal denticles, and introduce another parameter into the drag reduction model – the surface's degree of elasticity. Shark skin is not a static surface. It is affected by the sharks' movement in the water, and this fact seems to be missing from the model explaining the drag reduction function. In a series of experiments, they produced different surfaces with the structure of shark skin and attached them to rigid plates that had been dipped in a water tank and swung from side to side to simulate the swimming of sharks. They then repeated the experiment but this time on flexible membrane-like foils. The dramatic effect of the denticles was reflected on the flexible foils. In fact, the denticles even interfered with the motion when the base was static (a rigid foil plate).[105] Shark skin seems not only to reduce drag, as was known until now, but also changes the hydrodynamic flow near the skin in a way that produces thrust.

Sometimes the research laboratory is found in nature. For example, albatrosses can spend weeks over the oceans without returning to land. This remarkable feat led researchers from the Technical University of Munich to attach GPS loggers to albatrosses to trace their flight path with high precision.[106] The data collected from the loggers was processed and analyzed for building a model that describes the flight technique while considering various parameters, such as body weight and wind speed. They found that the flight path of albatrosses is not linear: they begin by flying close to the sea surface, continue with a sharp climb into the wind to gain altitude – reaching a height of about 15 meters – and a reverse turn back to the sea, surfing effortlessly downward. This cycle of motion lasts about 15 seconds and is called 'dynamic soaring.' This flying technique utilizes the wind gradient to extract energy by repeatedly crossing the boundary between air masses of different velocities (wind shear), where wind speed changes dramatically. The researchers concluded that the albatross extracts the most energy at the upper curve of the cycle, where the transition between air masses occurs. Could drones and gliders one day emulate this flying technique and fly over oceans for long periods of time? (*see 12).

Modeling the Functional Mechanism

Now is the time to present the knowledge accumulated during the stage of studying the biological mechanism through a simple and clear model that will support the transfer of knowledge to technology. The more coordinated the modeling is with engineering thinking, the easier it will be for engineers to advance to application. The solution for modeling in alignment with engineering thinking stems from the field of systems modeling, an accepted and basic field in the engineering literature. The idea is to take system modeling tools from the engineering world and apply them to biological systems, in order to understand and describe their functioning as a system. In fact, any model for analyzing a system can be applied to a biological system, since it is a system in every respect.

The most basic form of modeling is identifying all the parts of the system related to the function, assuming that any system's functioning can be described through its parts and the interaction between them. The term "system" implies an orderly structure or scheme. When children are given a new toy, they tend to disassemble it, as part of their investigation process, trying to identify its parts and understand how it works. Similarly, when we study a biological system, we want to identify its parts and the relationship between them. The basic assumption is that there is a connection between the system's parts, and if we understand the order or method that organizes them, we will be able to understand the system's functioning.

In the process of identifying the parts of the biological system, it is important to understand a less common principle in the engineering world: the system's parts can also be found **outside its physical limits**. For example, a drop of water is part of the mechanism that cleans the lotus leaf, even though it's not part of the leaf. This is part of the beauty and elegance of nature's solutions. In order to systematically identify all parts of the biological system, we divide them into the subsystem and the supersystem. Subsystem parts are components found within the physical boundaries of the biological system, and supersystem parts are components found in the biological system's environment that interact with it and help perform the action (function).

For example, the parts that make up the attachment system of burdock burrs, which inspired the invention of Velcro, are the hooks on the burrs, but also animal fur, plants, stems, and rocks found in the vicinity. Using these parts, we can describe the attachment and detachment mechanism. The animal passes by a bush full of burrs. The hooks of the burr entangle in the loops of the animal's fur and cling to it. The animal keeps moving and the burr remains attached to the fur. The burr may fall off eventually or get rubbed off by the animal when it advances and rubs against a rock or stem. The burr detaches and falls off. This simple story includes the system parts that were identified earlier and describes the interaction between them, which produces the actions of attachment and detachment.

To completely understand how the system operates, two additional aspects must be acknowledged. The first aspect is the control element that steers the system's behavior. What starts and stops the operation? The control element of a biological system can be outside the system. For example, changes in humidity levels in the environment is what triggers the opening and closing of pine cone scales. Changes in the sun's position causes the rotational motion of sunflowers. The control element can also be internal when the organism performs an action that initiates the functional mechanism. For example, bringing a gecko's foot closer to a wall produces attachment. Returning to the burdock burr example, the control element in this case is the contact of a nearby animal.

The second aspect is the energy source. What is the energy source operating the system? No system works without an energy source. Looking more broadly, we are talking about the system's input, which can also be information or matter and not just energy.

Returning again to the burdock burr example, the energy source here is the movement of animals (kinetic energy), which pass by the burr and detach it.

There are many methods in the engineering literature for modeling systems, and in fact, any modeling method that helps us understand the functioning of a system can also be used here. The benefit of modeling is revealed when the mechanisms are complex. As long as the mechanism is simple, understanding how the system operates is intuitive. When the mechanism is complex, modeling helps to crack the biological mechanism in an optimal way.

Abstraction Tools for Designers

Design students, who develop sketches, shapes, and forms during the design process, often encounter difficulty extracting the potentially complex functional mechanism in the absence of appropriate biological or engineering backgrounds. How will the inspiration from nature be translated into the blank page? How does one extract the meaning behind nature's design models? The beacon for designers in the abstraction process is to identify the design principle or conceptual idea.

For example, a design student from the Bezalel Academy of Arts and Design studied the closing mechanism of Dionea muscipula, popularly known as the Venus Flytrap. This carnivorous plant consists of two lobes connected by the leaf's midrib. On the edges of each lobe are long stiff outer edges that mesh together when the lobes close to prevent large prey from escaping. She was inspired to design a shoe that would "lock" the foot inside. The connection between the sole and the body of the shoe is similar in appearance and function to the two lobes of the plant. Another student studied crocodile skin and learned that it is made of bony scutes called osteoderms that are embedded underneath the dermal layers of the skin and create the appearance of scales. The layering, which consists of hidden material that emerges and gets exposed, has been translated into the world of silversmithing.

Another beacon for designers during the abstraction process is to notice the small details in the biological model and identify the interactions among them. This point in time of discovering connections is the starting point of the creative process – where the designer or creator begins to wonder and ask questions that advance the creative process.

One of the abstraction methodologies offered to designers is called From Inspiration to Sketches (FITS),[107] in which designers are directed to dismantle the source of inspiration into units of the design palette, units that make up the building blocks of product properties: color, shape, line, proportions, motion, joint, texture, material, and more. The dismantling allows the designer to understand what the function consists of, but also isolates the design elements in a way that enables their reassembly in the creative process, as the artist Paul Cézanne declared, "Painting from nature is not copying the object." The artist should realize his sensations by interpreting nature into the language of art, using form, color, structure, and relations.

Another tool launched for designers in 2020 is called *Nature of Form*,[108] a visual library of forms. The tool was developed by multidisciplinary designers who studied how forms in nature create meaning in different contexts. It was developed after its creators understood how vital inspiration from nature is to their work as designers, but experienced difficulty in utilizing it. They analyzed 275 organic elements and extracted 1,454 forms, textures, and colors from them. Several qualities were attributed as adjectives to each form, such as sharp, soft, symmetrical, asymmetrical, and more. In fact, Nature of Form is a database of models from nature that have been abstracted and refined for designers. The tool "bypasses" the abstraction process, and serves as an inspiration similar to Pinterest, but focuses on nature. It saves hours of searching and frustration over finding inspiration. The tool can also be used by architects and artists in design and creative processes.

Inventive Principles
in Nature and Technology

*In formal logic, a contradiction is the signal of defeat,
but in the evolution of real knowledge it marks the
first step in progress toward a victory.*

Alfred North Whitehead

Many times in life we want both: careers in both our interests; living abroad and in our home country; painting all day and building a startup; playing piano but also violin, clarinet, and drums. And then they tell us: you can't have everything, choose one, and focus. Is there a way to reconcile this apparent contradiction and manage the competition over our time, energy, and financial resources?

Nature excels in resolving such contradictions using inventive principles. For example, Brazil nuts. This nut grows on one of the tallest trees in the Amazon rainforest, which can reach a height of 50 meters. They grow in pods that range from the size of a grapefruit to that of a coconut with 12–25 nuts inside, each in its own shell. It is highly discouraged to stand under a tree while the two-kilogram pods are falling. Two contradictions make this story an enigma:

1) The pods fall from a great height, but also remain intact until their disperser arrives.

2) The pods are closed to everyone except agoutis, the rodent that exclusively disperses their seeds.

The mystery is solved using two inventive principles.

• **Local Quality:** This principle states that changing an object's structure from uniform to non-uniform can improve product quality. The outer shell of Brazil nut pods has specific protective qualities. It consists of several shock-absorbing layers that allow the pod to safely reach the ground.

• **Preliminary Action:** This principle refers to performing preparatory activities to expedite the execution of planned tasks, or more simply 'get it done in advance.' Just as you don't make a door without first designing how to open it; so likewise, Brazil nut shells have been designed with the feature that they can be cracked by agoutis. This rodent is equipped with the right key – exceptionally sharp teeth and a strong jaw. These features allow Agouti to gnaw a hole into the hard shell and retrieve the seeds.

Locating Inventive Principles

There is a memorial site in South Africa dedicated to Nelson Mandela. A statue on site is composed of fifty steel columns. From up close, you can only see the columns, but from a distance, looking at all the columns at once, you suddenly notice the form of an image: the face of Nelson Mandela. The experience is similar even when looking at a three-dimensional image. At first you see many details that seem unrelated. Then, from this blurry image, the details start to come together, and the three-dimensional image suddenly appears.

When looking at a large group of parts, we can discern a common element, a unifying principle, a repeating pattern. If we look at a large set of solutions, we can see a recurring principle common to solving the problems. This is exactly what Genrikh Altshuller did – a Jewish man living in Russia in the 20th century. Altshuller was an inventor and was offered a job in a patent office, with a very large stream of patents passing by his desk. At some point, he noticed that there were common and recurring inventive principles in the patents. No matter the field of the patent, the inventive principle was the same. And so began his life's work: he began identifying these inventive principles and laid the foundation for the Theory of Inventive Problem Solving, or TRIZ (its Russian acronym). At some point, due to criticism of the Soviet regime, he was sent to prison, and it was there of all places that he was granted the freedom to devote all his time to his life's work. He continued reviewing patents and extracting inventive principles from them. In total, hundreds of thousands of patents were examined.

Physical and Technical Contradictions

Altshuller recognized that the most striking feature of the problems he encountered was contradiction. For example, Brazil nuts, which must both fall from a great height and remain intact, must remain closed but also be open for agoutis. According to Altshuller, technological breakthroughs occur when contradictions are resolved. Contradictions are not signals of an impasse or defeat, as suggested by Alfred North Whitehead, a British philosopher and mathematician, but opportunities to produce evolutions of knowledge that develop from the resolution of the contradiction. In nature, too, the tension between opposing forces is an engine associated with the potential for growth and change.

Sometimes the contradiction is found in the values of a certain parameter: you want the system to be both hot and cold (temperature), both long and short (length), fast and slow (velocity), wet and dry (humidity). This contradiction is defined as a physical contradiction. Sometimes the contradiction is found between different parameters in the system: you want the system to be both strong and light in weight, fast and stable. This contradiction is defined as a technical contradiction. How are these contradictions resolved? Is it possible to have both?

• **The principle of separation:** Physical contradictions can be resolved using the principle of separation: separation in time or in space. How can cars move in different directions at one intersection at the same time? The solution is separation in space by means of interchanges, with each interchange built at a different height. And how can they move in different directions in the same plane of altitude? The solution is separation in time by means of a traffic light. The principle of separation also exists in nature. How can animals exist from the same resources in the same space? The solution is separation in space, such that every animal has its own territory. How can red flowers of different species be pollinated by the same pollinators? The solution can be identified in Israel by the blooming "red wave," a separation in time of blossoming: first the anemones bloom, then the buttercups, and finally, the poppies bloom last. Separation in space or time resolves physical contradiction.

• **Inventive principle**: Technical contradictions can be resolved using inventive principles. Altshuller identified 40 recurring inventive principles in the many patents he examined. These principles make it possible to reconcile contradictions between various parameters in a system. Using these principles to solve novel issues enables the creation of systematic innovation. The database of inventive solutions is concentrated in a matrix of conflicting parameters called the 'contradiction matrix,' which juxtaposes various system parameters, including length, weight, volume, velocity, temperature, strength, shape, and more. On one end of the matrix, is a parameter we wish to strengthen in the system, and on the other end, is a parameter that weakens as a result. At their nexus in the matrix, we can find inventive principles for solving this contradiction. For example, if we want to improve the strength parameter, but the weight parameter is harmed in the process, we can find inventive principles proposed to solve this specific contradiction at the meeting point between these parameters in the matrix. The contradiction matrix can be found on various websites, where we can select the parameters of the contradiction and receive inventive principles for solving it. The website, TRIZ40,[109] offers explanations and examples for each of the 40 inventive principles.

• **TRIZ, nature's inventions, and the abstraction process**: Altshuller did not examine nature's patents in his work, but nature's systems are systems in every way, so it makes sense to recognize in nature's solutions the same inventive principles that Altshuller identified in technological solutions. This was my assessment, and it turned out to be true. If so, then identifying inventive principles in nature is a wonderful way to understand, model, and refine nature's inventions, and to support the abstraction process. Although I won't be able to delve into all 40 inventive principles in this chapter, I have chosen a few to demonstrate how this fascinating knowledge base sheds light on nature's inventions, assists in their abstraction and refining process, and supports the innovation process.

The Segmentation Principle

Segmentation involves breaking down an object into several independent and repetitive parts. This increases the degree of segmentation, that is, the number of parts of the object. For example, insects like flies and dragonflies have eyes called compound eyes, which are made up of thousands of tiny independent photoreception units. The eyes resemble balls covered in tiny eyes from all directions. In this way, the insects can quickly detect movements around them, even though they do not see clearly.

Segmentation into small parts, bumps, twists, or folds is a

recurring strategy in nature to increase surface area without increasing volume. Lung alveoli increase the surface area of gas exchange in a small space; Cortical folds in the brain increase the information processing area within the volume limits of the skull; the human intestine is replete with folds to improve the efficiency of breaking down food. If we spread out the small intestine alone, the total surface area is about the size of a tennis court! The skin of large mammals such as elephants and rhinoceroses are full of folds, which increase the skin's surface area to optimize thermoregulatory processes.

Segmentation is a recurring inventive principle in the technological world, as well: tall ladders that fold up when placed in storage can both be tall during use and take up a small storage space. Dividing food into small packages allows you both to sell a large quantity and keep it fresh. Separating a long line into short segments allows moving a large number of people in a small area.

• **Silent flight:** A BBC video shows three birds flying over high-quality, super-sensitive microphones that record every noise.[110] First, a pigeon flew. Significant noise was recorded. Next flew a peregrine falcon, and again there was quite a bit of noise. Then came the turn of the barn owl. Its flight was completely silent. Almost no interference was recorded. The human ear can hear nothing. The barn owl, a nocturnal bird of prey, must move quietly toward its prey to surprise it. Noise can also impair its ability to spot prey. How can you achieve noise reduction in flight without damaging wing shape? The principle of segmentation resolves this contradiction: the ends of barn owl feathers located on the leading edge of the wing are separated by spaces, between which are tiny comb-like bristles called serrations. This design is absent in other birds. The air that meets these serrations breaks down into smaller currents called micro-turbulences which disrupt the turbulence and eliminate the sound.

This design does not involve altering the wing's shape or size. Today, this solution is implemented in low-noise wind turbine blade design. A similar principle is applied in the world of transportation: on the roofs of trucks, trains, and on aircraft wings are small metal blades called vortex generators, which break down turbulences created during movement into small currents and ensure quiet travel (*see 13).

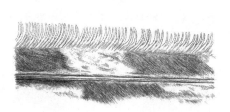

The Taking Out Principle

Taking Out is removing a part of the system that serves no purpose. If the part is required for the system's functioning, other parts in the system fill the role of the missing part. For example, the retama plant lacks leaves and it is the stem that replaces their role in photosynthesis. This allows the plant to live in arid and warm habitats and also to prevent fluid loss from the nonexistent leaves' surface.

Usually when we want to reinforce something, intuitively we tend to add material to it. But in nature, the contradiction between strength and weight is actually solved by subtraction, or more precisely, subtracting material where it is not needed. For example, bone is characterized by a spongy structure. Air cavities replace the missing material without compromising bone strength. Toucan beaks have a similar spongy structure. The beak is strong enough to absorb loads, but also light enough to minimize the energy required to fly. Bamboo, a particularly strong plant, grows as a hollow cylinder. Material was taken out from the center. The combination of strength and being light in weight makes bamboo an ideal material for scaffolding. In China, you can see modern buildings surrounded by bamboo scaffolding.

Even in the technological world, 'Taking Out' serves as an inventive principle. In the Far East, you can see people with umbrellas on their heads or backs. This is essentially an umbrella where the handle has been removed and the user's body replaces that function.

'Taking Out' is also a recurring pattern in every suspense plot, in which the identity of the killer is unknown, and it is an inventive principle used in the business world. For example, visiting a restaurant where the lighting has been removed offers a special experience for the diner. Suddenly the sounds, tastes, and smells take on new meaning. Another example is the retail company, Tesco, which increased its market share in South Korea despite avoiding opening up real stores. Instead, it launched virtual stores in subway stations to appeal to working people who are too busy or tired to reach the stores. The virtual display looks just like the real store. Purchases were made by scanning codes with cell phones and shipments would reach passengers' homes immediately after they arrived. Train waiting time turned into shopping time, and the shopping experience remained intact.[111]

• **A tire that doesn't go flat**: Beehives are strong and lightweight structures in nature, allowing strength on the one hand and space to store honey and sustain life on the other. An innovative biomimetic tire was developed inspired by the honeycomb structure,[112] one that implements the 'Taking Out' principle. The tire is airless. The honeycomb structure substitutes the air that used to support a vehicle's load in the past. The structure of the honeycomb tire is strong, which allows the weight of the vehicle to be distributed more evenly, and of course, eliminates the risk of getting a flat tire.

The Merging Principle

Merging or combining involves bringing two parts of a system closer together so that their two functions are performed by one part. This is one of nature's strongest design principles and is expressed in multifunctional design. For example, octopus arms serve as organs both for locomotion and gripping/adhesion. The arms include a system of suction cups, or suckers, which allow adhesion to different surfaces using a simple adhesive mechanism; Starfish have a system of tube feet called podia on the undersides of their appendages that help them both attach to surfaces via suction adhesion and move about on the ground; The ears of desert mammals such as rabbits and fennec foxes merge two functions: they serve as both auditory and cooling organs. Their ears are loaded with dense blood vessels that act as radiators, cooling and evaporating body heat. In this way, they manage to live in hot areas while regulating their body temperature.

In the world of business and technology, merging is a quick and simple way to generate innovation. From time to time, we encounter interesting business mergers: a café and a bookstore, an aquarium and a restaurant, a hairdresser and a clothing store. There are even products that realize the 'Merging' principle: a toothbrush with built-in toothpaste or a Swiss Army Knife that offers a variety of functions in one device. I once saw an emergency kit that included a whistle, radio, raincoat, flashlight, drinking water, and a plastic box, all packed into a 5 cm diameter tube that is water resistant and can float. But we needn't go far since we have access to instruments that can take on more and more functions at any given moment. All we have to do is open the app store.

• **Knotless sutures**: One day, a porcupine entered our garden, and within seconds I heard screams and saw our little dog full of quills. When we removed them, the screams only grew louder. The quills, used to deter enemies, are not smooth in some species, but are tipped with small barbs. When the quill penetrates the body, the barbs cling to the tissue, and any attempt to pull it out against the direction of the barbs causes pain. These barbs attracted the attention of a bio-engineer and professor of medicine who was searching for a way to improve the process of holding tissues together after surgery.[113] He gained much information about the barb structure and function from a biologist who was studying porcupines and was once even quilled in his bicep, feeling the actual pain. Due to his bio-engineering curiosity about the barbs, he began running experiments with his team. Current staples, made of metal, tear tissue on the way in and cause damage. Inspired by the quill barbs, a new type of barbed staple was suggested, one that would require much less effort to insert.

A Quill Barbed Suture is already on the market. It is a time-saving closure device that eliminates the need to tie knots to secure the closure. The solution replaces conventional threads, allowing surgeons to both have a better grip on the tissue while causing minimal damage and to close it. The process is faster and more efficient, and the resulting scar is even more beautiful since the tension gets evenly distributed. Both closing and gripping functions are merged in one device.

The Other Way Round Principle

The aim of 'The Other Way Round' principle is to invert the action(s) used to solve the problem, meaning perform an action opposite to the one expected or dictated by the problem, such as cooling instead of heating or a static instead of a dynamic solution. For example, Cape Ground Squirrels, who inhabit the deserts of southern Africa, venture out during the hottest time of the day instead of finding a shady shelter. Their large, impressive tails, which are erect and don't slump to the ground, provide a portable 24/7 shading service. Instead of the squirrel going into the shade, the shade comes to the squirrel. By reversing operating hours, night monkeys, also known as owl monkeys, have an advantage in accessing food resources. During a full moon, night monkeys become active at night and exploit the moonlight for nocturnal activity, giving them a relative advantage over daytime creatures competing for the same food resources.[114] Organisms in nature that cannot move also demonstrate 'The Other Way Round' principle beautifully. Instead of them moving toward the food, the food reaches them. For example, sponges trap food from currents of water that pass through them.

A classic example of a technological product that implements 'The Other Way Round' principle is the treadmill. Instead of the person moving, the floor moves beneath them. In this way, we can walk long distances without moving; There are also swimming spas, where the water moves and the swimmer stays in place. Another classic example is a boat lift, the most exciting event on river boat trips. The boat is placed in an enclosure, and instead of lifting or lowering it, they raise or lower the water in the enclosure. In this way, the boat is lifted and lowered in height.

A beautiful example of applying 'The Other Way Round' principle in archaeology occurred at Tel Eton.[115] Instead of the archaeologists excavating, the pottery sherds were brought up to them using mole rats. The director of the Tel Eton excavations, Avraham Faust, said, "We circled the mound to examine the area and noticed that where mole-rats had kicked up dirt is where we found pottery. The mole-rats informed us of a settlement in an area that no one thought had been settled." Thus, with the help of mole-rats, an "underground city" was discovered to have existed around the mound, and its boundaries were even marked – indeed outside the city limits, the mole-rat hills didn't have any potsherds.

• **From the depths of the sea to the depths of the skin:** A sea anemone is also a static animal. It doesn't move toward food, but waits for food to pass through its environment. Sea anemones have a system of stinging cells in their tentacles called nematocytes, which are capsule-like organelles. When triggered, the capsules launch venom-covered barbs at potential prey passing by. The discharge and injection process takes milliseconds! Sounds fictional? The internal stinging mechanism was studied and implemented in a skin penetration system for drugs and cosmetics to enable efficient absorption of the substances into the body.

Another Dimension Principle

Adding 'Another Dimension' to the system is another inventive principle. For example, adding a dimension of motion to a static system, a dimension of volume to a two-dimensional system, or height to a system on the ground. For example, sunflowers have an added dimension of rotational motion, which allows them to track the sun, a phenomenon known as heliotropism; desert snails have an added dimension of height, helping them retreat into an upper coil of shells on hot days, away from the scorching ground; flying fish, also called exocoetidae, do not fly like birds with wing movements but glide using their fins. Flying fish can remain in the air for 40 seconds, travel distances of up to 400 meters and reach speeds of 70 km/h (!) Adding the dimension of aerial movement helps the fish escape predators. Upon returning to water, the fins fold back against the fish's body, allowing it to swim.

The heart of innovation for many products is the addition of another dimension. Alarm clocks with added wheels (dimension of motion) that run away when they sound the alarms; toothbrushes with length and an angle added to its outer hairs so that it also wraps around the sides of the tooth while brushing; the addition of urinal target stickers to improve hygiene levels; tiny houses around the world, which have rotating kitchens that allow you to take advantage of the surfaces on their sides, as well; and if you're having trouble dieting, try the scale suggested by Dan Ariely, a professor of psychology and behavioral economics: adding a dimension of "weight trends" to the scale promotes successful diets. With the new scale, you weigh yourself every morning, but instead of getting a precise result, you only get feedback: if you lost weight, if your weight remained the same, or if you gained weight. It turns out that adding this dimension (and subtracting the precise weight measurement) helps with weight loss.

Sometimes all you need is to add a dimension of fun. Glass bottle collection machines designed as a game awarding points to recyclers have increased the number of bottles returned. Bins that make falling noises with every shot caused people to go looking for garbage to throw out, and piano stairs that sound a note with every step attracted people to walk instead of using escalators. These are some examples of behavioral changes achieved through fun, which have earned the title "Volkswagen's Fun Theory."

• **A Painless injection:** Female mosquitoes bite us without us noticing. In fact, we only notice we've been stung when it begins to itch. When they insert their proboscises into our skin, it is neither noticeable nor painful. Apparently, proboscises are not smooth but are covered with ring-like protrusions that add a dimension of height, thus separating the skin tissue from the proboscis. Another added dimension is vibration. During insertion, the entire proboscis vibrates to reduce the time of continuous contact with the tissue. The attenuated stimulation of the tissue reduces nerve stimulation, and hence the sensation of pain. Inspired by this mechanism, a less painful needle intended for injections and blood tests was developed in Japan; it's serrated and able to vibrate, and is to be incorporated into medical devices such as glucose-monitoring devices for diabetics.

Preliminary Action Principle

Another inventive principle is taking 'Preliminary Action,' such as cooling, coating, or prearranging objects so that the operation is more convenient and time-efficient. An action with foresight is another way of simply describing this principle of action. For example, waterfowl smear their feathers with oil before entering cold water to maintain body heat; migratory birds store fat in their bodies before embarking on their long journeys; bulbs store food before the plant grows; northern squirrels hoard nuts and acorns to survive the cold winter when food is scarce; tree frogs survive long, harsh winters through an unusual 'Preliminary Action' mechanism: they become like glaciers in their environment. Their hearts stop beating, they stop breathing, and two-thirds of their organs freeze completely. When the air starts to heat up, they thaw and resume normal activities. Prior to freezing, the tree frogs produce proteins that encourage freezing. Production is gradual to allow the body to adapt to freezing. They also produce their own type of antifreeze that prevents the cells from completely freezing so they don't get destroyed. This transformational ability is as impressive as a frog turning into a prince!

In the medical world, people are anesthetized before operations, sedated before injections, vaccinated before illnesses,
and sterilized before invasive operations. In the manufacturing
world, protective equipment is worn before exposure to ma-
chinery, kits are prepared with all the parts required for assembly ahead of time, holes are covered before being painted over to
prevent paint from entering them, and installations are set up to
collect the dirt before drilling.

• **'Nose house'**: The breathing process involves the loss of critical heat. Air inhaled into the body is generally colder than body
temperature, and animals lose heat when exhaling air that the
body has warmed up into the environment. Small birds and various mammals perform a 'Preliminary Action' before air is released when they exhale: they trap the heat in the pulmonary
artery walls. During inhalation, the trapped heat is released and
heats up the air entering the respiratory system. This is essentially a heat exchanger located in the nasal passageways.

Buildings face the same challenge: they must be ventilat-
ed with minimal heat loss in winter and minimal cold loss in
summer. Researchers from Duke University developed a model
based on natural heat exchangers, which aims to exchange air
with the environment without affecting indoor temperature.
The experiment results showed that using the heat exchange
model of different mammals vastly helps save energy in heating
and cooling buildings. The study also found that the longer and
narrower the ventilation ducts of the heat exchangers, the more
effective they operate – similar to pulmonary arteries.[116]

Inventive Principles are Everywhere

When you're familiar with the inventive principles, it's impossible not to spot their footprints everywhere – in nature and in
technology. When I visited a design exhibition, I immediately

noticed these principles applied in the designers' work. I saw a necklace from which the pendant was missing, and to replace this design element was a knot in the body of the necklace; I saw a lampshade with an added dimension that responds to light, such that when the lamp is lit, it begins to move; and I saw an umbrella based on the 'Merging' principle: its handle also being a drying rack. When done using it, the umbrella is placed standing on its handle, which was designed to stand firmly on the ground.

Even during the Covid-19 pandemic, I couldn't help but notice inventive principles. 'Segmentation' of students into smaller, monitored classrooms; 'Taking Out' crowds from football games and cultural performances; 'Merging' spaces: therapy clinics were opened in forests and synagogues in public gardens; 'The Other Way Round' principle on locomotion: instead of going out to lectures and performances, they "came" to our home; 'The Another Dimension' principle: the tracking of cell phones for epidemiological investigations and even the fashion dimension added to masks. See how quickly masks, which we used to see only worn in public in Asia, had become a fashionable accessory; and of course, the 'Preliminary Action' principle of measuring our temperature, wearing masks, and washing our hands before entering public spaces.

It turns out that nature uses similar inventive principles when dealing with epidemics: insect colonies have been able to defend against epidemics for millions of years.[117] Recently, interests have been piqued to study and mimic their epidemiological strategies to help manage human epidemics. How does an insect exposed to an infectious agent not infect the entire nest? The principle of 'Preliminary Action' includes maintaining cleanliness inside the nest and disposing of waste outside the nest. Some ant species collect tree resin with antimicrobial properties and disperse it in the nest, while others even extract antibacterial compounds from their bodies, dispersing it in their environment. The 'Segmentation' principle is another strategy they use: as soon as ants sense pathogens, the level of communication between groups in the nest decreases. Apparently, the principle of social isolation is naturally applied.

Inventive principles are based on thinking patterns that we all naturally follow, which is why they stand out in the solutions we observe. But the way to realize their great potential for innovation is to apply them systematically to the problem.

The inventive principles can also be found in nature's solutions, and usually, it is possible to identify several principles for every one solution. Their value also lies in the fact that they are design principles that can be transferred to the application. I have presented six inventive principles in this chapter, but there are many more, and a thorough familiarity with all of them will help refine nature's solutions during the abstraction stage.

Nature's Structural Language

"In general, no organic forms exist, save such as are in conformity with physical and mathematical laws."

D'Arcy Thompson

I have a friend who "plays" with evolution. He specializes in a method for designing products and processes known as an evolutionary algorithm – an AI-based computer application that solves problems by mimicking processes associated with biological evolution. A computer program runs a simulation of the evolution of solutions. We begin with an initial group of potential solutions to a particular problem (population). Then the population is tested for fitness – how well it solves a problem according to a selected criterion – and the most fitting solutions are selected to breed (to be the parents), and paired to reproduce new solutions (offspring). At this stage, some of the traits are randomly changed and are not inherited from the parents to ensure diversity in solutions (mutations). The best solutions among the offspring, according to the selected criterion, become the parents of the next generation. A few generations later, the method produces an optimal solution.

That friend set out to investigate the optimal shape for a beam. In the first stage, he started with a number of beams, from which he selected the ones that were more suited to the defined criterion – optimal strength-to-weight ratio. These selected beams were used to reproduce the next generation of beams through pairings and mutations. He repeated this cycle over and over again, running the program and never imagined the surprise that awaited him: the beam yielded by the simulation was very similar in structure to a tree branch. Later on, he searched for an optimal structure for a crane, and the structure obtained this time around was very similar to the head of a swan. Evolution ran fast in the computer program and converged to the same results that nature's design lab achieved after 3.8 billion years of evolution.

Shaping Forces

What exactly are the forces that shape structures in nature? Why do certain structures in nature exist and not others? If we examine the structures and forms identified in nature, we will find that the list is not very long. There are structural patterns in nature: structures and forms that repeat themselves identically or similarly in seemingly uncommon places, in different systems, and on different scales. D'Arcy Thompson, a Scottish biologist and mathematician, studied organic forms in nature and published his findings on the formation of structural patterns in his book *On Growth and Form*,[118] published in the early 20th century and still cited today. According to Thompson, "no organic forms exist save such as are in conformity with ordinary physical laws." Organic forms are subject to physical laws and are products of "invisible" forces in the physical world. The forces are invisible, but they act on matter and leave their impression. A similar idea was articulated by Steven Vogel, a zoologist who merged physics and biology and contributed to shaping the discipline of biomechanics. Vogel stated that all organisms are exposed to the laws of physics that limit the range of possible design solutions in living systems.[119] So if physical forces are affecting matter in a certain way, the expected result is also a certain result, just like inserting variables into a mathematical equation that acts on them and leads to a certain result.

A story I once heard illustrates this point. Test tubes with epoxy glue components were sent to a space station. One test tube contained a base material (resin) and the other a curing agent (hardener). The researchers on the space station were asked to mix the materials and to let the glue form and harden. When they did this on Earth, the resulting glue hardened and took on the test tube's cylindrical shape. But the glue that formed and hardened in space took on the shape of a coil. Other gravitational forces had acted on the material, and thus its shape was different.

A Quest to Search for Structural Patterns

Structures in nature have always fascinated me, but it took quite a while for them to become the heart of my PhD. I knew I wanted to develop a method that would guide the user, hand in hand, all the way from defining the challenge, to locating the solution in nature and abstracting it, to transferring it to the application. I started reading every citation and every mention. On the one hand, the subject at hand was virgin territory, and there was opportunity to innovate. On the other hand, there wasn't much to hold on to, because not a lot of research in the field had been done. For a whole year, I had been in an enquiring mindset. It's always inspiring to be in an enquiring mindset, and I'm all for it as a way of life, but even the most skilled miner needs a flashlight from time to time to show them the way, and such a flashlight hadn't been found for a long time.

As I was enquiring, I began to gather material. I put every biomimetic innovation I encountered into my database: both the biological systems along with the innovations which were inspired by them. At that point, I didn't know what I would do with all this information, but the samples began to accumulate and the database took up space, reaching several hundred samples. After about a year, I started to feel frustrated and stuck. I had a lot of information and didn't know how to turn it into knowledge.

At one point, my supervisor, Yoram Reich, tossed me the flashlight. "Check out TRIZ's content knowledge base," he told me, "it could have an interesting connection to biomimicry." TRIZ, as mentioned, is a theory of systematic inventive thinking based on problem-solving thought patterns. I started studying TRIZ, and I knew that I had found what I was looking for. I wanted to identify nature's patterns for solving challenges. Just as Altshuller had identified patterns of solutions in a large database of patents, so too I wanted to identify patterns in nature's patent database. When I searched for the definition of 'pattern' in the dictionary, I received the last bit of reinforcement I needed. A pattern, according to the Merriam-Webster dictionary, is a form or model proposed for imitation, and since my research is about imitating nature's inventions, it makes perfect sense to use patterns.

The database already existed. Several hundred examples of bioinspired innovations were just waiting for me, and at that point, I knew what I would do with them. I went looking for patterns. I decided to focus on structural patterns because I understood their critical role in shaping nature's solutions, and noticed that they had not yet been extensively studied in the context of biomimicry. I identified an opportunity for innovative research and application. Nature solves problems using intelligent and elegant structures, but they don't stand on their own – they are associated with functions. The connection between structure and function is a recurring concept in the worlds of engineering, architecture, design, and of course nature as well – wherever systems are designed.

Form Follows Function

'Form follows function' is a basic principle of design coined by architect Louis Sullivan in the mid-20th century.[120] It means that a structure or object's form is derived from and related to its function. For example, architects designing openings in a building to let in light. Changing the form will change the function. This principle is fundamental to all disciplines concerning the design of buildings and systems: architecture, engineering, and design.

This principle is consistent with Jean-Baptiste de Lamarck's theory of evolution, which posits that anatomy is shaped according to its related functions. For example, it is believed that giraffes have long necks to help them reach higher foliage on tree-tops. When treetops rose in height, giraffes needed to evolve by lengthening their necks, and according to Lamarck, this acquired trait is inherited. But according to Darwin's theory of evolution, the opposite principle is actually true: function follows form. The form preceded the function, and through small, random variations in form, the function also changes. The animal with the longest neck survives and reproduces more than those with shorter necks. This is why we often encounter the opposite phrasing of this principle in biological literature. So what came first? It's a bit like the chicken and the egg. It's a matter of worldview. Forms are related to functions and functions are related to forms. And in a broader sense – functions are also related to structures and structures are related to functions. My quest for patterns has thus been focused on identifying the relationship between forms and structures to functions in nature, from an assumption that this relationship is the basis of nature's structural language.

Nature's Structural Language

I vividly recall the moment I spotted the first structure-function pattern. I was sitting in the cafeteria of the School of Mechanical

Engineering at Tel Aviv University with Sara Greenberg, a biologist and lecturer on TRIZ who guided me through the pattern recognition process, and we identified the first pattern: repeated protrusions. We noticed that wherever the database has an example of a surface with bumps, the associated generic function is attachment and detachment.

The first pattern discovered opened the floodgates to other patterns. Slowly, they emerged, structure by structure. Since each structure is adapted to a specific function, every time a structure emerged, I asked whether a generic function was associated with it. It was a repetitive process of formulating hypotheses about the existence of structure-function patterns and returning to the database to confirm them. In the end, I had nine basic structures. At some point, each new biological system that entered the database corresponded to one or more of these structures, and new structures were not discovered.

Thus, I had in my hands the first words that make up nature's structural language – its building blocks. Just as words combine to form sentences, the generic structures I found combined to form complex sentences of function, which are the functional mechanisms of nature. At least one of these structures can be identified in every natural system, and it is usually a combination of several structures. In this way, we can understand how nature creates its functionality in response to various challenges. Here are the structure-function patterns I found – the basic words of nature's structural language:

1. Repeated protrusions

This structure is characterized by repeated protrusions of various shapes and substances at the nano, micro, and macro levels. The protrusions can be hair, denticles, bristles, epidermal bumps, scales, and more. Their generic function: to attach or to detach. Surfaces in nature are not smooth. They bear raised elements of varying shapes, sizes, and distributions, which transform the surface into a functional structure. Many biomimetic developments are based on this structure. The bumps on the surface of lotus leaves associated with the function of detaching water droplets and dirt; the hydrophilic bumps on the wings of the Namib Desert beetle are related to the function of attaching water droplets; and the half a millions hairs on gecko feet are used for attaching to and detaching from different surfaces.

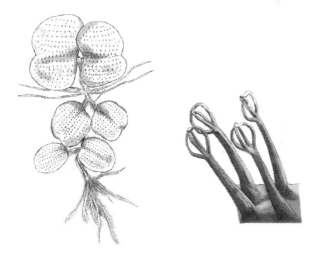

• **The Salvinia effect:** When the water fern, Salvinia molesta, is submerged in water by wind or animals, a layer of air quickly forms around it. One day, I brought this fern to my garden pond and saw it get covered in tiny bubbles after being immersed in water. The air layer insulates the fern and allows it to continue respiration even underwater. The layer remains stable even after spending several weeks underwater, and even in a state of flow and turbulence. When the fern floats back up and rises to the surface, it is completely dry.

The fern's leaves are covered with dense elastic hairs, called trichomes, that emerge in groups of four. The four hairs are grouped together in an egg-beater type of structure and stick out about two millimeters from the surface. The tip of the "whisk" facing away from the leaf's surface is hydrophilic, while the fern's surface itself is covered with a hydrophobic layer of wax. Water is repelled from the hydrophobic layer and gets caught in the hydrophilic whisks. The hairs actually form a gap trapping the air between the hydrophobic surface and the hydrophilic tips, creating an air layer that envelops the leaf over time. The one who revealed the mechanism is Barthlott, the botanist who also discovered the lotus effect. Barthlott proposed developing coatings for ships based on this effect as a stable and long-term solution for reducing the friction of the hull to the water interface. It is estimated that if all the ships in the world were covered with this coating, we would save about 1% of global CO_2 emissions.[121]

• **The mystery of the prune in the bathtub**: After spending a long time in an aquatic environment, the skin of the tips of fingers and toes fill up with grooves and resemble prunes. The scientific explanation for this phenomenon was described in an article I read in The Guardian: "Grooved skin provides a better grip, and may have helped our ancestors uproot wet plants while searching for food, as well as help feet better grip smooth surfaces."[122] Here is another example of the repeated protrusions structure and its connection to the functions of attachment and grip.

Familiarity with the structures and their roles can also help in understanding phenomena whose roles are not always clear, and moreover, perhaps even help researchers formulate hypotheses about these phenomena. Every time you come across a structure of repeated protrusions in nature, ask yourself: what attaches to or detaches from its surface?

2. Repeated tubes, channels, and tunnels

This structure is characterized as a system of tubes, channels or tunnels with or without valves. Their generic function: to channel (without valves) or regulate (with valves). Wherever there is a channel in nature, there is transport. In the circulatory system, oxygen is transported to the cells, and carbon dioxide is removed. Drainage basins consist of extensive systems of channels, canals, streams, and rivers, which carry water from high to low areas. The xylem system in plants is a network of conduits that transport water and minerals from the roots to the rest of the tree, and the phloem system transfers sugars formed during photosynthesis from the leaves to the rest of the plant. The repeated channels structure is often found in nature in conjunction with the repeated protrusions structure. There are channels between the protrusions. If something is attached to or detached from the bumps, it is then led to another location. For example, alongside the hydrophilic bumps on the wings of the Namib Desert beetle are hydrophobic channels that repel water. The drops that form on the bumps fall into the grooves and are led down the grooves into the beetle's mouth.

• **Termite mounds:** The termite mound is a wonderful engineering structure built by a creature the size of an ant. To illustrate the magnitude of the achievement, imagine building a skyscraper several kilometers high. But the engineering marvel doesn't end with sheer size. Termites live in areas where the temperature difference between day and night and between winter and summer is tens of degrees Celsius. Despite this, the inside of the termite mound is kept at a constant temperature of around 30.5 degrees Celsius, without air conditioners and without technology. The temperature is adjusted to the fungus living symbiotically with the termites in the mound. The structure of repeated channels is the explanation for this engineering marvel. The mound is built of air ducts that open and close during the day. When open, warm air rises up; and when closed, cold air penetrates from the depths of the earth and fills the mound cavity. Thus, by opening and closing the air ducts, processes of temperature and gas regulation take place between the mound and its environment. In one of the hottest countries in the world, Zimbabwe, a large commercial building called the Eastgate Centre was built in the capital Harare, mimicking this temperature-regulating mechanism. Instead of air conditioners, warm air is vented up through the ceiling and released by chimneys. In a way, the building cools itself with minimal energy investment, emulating the natural regulatory process and significantly reducing energy consumption in the building.

• **An intelligence officer in action:** Simcha Lev-Yadun, a researcher in the field of botany at the University of Haifa, is interested in branching systems in nature and has also served in the Intelligence Corps in the past. One day, while touring the desert as part of a course in desert ecology, he came across a plant that caught his eye: the desert rhubarb. Desert plants generally have a reduction in surface area to minimize moisture loss, which is expressed in leaves so small that sometimes they disappear completely. Amazingly, desert rhubarb boasts extremely large leaves. How does such a large surface area correlate with the need to minimize water loss in the plant's photosynthesis process? This fact puzzled him and prompted him to investigate the subject. Being an intelligence officer who was exposed to aerial photographs of terrain for many years, he was able to notice the great resemblance between the structure of the rhubarb leaf which is full of grooves, and the structure of the mountain range riddled with ravines that drain the rainwater to its foothills.

"Since interpreting aerial photography was one of my specialties, the moment I bent down to photograph the rhubarb, I immediately understood what was going on," Lev-Yadun said. The similarity in the three-dimensional morphology led him to speculate that the purpose of the large, ravined leaf structure was actually to serve as a drainage basin to transport rainwater directly to the roots. Lev-Yadun conducted the research in collaboration with his colleagues Gidi Ne'eman and Gadi Katzir, and they showed that rhubarb supposedly has a self-irrigation system. The concept of such self-irrigating plants was new to the scientific world and was demonstrated here for the first time.[123]

 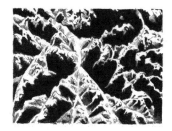

3. Asymmetry

"...symmetry is in a high degree characteristic of organic form, and is rarely absent in living things," wrote D'Arcy Thompson in his book, *On Growth and Form*, mentioned earlier. Symmetry is a prominent component of nature, but asymmetry is no less important. Asymmetry knocks the system out of equilibrium and drives change. An asymmetric component in the system is therefore related to a generic function of movement and change in the system: change in shape, volume, location, height, position, etc. In their book, *Fearful Symmetry: Is God a Geometer?*[124] Ian Stewart and Martin Golubitsky present a related idea: "... When systems have symmetry, there's a good chance that the symmetry may break. When it does, very tiny asymmetries play a crucial role in selecting the actual outcome from a range of potential outcomes." Stability and symmetry are closely related, and disruption in symmetry can lead to changes in the system. Several types of asymmetry in nature can be identified which drive processes of movement and change.

• **Geometric asymmetry:** Forms or structures are defined this way when they lack symmetry in at least one dimension. For example, the asymmetrical shape of the winged samara. The fact that one side is straight while the other is curved and that the center of gravity is asymmetrical relates to the seed's rotational motion. Another example are bird wings which typically have an asymmetric airfoil shape, where the upper surface of the wing is typically more curved than the lower surface, like airplane wings. When it moves through the air, the air pressure above the wing is lower than the air pressure beneath the wing as a result of Bernoulli's principle. This pressure difference (and other factors) creates the lift force and elevation. The basking shark's jaw is asymmetrical in structure. The outer part of the jaw is more curved and longer than the inside. These sharks swim open-mouthed in zooplankton-rich areas to capture its food, but there are no free meals in the wild: the incoming water must also come out. As with bird or airplane wings, the asymmetrical structure of the jaw produces pressure differences between the internal and external parts, making the water pressure greater on the inside. As a result, a passive flow of water is formed in the shark's pharynx through its gills, which release the water from the oral cavity without investing energy.

• **Material asymmetry:** Materials are defined this way when their properties are asymmetrical in space. For example, the pine cone effect is an opening and closing mechanism based on material asymmetry. Each scale consists of two layers that differ from one another both in directionality of the cells and the hygroscopic coefficient. When the moisture in the environment increases, the outer layer cells swell more than the inner layer cells and produce pressure causing the scale to close, and when moisture decreases, the opposite process occurs causing the scale to open. Another example is the bending mechanism of the bird-of-paradise flower, a beautiful and noble flower whose blossoms resemble a bird. When a bird lands on the blue petals, its weight exerts mechanical pressure that causes an interesting phenomenon to occur: instead of the petals being pulled back, they open to the sides. This phenomenon is due to material asymmetry. As we near the central line of the petals, the layer's thickness decreases until it reaches minimal thickness at the center. As a result, a natural axis is obtained, between the sides of which a flapping or bending process occurs. Inspired by this mechanism, a hingeless shading system called Flectofin was developed.

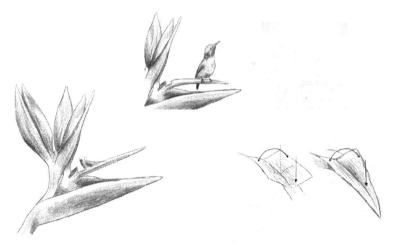

- **Temporal asymmetry:** An object is defined this way when it has pliable abilities that allow it to change shape, size, or volume at different points in time. Sometimes the ability to change is unrelated to geometric or material asymmetry, but to propulsion factors in the system acting on pliable material that is flexible and responsive to changes. Propulsive factors in nature are, for example, muscles, which produce movement in the joints. The ability of muscles to contract and expand in a medium that allows motion produces a change in the system.

As a rule, animals have miraculous abilities to change their shape and size. They swell, roll (like pill bugs aka 'roly polies') or shrink. For example, cockroaches manage to shrink to a quarter of their height without damaging their internal organs, which is why they can enter a room even when the door is closed; seahorse tails can be compressed to about half their widths before causing permanent damage to the vertebrae. Their tails consist of four bone plates surrounding the vertebrae that can glide over each other so that the tail can bend, turn, and twist over corals with a grasping motion; pufferfish inflate in times of danger in order to appear large and threatening; and pelicans' gular pouches can expand to hold up to 5 kilograms of fish and then shrink back to its original size.

Asymmetry was the final structure detected, since it requires more abstraction at the principle level. Asymmetry does not have a uniform physical appearance like bumps or ridges, and what led to recognizing the pattern in this case was actually the function (movement/change).

4. Layers

A layered structure is a kind of sandwich structure, consisting of alternating layers composed of different materials with different properties. The generic functions are mechanical protection – in the case of vertical pressure, and thermal protection. Abalone shells consist of alternating soft and hard layers, which give them mechanical protection against predators who exert crushing forces on them; nuts and drupes that fall from great heights, such as Brazil nuts or coconuts, are protected by their multi-

layered shells; and teeth are made of
layers that absorb the mechanical loads
exerted during chewing.

The layers protect not only from mechanical loads, but also from thermal
loads. For example, otters are marine
mammals that live in windy, low temperature, and cold water environments. Otter
fur has a unique layered structure that
provides thermal protection. The top layer
has waterproof hairs, so that the cold water does not come into direct contact with
their skin. Otter skin itself is covered with a
layer of water-repellent lipids, and the air that
gets trapped between the layers serves as an additional insulator. The British camping company, Finisterre, in
collaboration with the University of Bath, has developed a line
of storm jackets that mimic otter fur, with the aim of keeping
travelers warm and dry. The jackets are made of Pertex – a waterproof material that is breathable and recyclable. The fabric
developed contains several layers that prevent heat from escaping on the one hand and repel moisture on the other, similar to
otter fur.

5. Intersecting layers

Intersecting layers are a structure that resembles a network in
2D or a cellular, spongy, or hive-shaped structure in 3D. The generic function is mechanical protection in case of both vertical
and horizontal pressures. A classic example is the structure of
bone, which is built like a sponge. The cavities allow material to
be reduced where not needed, and to be reinforced where required. The Eiffel Tower, as mentioned, was inspired by the

structure of bone. Similar structures can be found in Toucan beaks, which absorb pressure and crushing loads from strikes against branches; insect wings that resemble nets, such as dragonfly wings; and in various plants such as the Victoria regia – a giant water lily that looks like a dinner plate. Its strength lies in its underside, which looks like a network of strong fibers, one that also traps air bubbles to help with buoyancy. This structure inspired the roof façade of the Crystal Palace, a glass structure designed by architect Joseph Paxton in London that burned down in the Great Fire of 1936. Paxton says he placed his young daughter on the giant lily to test its strength, and saw that it did not bend. He assumed that the crisscrossing layer structure was strong enough to bear the weight of glass, and chose this design for the roof.

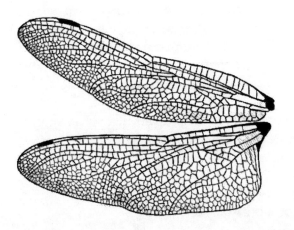

6. Cylinders

Cylinders are either full or hollow structures. The generic function is mechanical protection in the event of a peripheral load. Cylinders are commonly found in nature in stems, tree trunks, bones (the contour of a bone), insect legs, and more. For exam-

ple, horses' hooves are one of the strongest materials in nature. They are 20 times stronger than bone. The secret behind hoof wall strength has to do with the combination of hollow tubules that absorb peripheral loads and stop the spreading of cracks; The structure of a tooth resembles a cathedral, incorporating "columns" along the layers that prevent the development of cracks.

7. Helical structures

Helices are curves describing a circular transition in three dimensions while maintaining a constant diameter. Unlike spirals, helices do not start from a specific point and do not change their curvature. The generic function is mechanical protection in the event of variable loads whose directions are not fixed. For example, horns exist in a variety of shapes and sizes and are adapted for combat. Curved horns are adapted to butting during fights between males, a situation in which the load exerted on the horns does not have a predictable and fixed direction. Collagen, the most abundant protein in animals and humans, has a helical structure. It is the main component of fiber in connective tissue, blood vessels, cartilage, and other areas where loads are unexpected. The collagen that makes up our blood vessels is adapted to absorb the changing blood flow pressures.

8. Streamlined structures

These structures are characterized by contours that minimize resistance to motion through fluid, in air, or at sea. The generic function is stabilizing an object in the presence of fluid and drag reduction. For example, the fluid contours of boxfish, which led to the development of an energy-efficient concept car; and penguins, which look clumsy on the ground, but when they dive into water, they swim efficiently and quickly. Due to the streamlined contours of their bodies, drag is estimated to be reduced by 20–30% compared to other body shapes. These miraculous qualities led Festo's engineers to develop a bionic robot that looks just like a real penguin from far away. The bionic penguin is extremely energy efficient and can perform underwater tasks, such as tending ports, laying underwater cables, drilling, and more.

Spirals are also recurring structures in nature with fluid contours. They characterize shells located in aquatic areas. Spiral skyscrapers, such as the Turning Torso designed by architect Santiago Calatrava in Sweden, demonstrate greater resistance to wind at such heights.

Another fluid structure in nature is that of a network that splits open like a fan. River drainage basins, the alveolar ducts that split into bronchi in our lungs, roots and treetops, the arteries in a leaf—they all bear a similar structure of a network that splits open like a fan. For a system to flow over time, it needs to evolve in a way that provides broader and greater access to what flows through it. This design makes that possible.[125]

9. Containers

Containers are enclosed cavities surrounded by an external cover. The inside may be filled with gases, liquids, or solids. Containers are probably the simplest forms in nature. Their generic function is to hold or store. There are many examples of containers in nature: bird nests contain eggs and later chicks, providing them with protection and a place to hide from predators; pitchers of carnivorous plants, also known as monkey cups, contain digestive fluid that break down the essential food components from the insect's body; seed pods contain seeds in a neat and protective manner until time of germination, when they open up and release the seeds; and trapdoor spiders hide in holes underground beneath lids they construct from dense webs and dirt. When the time comes, when they sense vibrations, they leap out from hiding toward the prey.

Engines and Brakes

Those are the nine basic structures I identified in nature. Interestingly, the number nine is repeated in the context of creation and development. Nine is the last digit in the sequence of single-digit numbers and symbolizes the end of one cycle and the beginning of another. Nine months of pregnancy ends with the birth of a human being, and nine basic structures construct the whole of functionality.

After the intensive task of identification was complete, I suddenly noticed an interesting feature related to the structures' functionality: some of them are essentially engines. Engines are machines that convert energy into motion. Similarly, engines in nature are structures that convert energy sources into motion; they harvest energy fields and produce action. The structures that function as engines are repeated protrusions, repeated channels, and asymmetry. And the generic functions associated with them are dynamic functions: to attach and detach, channel, regulate, change, or move. For example, lotus leaves with their repeated protrusions are structures that harvest intermolecular fields to detach water droplets from their leaves. The air vents in termite mounds harvest thermal fields and transport warm air out of the nest. The asymmetry of pine cone scales harvests hydrostatic fields to open and close the scales.

Conversely, some structures are brakes. Brakes are machines that inhibit movement. Similarly, brakes in nature are structures that inhibit undesired movement, in cases where the change can cause mechanical or thermal failures. The structures that function as brakes are all the structures that are designed to provide a wide range of mechanical or thermal protection and to stabilize the organism in its environment: layers, intersecting layers, cylinders, helices, streamlined structures, and containers. For example, integrating cylinders into hoof walls prevents the development of cracks, and the streamlined contours of kingfisher beaks prevent the undesired motion of noisy water. The generic functions associated with these structures are static functions: to protect, stop, absorb, stabilize, or contain.

Abstraction using Structures

Today, when I take nature walks, see pictures of nature, or read about mechanisms, I immediately recognize the structures and 'listen' to their functional stories. There are structures that whisper small functions, and others that have joined together to shout large functions. The study of nature's structural language makes it possible to refine and understand the functional mechanisms and carry out abstraction.

How can we speak "structurally" in nature? The nine basic structures are the first words that make up nature's structural language. The capacity for functional expression deepens as more words are incorporated into a sentence. During the abstraction process, we refine the functional mechanisms by identifying the structures. It is generally possible to identify several structures in a single biological system, and their unique combination explains the studied functional mechanism.

For example, hives both contain (store honey) and provide mechanical protection through honeycomb structures (intersecting layers); arteries are both transport systems (repeated channels) and provide protection from changes in blood pressure through helical collagen structures; bamboo are built as hollow cylinders that absorb peripheral loads, and the cylinder shells grow spongy to absorb vertical and horizontal loads; Namib Desert beetles have hydrophilic protrusions to attach and condense water, channels to transport the water, and geometric asymmetry formed by lifting their hind legs to move the water into their mouths; termite mounds contain ventilation channel systems to regulate temperature, and each channel is built as a cylinder that gives mechanical strength to the mound itself; lobster exoskeletons consist of chitin fibers that form one-way layers to withstand loads, but in areas where loads are not unidirectional, helical structures exist. This combination of layered and helical structures optimizes load absorption.[126]

Another example is the sea sponge – simple marine creatures lacking vertebrae, organs, and tissues. They can be very small or extremely large – they can be about three meters high and even host a person in their chimney. My curiosity was piqued when I saw a video of a "smoking" sponge: the sponge was injected with colored ink, which passed through it and turned up through its chimney. Unlike SpongeBob's character, sponges are immobile, so they filter their food from the water passing through them. The byproducts of this filtration process are released from the chimney. A light investigation revealed the structures responsible for this process: the sponge's surface is covered with small, protruding holes (repeated protrusions) and connected to a central chimney (cylinder). There are pressure differences between the ends of the chimney due to the differences in height (asymmetry). The small holes catch oxygen and food particles from the water that flows through them, the waste products are passively transported through the chimney, along the pressure cascade, and are released. In this way, we can abstract each biological system, identify the recurring structures in it, and understand how they together form the functional mechanism being studied (*see 14).

THE PAX SCIENTIFIC STORY:
ONE STRUCTURE, ONE PRINCIPLE,
GREAT INNOVATION

*Pretty much everything in the industrial world can
be improved by taking these shapes from nature and
reconfiguring what engineers build today.*

Jay Harman

One day, I discovered that a good friend of mine was walking around with pebbles in her bag. She usually holds them during meetings, and even gave me one as a gift. They really do give off a good feeling. The smooth edges and coolness of the stone are pleasant and relaxing. "But why pebbles?" I asked, and she shared with me her personal BIO-WOW. As an architect involved in design, she was surprised by the pebble's smoothness and set out to investigate why this is the common form of pebbles in nature. Her research led her to Viktor Schauberger and his discoveries about living water. How can water be alive?

Schauberger was a simple man, from a traditional family of foresters, who lived in the Austrian forests in the 19th century. He used to traverse forests where almost no human had ever set foot and observe the water sources in and around the forest. At one point, he noticed that fields irrigated with water flowing from mountainous, shady areas yielded more crops than fields irrigated with water flowing from other sources, and assumed that the quality of mountainous water was better. One night, he noticed trout jumping toward the top of a waterfall as the moon rose, almost effortlessly. He assumed they were using an energy source found in water. He continued observing and searching for this energy source, until he found it in the motion of water. Schauberger understood the laws of natural movements and described the connection between the water's movement and its vitality. In order for water to conserve its natural, inherent energy, it must move in a vortex manner. Vortexes occur naturally at low temperatures, which is why streams that wind around shady banks without the power of direct sunlight are a higher-quality water source than sun-exposed water. This circular motion is the force that shapes the quality of water.

Schauberger said that "Water in its natural state shows us how it wishes to flow, so we should follow its wishes,"[127] and didn't stop there. He registered several patents for harvesting water's natural energy and even invented devices for purifying water and charging water's living energy. Schauberger concluded: "first understand nature, then copy it...Nature is our foremost teacher." My friend received an answer to her question about the slippery pebble: it was repeatedly eroded by the vortices of water from all directions.

But I was left with a new question: Why specifically vortex movement? The one to supply the answer was Jay Harman, an entrepreneur and founder of Pax Scientific, which designs and develops products and technologies based on the streamlining principle of nature: fans, impellers, pumps, turbines, heat exchangers, propellers, and more. The company was founded in California in 1997 and has several subsidiaries.

Harman is committed to environmental preservation and has a deep connection to nature. He grew up off the coast of Australia, and as a child noticed that seaweed is designed with curvilinear lines that allow water to pass through and reduce resistance to water flow. As an adult, Harman specialized in fluid dynamics, an extensive field of research in applied mathematics. At one point, he noticed a recurrent geometry in nature. Forms and shapes existing in liquid flows, such as shells, often exhibit a three-dimensional spiral shape, following parameters similar to the golden ratio. Pax Scientific's innovation story is linked to the spiral form, one of nature's recurring structures. One structure, one principle, great innovation.

The Golden Ratio in Nature

The golden ratio is a mathematical constant discovered in the Pythagorean period, probably by one of his students, as a recurring ratio in nature between two numbers roughly equaling 1.618. The ratio is derived from the famous Fibonacci sequence, in which each integer in the series is equal to the sum of the preceding two numbers, and the quotient between each successive pair of numbers in the sequence approximates the golden ratio (1, 1, 2, 3, 5, 8, 13, 21...). Already in ancient Greece, mathematicians, architects, and artists worked with this ratio, saw in it perfection and assimilated it in art and architecture, in sculptures, paintings, and the structures they built. The ratio has been called the "divine proportion" due to its recurrent imprint in nature, and indeed, the numbers of the Fibonacci sequence are found nearly everywhere in nature. Bananas come in three forms – a single banana, several bananas known as a 'hand,' and several hands of bananas known as a 'bunch'; apples have five seeds; flowers almost always have exactly 3, 5, 8, 13, or 21 petals. The arrangement of leaves around a stem, the distribution of scales on a pine cone, and the number and distribution of seeds in a sunflower are also based on the Fibonacci sequence.

When you use Fibonacci numbers in geometry, you get a spiral that can be found everywhere in nature: in shells, in the anatomy of human ears, in hurricanes, and even in the arrangement of galaxies. Even if we remove the drain stopper in a bathtub, we will see a vortex, and its geometry will be identical to that of a hurricane or tornado. This spiral shape is the recurring archetype of nature that appears in states of flow. Spirals are associated with efficiency in nature. Hurricanes spread with minimal energy. Snails build their shells with minimum effort. In fact, the spiral is a mathematical expression of efficient growth and replication processes in nature.

Jay Harman, of course, was not the first to investigate the mathematical principles that explain the golden ratio. Many mathematicians, philosophers, scientists, and artists did this long before him. But he was the first to recognize the connection between spirals in nature, which are associated with the golden ratio, and flow efficiency.

Nature's Streamlining Principle

Movement in nature follows a spiral path. There is no linear movement in nature. The path of least resistance in fluid environments is not a straight line, but a spiral line. The reason you see so many vortices in nature is because they are the path that is least resistant to motion. In nature, gases and liquids move in spiral formations, in contrast to the conventional technology for producing gas or liquid propulsion systems that is based on straight lines. Attempts to transport gases and liquids in straight lines produce pressure, increased friction, heat loss, and cracking. Vortex management is therefore the key to energy efficiency.

Harman moved from Australia to the United States, equipped with his insights on nature's streamlining principle and a strong affinity for environmentalism. In 1997, he founded Pax Scientific with the goal of translating nature's streamlining principle into industrial flow technologies. He realized that if fluids always tend to follow a particular path, there must be a way to design equipment that takes advantage of this property.

A necessary step in any bioinspired innovation process is the abstraction stage. Using mathematical tools and computational fluid dynamics, they studied spiral objects in nature in the context of flow. During the research, they built a propeller with the geometric structure of a seashell, which includes curved lines on several axes, according to the parameters of the golden ratio. When the propeller is rotated backwards, a vortex pattern similar to a hurricane is formed. The drag and resistance to the propeller's motion decreased, and as a result, so did vibrations and noise, while energy efficiency increased. In light of the success, they began to examine the effectiveness of the seashell's geometric structure in aerial environments, as well, with the understanding that any system in a fluid medium could benefit from this design. At this point, the patents were registered and work began on applications.

Traditional fans, impellers, and propellers consist of flat surfaces with a curved line on only one axis, unlike geometry in nature, which is based on curved lines on several axes. Their redesign according to the streamlining principle guarantees energy efficiency.

The first subsidiary to open based on this principle was a fan company, which marketed home and industrial fans with impressive energy efficiency.

The second subsidiary was an impeller company. In fact, the design of impellers has changed very little since ancient Egypt – around 4,000 years ago! Modern mixing solutions are not fundamentally different from those of antiquity, and they also suffer from drag, energy inefficiency, noise, and abrasion. The flagship product of the impeller subsidiary is the Lily Impeller, designed with spiral lines similar to the structure of the calla lily flower. This impeller produces a jet that sweeps the entire tank volume into a large vortex ring, bearing the geometric characteristics of spiral vortices in nature. It reduces drag and energy consumption relative to other mixing technologies.

The third subsidiary engages in water technologies. The main challenge they tried to solve was the issue of bacterial growth in water tanks and the need to neutralize it despite regulations restricting use of disinfectants. In static water, a process of thermal stratification occurs: the surface layer heats up and becomes fertile ground for the development of a layer of bacteria and nitrates (biofilm). The use of antibacterial disinfectants treats the symptom (biofilm) rather than the root of the problem (temperature stratification). The only solution for fixing the root of the problem is to mix the water in the container, thereby dispersing it and maintaining a uniform temperature. Mechanical mixing systems proposed for this purpose underperformed and consumed a lot of energy. Where others have failed, the Lily Impeller has succeeded. It was installed at the bottom of a tank and led to unprecedented performance: heat uniformity was achieved within 24 hours, and the biofilm layer disappeared within two to three weeks. The impeller mixes 24 hours a day using minimal energy. In fact, the ratio between the size of the impeller and the volume of mixed water has never before been achieved.

Harman commented on this performance saying that it was not even perceived as possible from an engineering perspective. Nature has set a high performance bar, beyond what engineers could even imagine. What will be the next challenge that the spiral structure will solve? Harman says that for him, biomimicry is a love story, the love of life. This love is taking him to the next vision. He described an enlarged Lily Impeller that would be positioned near cities suffering from air pollution, mixing up pollution and keeping it away from residential areas. Perhaps one day, the streamlining principle will indeed solve the problem of air pollution, which is one of humanity's greatest issues. Harman concluded: "Nature has already solved every problem humans face and have ever faced."

Bioinspired Tools for Sustainable Design

*The natural environment sustains the life
of all beings universally*

Dalai Lama

Our understanding of the concept of sustainability has evolved and deepened over the years, and in a sense is getting closer to the meaning of sustainability in nature. Nature not only exists; it also renews itself every moment, thrives and develops.

The initial definition of sustainable development – "development that meets the needs of the present without compromising the ability of future generations to meet their own needs,"[128] adopted at the UN Brundtland Conference in 1987 – is a modest definition that deals with the question of existence over time. But it's not enough just to exist. We also strive to exist in a state of well-being and prosperity, we strive to develop.

The World Health Organization defines 'health' as "a state of complete physical, mental, and social well-being and not merely the absence of disease or infirmity." Similarly, it is not enough just to exist, the question is how to exist. Today, there is already discourse about regenerative sustainability, that is, life that can be renewed, like in nature. Regenerative sustainability does more than just reduce harm; it attempts to rejuvenate systems. For example, regenerative agriculture does not reduce soil fertility and does not damage water sources. It views the field as part of an ecosystem that must be preserved and renewed. The word 'regenerative' is slowly replacing the word 'sustainable' and moving us from the passive role of preserving what exists to the active role of gaining ground in the midst of regeneration.

Designers and engineers have a very big impact on sustainability in our world. They stand at the critical junction of the energy and matter cycle. They decide which materials will be used to create systems, which processes will be used to build them, how long they will be in use, and what will happen at their end-of-life.

However, practicing sustainable design is not simple. There are many design parameters that affect sustainability. For example, which coat is more sustainable? The first is made of organic wool, the second of recycled fabric, and the third was made in your home country. The answer is not simple. Each coat presents a different aspect of sustainability. The first presents crop growth without the use of pesticides, which harms the well-being of neighboring residents and may seep into the soil, penetrating groundwater; the second makes full use of the material by reusing it; the third prioritizes local production and saves the energy waste involved in shipping overseas.

The definition of sustainable development adopted at the Brundtland Conference is a qualitative one – a general indicator that anchors an ethos and mindset that can serve as a compass for serious decision-making. But it also causes discomfort among engineers and designers who need to translate it into practice for the design and production of sustainable environments, systems, technologies, and products. Clear benchmarks and practical design tools are required.

If to be or not to be is the question, then nature has answers that have been translated into a series of tools for sustainable design, which also expand the concept of sustainability from mere existence to existence for regeneration, well-being, and prosperity. These tools, which were developed through inspiration and observation of nature, offer sustainable design strategies and principles. These strategies and principles were refined after studying and abstracting biological systems. Their application helps in transferring sustainability from nature to technology and engineering. Just as functionality in nature is achieved in different hierarchies and on different scales, so too is sustainability. Implementing sustainability requires a holistic approach, one that views the solution as part of an entire system; an approach that addresses sustainability at the level of material, structures, production processes, and adaptation to the system. That's why it's a good idea to integrate bioinspired sustainable design tools into the Framework for Strategic Sustainable Development (FSSD), which has gained broad scientific consensus. They should also be combined with other tools, such as the life cycle analysis (LCA) tool, which allows us to evaluate and quantify environmental impacts at every stage of the life of a product or service: raw material extraction, production, distribution, use, and end of life.

In the next three chapters, I will present bioinspired sustainable design tools: Cradle to Cradle, Life's Principles, and principles of ideality in nature. These tools are practical design tools that support the implementation of sustainability during the design process. They are based on nature's concepts of sustainability and regenerative sustainability, and lead to sustainable innovation.

FROM CRADLE TO CRADLE

*Waste is any human activity which absorbs
resources but creates no value.*

Taiichi Ohno

Imagine a world where cars emit air-purifying substances; carpets function as leaves and release oxygen into the air; food packaging gets buried underground and sprouts seeds that give rise to life; factories at the end of the production line dump quality, drinkable water; cities function like forests and provide clean, balanced, and diverse environments. All these examples describe systems that not only cause no harm to the environment, but nurture it. Just like in nature, systems create conditions conducive to life. You don't have to imagine these systems. They can be designed using a "Cradle to Cradle" approach – a design philosophy based on natural principles. The approach was born from a deep understanding that there are design failures in the way we design our systems today.

Michael Braungart, a German chemist, and William McDonough, an American architect, claim that the new industrial revolution is a **design revolution** that refers to the ongoing design failure of the industry, and is based on the belief that materials are only moving in one direction – toward the nearest landfill. If design is a signal of intention, as McDonough said, it is about time we rethink our intention. They propose an alternative design philosophy and approach based on a new set of products that move "Cradle to Cradle."[129]

When my eldest daughter was born, I was given a beautiful straw cradle with a small mattress inside as a gift. For the first month of her life, my daughter slept in that cradle next to us and was moved around from place to place, until her body, which grew rather quickly, was moved to a more permanent cradle, which soon became a bed. For me, the image of a cradle, more than anything else, connotes where it all began.

This is the exact concept of Cradle-to-Cradle design: the raw materials used for the product are mined from the cradle – from the place they were formed – in nature or in the industry, and return to the cradle at the products' end of life to be used as raw materials for other products. A cycle is formed in which today's raw material is also tomorrow's raw material. Taiichi Ohno, the father of the Toyota Production System, defined waste as "any human activity that absorbs resources but creates no value." That is why in nature, there is no waste. In nature, waste from one organism is valuable to another organism. Waste = food.

Plants are the first producers in nature. They feed on raw materials found in the air (carbon dioxide) and in soil (water and nutrients) and produce the first energy currency – carbohydrates – which are created in the process of photosynthesis. The carbohydrates, in turn, are passed onto the herbivores and later to the predators. But every ecosystem also has decomposers. Bacteria and fungi break down the remains of animals and plants after they perish and return them to soil. In this way, matter returns to nature's cradle over and over again, and supports the continuation of life.

McDonough outlined the design principles for the approach. He said that one day, while he was in Japan, he was amazed by the magnificent cherry blossoms, and then a thought occurred to him: cherry blossoms produce so many flowers, but even if just one seed fell to the ground, took root, and grew, it would be enough. At first sight, the process seemed incredibly inefficient and like a waste of energy. So many flowers produced for nothing. But then he realized that nature's redundancy strategy (producing excess flowers to increase the chance of successful fertilization) was supported by a strong design principle in nature: waste = food. McDonough said: "When a cherry tree grows, it enriches far more than the soil." It enriches the whole environment. The waste of one system becomes food for another.

When the flowers fall to the ground, they decompose, and the nutrients return to nourish microorganisms, insects, plants, and animals, and improve the soil.

A similar design principle is identified in ant nests. The biomass of ants is larger than that of humans, but they are an example of a dense population that not only poses no threat, but makes the world a better place. Leafcutter ants collect waste, such as freshly cut leaves, and transport it to their colonies, where it is used to feed fungi that live symbiotically with the ants. Ants transport nutrient minerals to upper layers of the soil, ventilate the soil as they move, form drainage pathways for water, and support soil productivity. Ants may be "the little things that run the world," as ant biologist Edward Wilson suggested, but they certainly do so beneficially.

Armed with insights he gleaned from cherry blossoms and ants about how nature works, McDonough teamed up with Braungart to help him translate the principle of 'waste = food' into an organized doctrine of design. Since these are materials that need to be managed differently, a professional familiar with processes in the material world, including decomposition processes, is a natural choice for the task. Together, McDonough, the architect, and Braungart, the chemist, formulated a new vision for the industry: to design an industry that enriches its environment, inspired by nature. There is no need to reduce the industry, just as the cherry tree does not reduce its blossoming, but there is a need to design it so that it becomes beneficial and nutritious to its environment.

The design revolution will allow materials at the end of their life cycle to return to the cradle and prevent them from reaching the grave (landfills). Just as it is difficult to put toothpaste back in the tube after squeezing it out, it is very difficult to clean contamination from water or soil after it has already formed. A more correct solution is to prevent the formation of the contamination in the first place with the help of design.

The prevailing approach to sustainability management today is to reduce the use of pollutants or toxic substances by reducing use, by reusing, or by recycling. But according to the Cradle to Cradle approach, **being "less bad" is no good**. Braungart explained this principle in a lecture I attended, in a way I will never forget. He compared it to a man striking his wife and asked: If instead of hitting her five times a day, he hit her three times a day, would that be the right approach to solving the problem? In a Cradle to Cradle approach, it isn't about reducing waste, it's about eliminating the entire concept of waste and turning it into something good.

Another conceptual principle that is challenged by the Cradle to Cradle approach is the perception of industry as a harmful factor, whose very existence produces "evil," which inevitably produces "waste." If we go back to nature's production plant for a moment, we will see that flower production consumes a lot of energy. From the tree's point of view, it makes sense to reduce flower production, but then the environment will lose out. The flowers provide a source of nourishment for insects and birds, and at the end of their life, enrich the soil. Similarly, a Cradle to Cradle approach invites systems to be designed so that they not only cause less damage, but also support economic, social, or environmental well-being. This is the heart of the approach's concept.

Instead of viewing the industry as harmful and polluting, it can be seen as beneficial. Instead of reducing toxins, emissions can be designed to benefit and nurture the environment. Instead of designing with a linear approach, in which resources from nature are mined, used, and buried, it is possible to design a circular industrial system that returns its resources to the cradle of their formation. In this way, developing the industry is not limited in the long run, because it is associated with economic growth. This is the new industrial revolution.

The term used today, "circular economy," is based on Cradle to Cradle ideas and extends them to an alternative economic approach that strives to exhaust material and energy resources. According to the circular economy model, one should strive to create circular systems that replace linear "take-make-waste" systems, since linear perception is not sustainable in a world of finite resources. Economic growth in the circular approach is not necessarily linked to the consumption of perishable resources. Instead of tossing the resources at the end of the product's life cycle and mining new ones, they can be reused again and again. In nature, circles are constantly being opened and closed, and material resources swirl about within the system. Sustainable economic growth will be achieved in a similar way. Cradle to Cradle is therefore a design approach that allows the concepts from the circular economy model to be applied in practice; the circular economy philosophy is translated into a practical design method.

Material Cycles

McDonough and Braungart know that not all industry needs can be met with natural raw materials alone. For example, the days when textiles were produced just from natural fibers are over. It is not possible to supply billions of people with clothing made only from natural fibers. Therefore, to practically apply the Cradle to Cradle approach, two cycles are defined: a biological cycle and a technical cycle. All products produced by humans belong to one of these two cycles.

• **The biological cycle:** includes natural and biodegradable components taken from the biosphere: plants and biopolymers (polymers synthesized by living organisms). All ingredients should be safe for consumption by living organisms. Products should be designed so that their biological nutrients safely return to air, water, or soil at the end of the product's life to nourish biological processes. Products consisting of biological ingredients are referred to as **consumer products**.

• **The technical cycle:** includes synthetic components taken from the technosphere: for example, industrial polymers that cannot be safely returned to air, water, or soil, but have the potential to remain safe in a closed system. These products should be designed in such a way that their technical nutrients are reused in a closed production cycle, without polluting the natural environment. Products that contain valuable technical components, such as cars, televisions, carpets, or computers, are referred to as **services** that people consume. At the end of use, these ingredients, according to the vision, return to the manufacturer for reuse. For example, a washing machine will be offered as a laundry service to the customer. At the end of a predefined period, for example after 3,000 washing cycles, the manufacturer will replace the product and use its components for the safe reproduction of new products. The manufacturer remains the owner of the material, and has an interest in providing a quality product to win another service cycle. The customer has no need for the material, just the service.

During the Cradle-to-Cradle design process, we focus on several design aspects, including: materials as nutrients, material reutilization, clean energy, clean water, and social fairness. Let's elaborate on the first two aspects.

• **Materials as nutrients**: Materials in a product must be reconsidered to ensure that each one of them is a nutrient for the system. Begin by mapping out the materials from which the product is made. Identify harmful substances and find alternatives for them. When choosing alternatives, consider criteria such as toxicity, carcinogenicity (how cancerous the substance is), allergenicity, and compatibility with the biological or technical metabolism. For example, there are products that are safe to use, which only become dangerous during the decomposition or disassembly phase. Later, improvements are made and an optimal list is reached. The way we use harmful substances in our living environment raises questions. How is it possible that we accept with full understanding the presence of carcinogens or even suspected carcinogens in our dishes, textiles, house walls, and even the food itself? The time has come for our living environment to be free of substances that endanger our well-being, health, and existence – just like in nature.

• **Material reutilization**: Natural products are not only made of harmless materials; they are also designed for decomposition to enable potential reuse. Seeds, for example, are connected by connective tissue that dries out and weakens over time, allowing the seeds to be easily detached at the appropriate time. Similarly, products should be designed for quick and easy decomposition or disassembly: biological decomposition that returns biological nutrients to the natural cycle or mechanical disassembly that returns technical nutrients to the industrial cycle. If the decomposition process is complex or requires a lot of time and money, it will not likely take place. Companies that design products in such a process can receive a Cradle to Cradle Standard from the International Organization for Standardization (ISO) after they pass a stringent series of tests.

The Imagination is Already Here

I began by describing an imaginary world, but similar products already actually exist, developed using a Cradle to Cradle approach. For example, the American company Method closes a biological cycle in the production of cleaning products and cosmetics based on non-toxic biodegradable substances. The approach used by the company to develop and design their products involves searching for materials that are safe for people and the environment, design that takes into account the product's end-of-life (recycling, composting, etc.), and saving water and energy throughout their production processes. The company's product packaging is made from 100% recycled and recyclable plastic. Even the glue used to stick labels on the packaging does not impair their recyclability.

Another example of a biological closed-loop product is produced by Trigema, Germany's largest manufacturer of sports shirts and tennis apparel. In 2005, the company began developing the world's first T-shirt that decomposes safely into compost. They selected thread, pigment, and material suitable to produce the shirt, which can be composted according to the design criteria of the Cradle to Cradle approach. By using only biological nutrients, the shirt becomes food for the environment.

Naturally, alongside the environmental benefit of circular design, there is also the economic benefit in utilizing material resources. The process is often referred to as "turning waste into gold" in the symbolic sense of its value in money, but also in the literal sense: the company Apple generates tens of millions of dollars each year from breaking down the gold components of their cell phones which are collected for recycling.[130]

In the film, *The Next Industrial Revolution*, available for viewing online,[131] the Cradle to Cradle design approach is presented in detail, as well as its sources of inspiration from nature and practice. In the film, William McDonough articulates the essence of the approach: "The question is can we follow nature's laws? If we do, then growth is good. Well then the question is: what do you want to grow? Because in nature, if a tree grows, that's good. If a child grows, that's good. So the question would be: what would good growth look like?...How about we grow health instead of sickness...how about we grow intelligence instead of stupidity..." What would you want to grow?

LIFE'S PRINCIPLES

Life creates conditions conducive to life.

Janine Benyus

B ig Brother – the television reality show that first aired in
1997 and has since been broadcast in many countries around
the world – has an even bigger brother. In 1991, eight scientists
and engineers – four men and four women – entered a 3.14-acre
sealed glass structure in Arizona and stayed there for two years.
But instead of a luxurious villa, the glass structure contained a
closed ecological system, or vivarium. The project is called "Biosphere 2." The biosphere is the sum of life on Earth that includes
all ecosystems occupied by living organisms.

Inside the glass structure were various biological biomes,
including a fog desert, tropical rainforest, savanna grassland,
mangrove wetlands, agricultural system, and an ocean with a
coral reef. The ecosystems inhabited approximately 3,000 species of plants, insects, pollinators, fish, reptiles, and mammals
chosen to represent as best as possible the diversity and abundance of true natural environments. This Big Brother didn't
look at social interactions but at ecological processes. All recycling processes of air, water, and nutrients took place within the structure, and the scientists had to live inside the closed
dome and provide for all their needs. Like Earth, Biosphere 2 is
a closed-loop material cycle, so nothing went in or out, but it
was open to energy.

The idea was to build a world impervious to the external environment, a place that produces everything by itself and for itself – a kind of Noah's Ark. The name "Biosphere 2" implies the purpose of the study. We all live in Biosphere 1; the question is whether it is possible to create and sustain another biosphere. If humanity needs to move to another planet, will we be able to mimic the characteristics of the biosphere that sustains us here on Earth and create a resilient living environment? This was the most ambitious project ever undertaken for learning about life in a closed system and it cost about $200 million. Was it successful?

Jane Poynter, one of the residents of Biosphere 2, recounted her experiences in a TED Talk.[132] To make her own pizza, she harvested the wheat to make the dough and milked the goats to make the cheese, a process that took four months! The carbon dioxide she exhaled fed the sweet potatoes she grew, so she actually ate the same carbon dioxide over and over again. In a way, she was actually eating herself... But as the carbon dioxide was being repeatedly consumed, the oxygen began to disappear. Oddly, large amounts of oxygen were lost, and the crew began feeling unwell. The life system was failing in its basic function: to supply oxygen to its inhabitants. After 17 months, due to the decline in oxygen levels, the people lived at an oxygen level equivalent to being at a height of about 5.3 kilometers and required medical attention. The ecological balance among species was also not maintained. The number of cockroaches doubled, and they took the place of pollinators, since many other insects died. Of the 25 species introduced, 19 became extinct.

Two hundred million dollars and some of the world's best scientific minds went into building a functioning ecosystem, but it struggled to keep eight people alive for 24 months. By comparison, eight new people are added to Earth in less than four seconds. Today the building serves as a tourist attraction, but we have no other biosphere to escape to. The experiment failed to create an environment that supports and maintains life and showed how complex the living environment is. In nature there is a delicate balance between different factors that can be easily disturbed. Biosphere 2 is modeled after Earth's environment (Biosphere 1). Though this experiment failed, learning how to sustain life from nature is a promising path.

So how can we understand how natural systems are built and function sustainably? This question was first asked by Janine Benyus in the 1990s, who along with Dayna Baumeister founded the Biomimicry Institute (2006) and Biomimicry 3.8 (2010; formerly the Biomimicry Guild 1998-2010), a leading bio-inspired consultancy offering biological intelligence consulting. Their research led to the development of a knowledge base titled "Life's Principles."[2]

This name may evoke an association of principles for leading a better life, and there is an element of truth to this. Implementing nature's concept of sustainability leads to development and regeneration, not just survival. Life is emerging and transforming every moment. When external conditions change, organisms must respond with change, development, and readjustment to their environment to survive and thrive. So how can we live in a way that allows us not only to continue to exist – but also to evolve? What is the secret behind nature's sustainability?

The study involved observing biological and ecological systems and identifying existing principles in nature that allow these systems to survive within the limitations of life on Earth. The principles repeat among different organisms and represent nature's sustainable design patterns. The 26 identified principles were developed and enhanced over the years (now 27 in 2023).

---

2. This chapter describes a knowledge base developed by Biomimicry 3.8 and is written in a way that I understand life's principles. In the chapter, I present my own interpretation of the subject. This interpretation has not been validated by Biomimicry 3.8.

Their graphics organize the principles into master and sub-principles to make the collection more manageable, but all are equally important. The graphic representation also underwent development. Around a decade ago, these principles were presented on a butterfly-shaped graph, later the butterfly turned into a chart, and today the chart is a wheel graph (*see 15).

Presuppositions

The strategies identified in the knowledge base of Life's Principles are derived from operating conditions of Earth and the fundamental characteristics of life.

Operating Conditions of Earth

Life runs on sunlight, water, and gravity. The vast majority of life forms depend on energy from the sun and the presence of water for all life processes. All organisms adapt to the conditions of gravity, as well, and even make use of it.

Earth is in a state of dynamic non-equilibrium. This means that nothing remains constant. All conditions change over time, and organisms which lack the ability to change and adapt will not be able to survive. Balance is achieved over a long period of time, between cycles, seasons, and epochs. Overall, equilibrium is sought, but no state is fixed, like a small marble moving in a bowl. Each action will move it away from the center of the bowl, but eventually it will return to the center.

Earth is a system almost completely closed off to mass, but is open to energy. This means that all life forms are subject to the limited amount of resources and availability of energy, and act in accordance.

Nature also operates in circular and cyclical processes. For example, cycles of water, nitrogen, carbon, tidal processes, and seasons.

A Fundamental Characteristic of Life

"Life creates conditions conducive to life," said Benyus. Living things are not only adapted to the operating conditions of Earth to survive, but by their very existence, they support life processes and contribute to the formation of life. For example, a tree can't grow without also growing its environment. When it grows, it creates regenerative abundance. It supports many life systems. It stabilizes the soil, enriching it by cooperating with nitrogen-fixing bacteria living in its roots, produces oxygen needed by many organisms and is itself a habitat for a wide variety of animals. One cannot ignore the similarity between the words 'nature' and 'nurture.' Nature nurtures by its nature.

Life's Principles[133]

1. Evolve to Survive: *Continually incorporate and embody information to ensure enduring performance.*

Change is life. A living system is an evolving system that must incorporate new information. Change occurs both at the behavioral level, by adopting new patterns of behavior, and at the genetic level, when new traits are embedded into the genetic code. The road of evolving passes through several sub-principles:

- **Replicate Strategies that Work** – *Repeat successful approaches.* When something succeeds and works, it pays to replicate it. Successful solutions in nature that aid survival are replicated and repeated both by appearing in the genome and by imitation and learning. For example, crows learned to crack nuts in an original way. They throw nuts down from great heights onto busy roads, let passing cars run over them, and then, when the traffic light changes to red, they jump into the road and indulge. Apparently, it began when a nut fell and cracked open, but later, this strategy turned into an innovative cracking method.

- **Integrate the Unexpected** – *Incorporate mistakes in ways that can lead to new forms and functions.* Even failures and malfunctions can bring about change. Mutations are a one-time malfunction in genome replication. Some lead to failures and even death, and some lead to improvements and break-throughs. For example, the larger mammals are, the more heat they need to lose to maintain a constant temperature, so the surface area through which heat loss occurs limits the possible physical size of the organism. A mutation that causes skin to wrinkle significantly increases the skin's surface area and allows life to exist in even larger physical sizes, relative to the size that is possible when the skin is smooth.
- **Reshuffle Information** – *Exchange and alter information to create new options.* Mixing, merging, and replacing is a quick and safe way to bring about change. At the genetic level, this is how new traits are formed. For example, bacteria can trans-fer plasmids – circular pieces of DNA that are not part of chro-mosomal DNA – and thus transfer traits and genes from the bacterium that donated the plasmid to the bacterium that receives it. The transferred genes can, for example, contain information about resistance to different types of antibiotics. Then those resistant bacteria will pass on the resistance they developed to their offspring, and they too will be partially or fully resistant to the same types of antibiotics. This is an ex-ample of rapid evolutionary processes within bacterial popu-lations, carried out by genetic shuffling and is what led to a race against antibiotic resistance.

2. Be Resourceful with Material and Energy: *Optimize the use of resources and take advantage of opportunities.*

Using resources in a creative yet calculated manner and tak-ing advantage of opportunities to use resources and support life. Surviving organisms learn to utilize material and energy efficiently and effectively, while creating minimal by-products and "waste." So, what makes a natural system resourceful?

- **Use Low Energy Processes** – *Minimize energy consumption by reducing requisite temperatures, pressures, and/or time for reactions.* In nature, construction and production are energy efficient, because they take place in the living environment, without the need for energy consuming processes such as applying heat or pressure.

- **Use Multi-Functional Design** – *Meet multiple needs with one elegant solution.* As mentioned, one structure or material in nature often has several functions. This leads to material and energy savings, eliminating the need to create several structures to perform different functions. This solution is elegant, meeting a number of needs. For example, the fat that ducks spread on their feathers with their beaks, extracted from a fat gland above their tail, keeps pests away, isolates from cold water, and is broken down by the sun into vitamin D – an important nutrient for ducks; the tusks of walruses are used for clinging to ice shelves, fighting with other males, and digging at the bottom of the sea.

- **Recycle All Materials** – *Keep all materials available in connected flows.* In nature, one organism's "waste" is another organism's treasure. Recycling often occurs within systems of biological interaction, and the quality of recyclability does not diminish, unlike industrial recycling processes, in which many times the recycled product is inferior to the previous one. For example, the lives of many trees end suddenly. But in the forest, the dead body is essential to the cycle of life. For hundreds of years it has absorbed nutrients from the soil, storing them in the branches and bark. Decomposers, such as bacteria and fungi, break down the organic matter, and release the stored nutrients back into the soil. These nutrients become available for other plants and organisms in the ecosystem, helping to support their growth and survival.

- **Fit Form to Function** – *Select for shape or pattern based on need.* Organ or system designs (structure or form) stem from needs they are supposed to fill – from a tiny seemingly negligible stain to a sophisticated and complex structure. For example, tigers have white spots on the tips of their ears.[134] They are assumed to function as "fake eyes," creating the false impression of a larger head. Tigers also seem to be watching and alert even when their eyes are turned to the ground.

The beaks of different birds are adapted in form to the types of food they rely on; the fruit of the common storksbill flower bears a corkscrew tip that straightens out with moisture, and this movement allows it to insert its seeds into the ground; the Venus Flytrap is a carnivorous plant. Closing the trap consumes a huge amount of energy and reopening it takes several hours. There is no room for error. The trap is only closed when it is confirmed that the insect crawling on it is large enough to be worthy of closing the trap. The Venus Flytrap has large trigger hairs, which allow it to sense its prey. If the insect touches just one trigger hair, the trap will not close, but if the insect is large enough to touch two trigger hairs, the trap will be activated within about 20 seconds – Fitting Form to Function displayed at its best.

3. Adapt to Changing Conditions: *Appropriately respond to dynamic contexts.*

Life takes form in changing and often unpredictable environments. When environments change, organisms must evolve accordingly to survive. The change required can be an immediate response, for example as a response to injury or danger, or a long-term change that is expressed in genetic evolution and adapted to the degree of change in the organism's environment. Backup systems enable risk management and making the most of opportunities in dynamic contexts. Managing change is carried out in several ways:

- **Incorporate Diversity** – *Leverage a variety of forms, processes, and systems to interact with one's external environment.*
  When a species employs different strategies to meet its functional needs, it raises its chances of survival during environmental changes. Being armed with different ways to interact with the changing environment is key for survival and prosperity. For example, when bees adapt to a diverse range of flowers, they increase their chances of obtaining nectar even when certain flower species are unavailable.
  Diversity has value at the ecosystem level, as well. Every small slice of nature contains a huge variety of life, and diversity is the secret behind nature's resilience. For example, In the gentle war between pests and plants, a single pest can wipe out an entire species and leave an area barren of life. Having a variety of species in the habitat ensures that at least some of them survive even if there is a pest infestation or extreme weather, and then the entire system can recover more easily. This is in contrast to the modern agricultural system of

monoculture, where fields only hold a single species that are indeed extremely vulnerable. In this context, Darwin said that a plot of land which grew grasses that were not closely related, would be more productive than a plot with a single species of grass.

- **Maintain Integrity Through Self-Renewal** – *Persist by constantly adding energy and matter to heal and improve the system.* Living systems are constantly being renewed, replacing and rebuilding parts of the system, not waiting for malfunctions or parts to collapse. This maintains a constant level of functioning over time, and adjustments can occur gradually without disabling the system. Simply put, you don't have to "restart" to upload new software. For example, all the cells in our body are routinely replaced in a controlled manner. When organisms are harmed in nature, self-repair mechanisms get activated: when the body receives a cut, the natural coagulation mechanism is activated and stops the bleeding; during a fire, in the heat of hundreds of degrees, pine cones open, and after the fire is extinguished, they sprout and form a new forest; in our plastic brains, new connections are formed in response to damage that has caused cellular destruction; Some organisms have a particularly impressive ability to regenerate, to the point of regrowing entire limbs that have been amputated.
- **Embody Resilience** – *Maintain function following disturbance by incorporating variations, redundancy, and decentralization.* Variation is the assignment of different roles to different parts of the system in order to respond to different situations. For example, a dual root system that stretches both deep and across to absorb runoff and groundwater. The circulatory system includes both white blood cells whose function is to identify and destroy various threats invading our body, and red blood cells whose primary function is to transport oxygen

to all cells in the body and to remove carbon dioxide from body tissues and organs.

Redundancy is the performance of the same function by a large number of units in the system in order to provide a response even when some units fail. Female sea turtles lay many eggs, but only a few turtles will survive the expected dangers and reach adulthood; the circulatory system contains large amounts of red and white blood cells, so that there is backup if some of them fail; excess blooming of flowers increases chances of pollination.

There is also decentralization in nature: assigning the same role to several external factors. For example, there are several different pollinators for the same plant, so that the plant will continue to exist if one pollinator goes extinct. Nature never puts all its eggs in one basket.

4. Integrate Development with Growth: *Balance investments to move toward an enriched system.*

The forms of everything in nature come into being as organisms grow, until they reach their final form. In nature, there is no separation between physical growth and the system's development and its functions, because development supports growth, and both occur simultaneously and in a balanced way. For example, when a snail grows inside its shell, the shell grows along with it and supports its maturation. Unlike nature, when our "shell" is too small for our size – when the number of members in our family or organization increases – we usually move to a new structure with adapted physical dimensions. Construction methods in nature enable modularity, spontaneity, and adaptation to the design that emerges as it grows, using several principles:

- **Self-Organize** – *Create conditions to allow components to interact in concert.* Development in nature is the product of self-organization due to interactions among system components. The process is spontaneous and is not controlled by any factor outside or inside the system, and is therefore called self-organization or self-assembly. The process explains using simple elements to form complexity. Simple building blocks join together, creating a system-level functioning on the macro level.

The idea of self-assembly was explained succinctly by Oded Shoseyov – a researcher, entrepreneur, and inventor from the Hebrew University of Jerusalem – in his TED talk: *How We're Harnessing Nature's Hidden Superpowers*.[135] "In nature, there is no one there that actually takes my head and screws it onto my neck or takes my skin and glues it onto my body. In nature, everything is self-assembled. So, every living cell, whether coming from a plant, insect, or human being, has DNA that encodes for nano bio-building blocks, many times they are proteins; other times, they are enzymes that make other materials like polysaccharides or fatty acids. And the common feature about all these materials is that they need no one. They recognize each other and self-assemble into structures, scaffolds on which cells are proliferating, to give tissues. They develop into organs, and together, bring life."

Nature creates optimal conditions so that components can react with each other and create complex life. For example, the first algae were formed from the combining of single-celled organisms, which led to resource sharing and energy efficiency in the multicellular state, where each cell already had a specialization and role; ecological habitats are the result of many species assembling together, resulting in a system that is more complex and richer than the sum of its parts.

- **Build from the Bottom-Up** – *Assemble components one unit at a time.* Systems in nature are built from the bottom up and their construction is modular. Trees don't create large surfaces and then cut leaves out of them, but cells join other cells until the leaf's margin is formed. The margin then grows with the leaf to a certain size and then the growth stops. Thus, there is no waste nor surplus of material, and all of the leaf's needs are met as it grows.

- **Combine Modular and Nested Components** – *Fit multiple units within each other progressively from simple to complex.* Most of life is made of simple base units that connect to each other and contain each other. Diversity and complexity are created through different combinations: four DNA bases code for 20 amino acids that make up thousands of proteins. For example, keratin is one type of protein that forms hair, scales, feathers, beaks, rhinoceros' horns, horse hooves, and more. The same protein only in different spatial forms produces a wide variety of products. Of course, complexity increases when several proteins are used as basic building blocks.

5. Be Locally Attuned and Responsive: *Fit into and integrate with the surrounding environment.*

Locality is a value in nature. The locality is home, the local environment is Mother Earth that provides resources, the "neighbors" are partners, and the environmental cycles of activity are the local clock, which dictates the pace and drives development and change. Organisms are in constant "dialogue" with their local environment; they are attentive, connected, and responsive to threats, and seize opportunities. This "dialogue" is conducted in several ways:

- **Leverage Cyclical Processes** – *Take advantage of phenomena that repeat themselves.* Cyclical processes in nature offer the value of survival. For example, the number of leaves on a tree decreases with the drop-in daylight hours until all the leaves fall, according to the cycle of daylight hours and seasons.

There is no point in maintaining many leaves when the ability to produce energy decreases. The life cycle of certain plants is matched with the life cycle of their pollinators to maximize the chances of a fruitful encounter. Some cicada species operate in life cycles such that all individuals in a local population reach maturity at the same time, say, once every 13 or 17 years. Researchers hypothesize that this cycle is a defensive method known as "predator satiation" – since the food is concentrated in a small area and over a short period of time, potential predators get satiated long before they have devoured even a small percentage of cicadas. It is also hypothesized that the use of prime numbers in life cycles (13 and 17) reduces the chance of synchronizing with the life cycles of predators, which are cycles of two, three, four, or six years.[136]

- **Use Readily Available Materials and Energy** – *Build with abundant, accessible materials while harnessing freely available energy.* Organisms will always prefer to use resources from their immediate environment as energy sources, food reserves, and material solutions for building nests and shelters. Birds in Israel will not build their nests from twigs they bring from Italy. Only if they have no choice, will organisms distance themselves and migrate far and wide to get a significant and vital benefit to their lives that they cannot receive from their immediate environment.

  Another example, prairie dogs – a rodent species common in the North American prairies – position the burrow openings they build to create passive ventilation for cooling and air exchange.

- **Use Feedback Loops** – *Engage in cyclic information flows to modify a creation appropriately.* Organisms maintain feedback cycles with their environment. For example, the color and thickness of animal fur varies between winter and summer; the hours when tiny mammals operate vary according to the presence of predators in the field; and squids change color rapidly to communicate or camouflage. A gorgeous example of instant feedback can be seen in the scallop-leaved mullein flower, which snaps and falls off around 30 seconds after being touched. If anything touches a flower in nature, it's an insect, and after visiting the flower and satisfying pollen exposure, there is no need to continue maintaining the flower.

- **Cultivate Cooperative Relationships** – *Find value through win-win interactions.* In nature, it is common for there to be collaborations among individuals in a mutualistic relationship. Such cooperative systems yield mutual benefits for both parties and support their survival. There are many examples of symbioses and win-win relationships in nature. When a jay eats an acorn, the oak tree receives a dispersion service for its acorn, and the jay receives a source of nutrients rich in minerals and proteins. Female boa constrictors, which live in open deserts, receive shading services for their eggs from shadow birds – birds with large, fan-like tails. The female shadow bird benefits from the cooperation as she can lay her own eggs in the nest, protected from predators. Clownfish hide from predators among anemone tentacles while the anemone absorbs the nitrogen from the ammonia excreted from the fish's excrement and enjoys the protection the clownfish provides by chasing away predators.

6. Use Life-Friendly Chemistry: *Use materials and processes that support life's systems at all scales.*

Nature performs sustainable chemistry that is biodegradable, water-based, and life-friendly. Observing nature reveals how life-friendly chemistry works.

- **Employ Elegant Processes** – *Build and regulate using shape complementarity and easily reversible interactions.* Chemical processes in nature are perfected, well-designed, and well-tuned – just like a puzzle piece that perfectly fits the pieces around it, but can be easily disassembled.

- **Use a Small Subset of Elements** – *Achieve functionality by using relatively few elements in key proportions and positions.* Using a limited number of elements allows for efficient assembly and easy breakdown at the end of the life cycle. The most essential substances for life to exist are simple compounds of carbon, oxygen, hydrogen, and nitrogen. Relatively small amounts of metallic elements are also used in life processes, including magnesium, calcium, iron, copper, and zinc.
- **Do Chemistry in and with Water** – *Leverage the multifunctional properties of water.* One of the properties is being a benign solvent. Water is the common solvent for most compounds in nature, unlike industrial solvents which can be hazardous substances. For example, the biochemical processes occurring in a cell take place in an aqueous environment. Water is also a fundamental component of photosynthesis, all of whose products are used for life.
- **Break Down Products into Benign Constituents** – *Use components that readily decompose into life-friendly by-products.* Sometimes organisms produce toxins deliberately, for a specific purpose and in limited quantities. Even these compounds, when eventually released into the environment, decompose naturally and without energy investment into harmless basic materials. For example, snake venom is deadly to their prey, but after the venom has achieved its goal and the snake digests the prey, the venom decomposes into the snake's body and causes no harm. In contrast, DDT or other fabricated pesticides that don't break down, accumulate in the ecosystem and cause severe cumulative damage.

Using Life's Principles as a Design Tool

Once Life's Principles have been studied and understood, their traces will be felt in every encounter with nature. In order to delve deeper into these principles, it is worth getting to know the visual report titled *Genius of Biome*,[137] published by HOK, a global design firm, in partnership with Biomimicry 3.8. The report describes strategies and designs adopted by living organisms in various ecosystems, based on Life's Principles. It is essentially a large repository of examples of Life's Principles in the context of various environmental challenges.

During the bioinspired design process, it is important to identify Life's Principles within the studied biological solution. This act of identifying helps extract principles of sustainability that deserve to be put into practice. Designers who wish to design a sustainable system following nature's path can implement Life's Principles as design principles.

Let us return to the coat example I presented in the introduction to these chapters. Each coat expresses a different Life's Principle. An organic wool coat expresses the principle of using life-friendly chemistry and the sub-principle of breaking products down into benign constituents. A coat made of recycled fabric expresses the principle of being resource efficient and the sub-principle of recycling all materials. A coat made in your home country expresses the principle of being locally attuned and responsive and the sub-principle of using readily available materials and energy.

What would a coat that expresses other Life's Principles look like? For example, could it be: a coat with self-repair and renewal abilities, a coat that maintains feedback loops with the environment, or a modular coat that integrates development with growth? Each principle aims at design innovation that is also identified with sustainability. The more sustainability principles we implement in the designed product, the more sustainable it will be, and the greater its potential to be innovative.

Life's Principles are an excellent framework for guiding thought processes around system redesign. They can be used both to design a new system from scratch and to improve an existing system of any kind: technological, engineering, organizational, or social. In fact, any organization, process, or product can benefit when we look at it through the prism of Life's Principles. Social organizations like schools can also be redesigned in this way. Perhaps we should start by designing Biosphere 2 according to Life's Principles, in the next season of Big Brother.

PRINCIPLES OF IDEALITY IN NATURE

*People tend to be attracted
to what most benefits them.*

Indonesian proverb

Who among us wouldn't want to marry an ideal partner, live in an ideal home, engage in an ideal occupation, go on an ideal vacation? In fact, we can attach the descriptor 'ideal' to any facet of our lives, savor the possibility, and perhaps even strive to get as close to it as possible. Ideal according to the dictionary is a standard of perfection, beauty, excellence. The word 'ideal' is derived from the word 'idea,' and implies an imaginary state that exists only as an idea to which one aspires. An ideal is like the moon: it cannot be touched, but it illuminates the path.

Is nature ideal? Natural systems are certainly not ideal because ideality is a static state in which everything is "perfect" and where the work of design and improvement is already done. Design in nature will never be done. Natural systems are constantly being designed, but in a way that increases their ideality.

The concept of "ideality" is interesting not only in the context of our personal lives or that of nature, but it's also fascinating in technology. Can we design ideal systems or at least strive to design and produce ideal systems during the design process?

Let us return for a moment to the knowledge base of TRIZ, the theory of inventive problem solving developed by Altshuller that presents inventive principles which are repeated in hundreds of thousands of patents. Beyond these principles, the TRIZ knowledge base also includes laws of technical systems evolution – general trends and patterns observed in the development of technical systems. These laws have been identified after reviewing a vast number of patents describing various systems.

I recall hours in the darkroom, developing negatives of pictures I'd taken, stirring a bath of chemicals and watching the picture emerge in the light of the red lamp. I remember the big trip to the Far East where I walked around with a pouch full of film, praying they wouldn't get lost, waiting for the moment I could hand them over for development. I remember the first digital camera I purchased, and the awe I felt that masked the poor quality of the pictures. I also remember the next camera I purchased, which is now lying at home, because my cell phone, which is always on me, shoots in just as good quality. For a short period of time, photographic technology underwent a rapid evolution, and photography became simpler and simpler.

We capture small moments of memory, often only captured by time, which connects and traces the trend, the evolution. Altshuller captured moments like these but of technological leaps in time. He observed technical systems at different points in time and identified laws of evolution that dictate their development. A total of eight laws were formulated that dictate the evolution of technical systems.

One of the laws of technical systems evolution is the law of increasing the degree of ideality of the system (from here on referred to as 'the law of ideality'). Ideality has been defined as "a qualitative ratio between all desirable benefits of the system and its cost or other harmful effects,"[138] or simply put, a benefit-cost ratio. Desirable benefits are the value that the system provides, and harmful effects are the unwanted costs associated with the operation of the system, such as the cost of resources, noise, garbage, pollution, etc. According to the law of ideality, a technological system becomes more ideal over time and over the course of its development, such that it provides more benefit at less cost. The final ideal outcome is a hypothetical situation in which all the benefits of the system are provided at zero cost.

One just has to look at a smartphone, and compare it to all the other devices from the early 1990s that provided the functions it provides today, to understand the law of ideality: a phone, watch, computer, camera, camcorder, MP3 player, media player, electronic organizer, flashlight, and much more in one small device that provides all of these benefits.

The pursuit of benefit is a shaping force that directs people's behavior, as suggested by the Indonesian proverb, and also the development of systems, as the law of ideality suggests. The quest to increase the benefits over time and reduce the costs dictates the evolution of systems. This definition also illustrates mathematically that ideality is something to aspire to and to be approached, but never to be reached, because it doesn't exist. System costs can aim at zero, but will never reach zero. In a hypothetical and mathematically impossible situation, system costs are zero and ideality is infinite.

$$\text{IDEALITY} = \frac{\text{benefit}}{\text{cost}} = \frac{\text{all desirable benefits}}{\text{all harmful effects}} \longrightarrow \infty$$

In fact, there is a direct and clear connection between the definition of ideality and the definition of sustainability. Given resource constraints, the strategy relevant for sustainability (continued existence) is to "achieve more with less," i.e., to get more benefit with fewer resources. Sustainability can also be achieved with ideal systems that provide more benefit with fewer resources. If you minimize the negative effects of the system you designed and maximize the positive effects, then you design a more sustainable system that strives for idealism.

When I was exposed to the definition of ideality and understood its connection to sustainability, I realized that there was an opportunity here to develop an ideal tool for sustainable design inspired by nature. Instead of analyzing sustainability, which is an abstract concept, we can analyze ideality. While writing my doctoral dissertation, I set out to search for the principles of ideality in nature, and I asked what makes systems in nature ideal systems. How does nature provide more benefit with fewer costs? Biological systems exposed to competition over resources demonstrate ideal strategies for survival. I expected there to be some overlap with the knowledge base of Life's Principles, which also reflect sustainable principles in nature, while looking at nature through the lens of ideality has several advantages.

First, while it is unclear how to perform a search for "Life's Principles," the search for ideal strategies is guided by a simple rule – increasing the benefit of the system while reducing its costs, meaning that this tool offers a pattern of thinking and search method, rather than just a closed set of principles. Second, the ideality tool is derived from an engineering knowledge base and is based on engineering thinking patterns, and therefore can serve engineers in sustainable design processes. Third, there is an opportunity here for a reverse learning process: while biomimicry is based on the transfer of knowledge from nature to engineering, here we have a solid knowledge base concerning ideality in technological systems. I assumed I could use these findings to better understand the ideality of natural systems. I set out to explore. I looked at biological systems through the prism of ideality and identified strategies in nature that increase benefits and strategies that reduce costs. I formulated the findings as design principles.

Increasing the Benefits

Functions are a major part of the benefits that a system provides, ergo an increase in the benefits will happen with an increase in the range or intensity of the functions. The more functions a system provides and the stronger the effect of each function, the greater the benefits and the greater the ideality. The way to enhance functionality is highlighted by two principles:

1. Increasing the number of functions: Increasing the number of functions associated with one structure is made possible through multi-functional design. For example, a root system that provides both anchoring and transportation.

2. Enhance the effect of the function: Increasing interaction with the environment will enhance the effect of the function. This is carried out through segmentation, that is, repeating elements that increase the surface area and interface with the environment. For example, alveoli in the lung increase the surface area and allow for greater gas exchange.

Reducing the Costs

Reducing costs in nature happens in a variety of ways:

1. Protection Strategy: Malfunctions are directly translated into costs, wasting material, and creating the need to rebuild what has already been built. Therefore, having a defense strategy and preparing for malfunctions will reduce costs. Protection is achieved through means of prevention and repair.

- **Prevention** – Nature prepares for malfunctions ahead of time. Amniotic fluid protects the fetus in the womb from shocks and bruises; beaver teeth are self-sharpening, which prevents their erosion while gnawing on trees; the surface area of leaves in the desert is smaller to reduce water evaporation; migratory birds store fat before the journey to prepare their bodies for the anticipated effort; when lizards feel threatened, they voluntarily cut off their tail in an act called caudal autotomy, and while the fluttering tail attracts the predator's attention, they escape. The tail is not cut at a random location, but at fracture planes, mechanically weakened areas that allow for quick and precise cutting. Not every malfunction comes as a surprise and inevitably ends in failure. They can be designed and managed.

- **Repair** – Natural systems are renewable and excel when it comes to healing and self-repair. For example, rhinoceroses use horns to locate plants and minerals hidden under soil and as a means of defense and attack. These functions expose the horn to mechanical forces of torsion and compression which may cause fissures and damage, but this is prevented thanks to a microscopic self-repair mechanism. When tiny cracks begin to form, a protein in the horn fills the space and solidifies when exposed to air. In this way, the horn continues to function.

2. Opportunistic Strategy: Utilizing available resources, which offer free benefits, increases the ideality of the system. Organisms are adapted to take advantage of every opportunity to obtain life resources in their environment. Green tree frogs, which live in the deserts of Australia, use small holes in trees as water-condensation stations to harvest water from the air. In the early morning, when their bodies are still cold from the night air, they enter small, warm holes inside trees and slurp up the water that gets collected on their bodies as a result of the temperature difference between their cool bodies and the warm chamber; Birds use abandoned nests found in fields instead of building new ones. There are two aspects of opportunism in nature, each associated with a different design principle:

- **Taking advantage of energy sources** – Utilizing free energy sources such as physical, chemical, geometric, and other gradients (differences) enables operation at no energy cost. For example, temperature gradients are used for heat transfer, and pressure gradients are used for the passive transport of gases or liquids.

- **Taking advantage of material sources** – Utilizing material resources from the environment to perform required functions increases the benefits at no cost. For example, puffer fish use water from the environment to inflate their bodies; snakes rub against elements in the environment to move forward; drops of water are used to remove dirt from lotus leaves. In addition, utilizing materials to create structures yields benefits (functions), and eliminates the need to constantly invest energy in performing the function since it is already provided by the structure.

3. Utilization Strategy: Utilizing material and energy resources, while reducing waste, leads to cost reduction. If it is possible to extract the energy and material to the fullest, to be precise in the use of material and prevent excess, then you have exercised efficiency. A number of design principles will lead to the much-anticipated utilization strategy.

- **Synchronization** – Synchronizing system parameters with environmental parameters prevents waste and leads to efficiency. For example, synchronizing the germination time of seeds with the humidity level in the environment will increase chances of germination and prevent seed waste; synchronizing the position of flowers with the position of the sun (heliotropism) will lead to optimized use of solar energy. An amazing story of synchronization occurred at the end of 2020, when dates were picked from a date tree that sprouted from a 2,000-year-old seed! Israeli researchers from the Arava Institute for Environmental Studies succeeded in germinating dates from seeds found in archaeological excavations, reviving the extinct date species from the Second Temple period.[139] It seems miraculous to us, but the seed actually preserves its creation plan for long periods of time, until the very moment when conditions for germination are met.

- **Transmission** – improving energy transmission in the system to provide easier access and prevent energy waste. For example, tree transport systems have a network structure that provides good conduction with minimal resistance.
- **Giving up unnecessary parts** – reducing material where it is not needed, such as spaces in the frame of a beehive or the space inside a cylinder.

An Ideal Encounter

An article in *Nature* described a beetle with an intriguing name: the diabolical ironclad beetle.[140] It is a particularly durable beetle common in the deserts of western North America. If animals step on it, it will emerge unharmed, and even survives if run over by a car. The study found that the beetle was able to carry 39,000 times its own body weight! This is an unimaginable ability. In human terms, we are talking about a person weighing 75 kilograms who can carry about 3 million kilograms. Since particularly strong materials are required in the engineering world, this beetle aroused great interest.

Observing the beetle's crush-resistance mechanism through the lens of ideality clarifies its uniqueness. The ironclad beetle cannot fly, and like other flightless beetles, over the course of evolution, their forewings which allow flight, have degenerated. These forewings have hardened to provide the necessary protection in the absence of flight. The forewings consist of several layers joined together like a jigsaw puzzle. These beetles carry a type of three-dimensional multi-layered puzzle on their backs. When compressed, the armor slowly breaks, and instead of hopelessly cracking open all at once, it only loses some of its original shape. This is a cost-minimizing protection strategy that prevents expected malfunction due to crushing loads. The armor excels in adapting structure to function in an optimal way, and provides the necessary protection. Additional costs are saved through a strategy of preventing waste by giving up unnecessary parts. The flight-enabling hind wings, which are no longer needed, are atrophied.

From the perspective of increasing the benefits, it can be identified that the armor, like other structures in nature, is multifunctional. Beyond mechanical protection, it also provides thermal protection and is permeable to oxygen and impermeable to water. The fact that there are several layers joined together like a jigsaw puzzle in the forewing enhances the effect of the crush-resistance function by better distributing the weight.

Joining dissimilar materials in engineered structures is a challenge. Engineers often use welding, adhesive bonding, nailing, pegs, or screws to connect parts, but these areas remain mechanically weak. A structure that breaks accurately and predictably, like the armor of the diabolical ironclad beetle, has many advantages: it is easier, for example, to find the source of any cracks since they will likely develop among the intersecting parts.

Is this the strongest beetle in the world? Perhaps, and perhaps we will find stronger beetles in the future. Either way, "We're trying to go beyond what nature has done," said material scientist and engineer David Kisailus, who participated in the study. The law of ideality continues to work, and it is quite likely that in due time we will see crush-resistance systems that provide more benefit at lower cost. Perhaps human design will reach this faster than nature. The evolution of technological systems is much faster than the evolution of biological systems.

The law of ideality works in both nature and technology, but at different intervals. The ability of the human race to change rapidly is incomparable to the rate of change in nature, and therefore our potential for repair is also high. Humankind is able to manage and accelerate processes of change that occur spontaneously and slowly in nature. We have the ability to connect an element from the depths of the lowest sea with an element from the top of the highest mountain – what seems to be elements at the greatest physical distance – if we choose to do so. Their encounter in nature would probably never have occurred. We have the ability to join forces and share knowledge to find a quick solution to a global pandemic that has befallen us. Humanity's ability to change rapidly is a source of hope in light of the environmental crises we are experiencing – the climate crisis and global waste crisis – which often arouse a sense of despair and frustration.

Using the Ideality Principles as a Design Tool
Like Life's Principles, the ideality principles can also be applied to the design or improvement of any type of system. The basic assumption is that applying as many ideality principles as possible to the designed system will increase its ideality and, by extension, its sustainability. Ideality in everyday life is a subjective value. What's ideal for one is not ideal for the other, but the concept of what ideality is, borrowed from the engineering-technological knowledge base (TRIZ), presents a clear criterion for ideality: increasing benefit while reducing cost. One thing is clear: the quest for ideality produces movement and development in technology, nature, and personal life.

PART IV

WHERE?

BIOINSPIRED INNOVATION
IN THE CORPORATE WORLD

Those who do not want to imitate anything,
produce nothing.

Salvador Dali

It's hard to imagine a company that wouldn't want to reach nature's patent database, especially if it has a road map that shows it how to get there. And yet, many companies are still not searching for the way there. I am often asked, if the field of bio-mimicry is so successful (everyone is convinced of its potential), why don't we see it more integrated in the industry and business organizations?

Apparently, the primary barrier is skepticism – a natural barrier when it comes to new approaches. But the more success stories there are, the more biomimetic activity there will be in organizations. Companies that have already broken through the barrier of doubt are imitating nature and generating innovation. Bioinspired innovation spans industries: not just one segment of the market benefits from it, for the simple reason that many of life's challenges have already been solved by nature, and these challenges are related to areas of activity of many organizations. The challenge can be technological, operational, productional, managerial, or organizational. Looking through the appropriate lens will lead to identifying the appropriate solutions in nature.

The big opportunity for the business sector has already been identified. "If you're not incorporating the most brilliant ideas from the natural world into what you sell, you're leaving money on the table," Fortune magazine wrote in a 2017 article on identifying business trends.[141] But the opportunity isn't just the money on the table. The opportunity is also a paradigm shift – perceiving the organization as a living organism, whose very activity fosters the business ecosystem. The opportunity is also to introduce the code of nature into the organizational DNA and its conduct, which leads to sustainability, resilience, and prosperity.

The Biologist at the Design Table

In Benyus' words, "for businesses, biomimicry is about bringing a new discipline – biology – to the design table." Companies integrate biology into design processes in various ways, depending on their size and budget. Some of them establish large internal teams for bioinspired innovation, and sometimes it is a "team" of one, crazy enough individual who was turned onto the field and actively inserts it into the organization. Biology is introduced at the engineering table through biologists who accompany the design processes, biomimetic consultants, or cooperation with academia.

NASA, America's space agency, established a dedicated unit for biomimetic research and development.[142] NASA's interest in nature is broad and related to solutions in the fields of aeronautics, propulsion, safety, and more. One of the projects developed is an innovative wind-powered concept vehicle, for the purpose of mobility and research on Mars. The Martian surface is covered in rocks and sandy dunes, and in 2005, one of the wheels of the Opportunity rover got stuck there for a month before being retrieved. NASA searched for a concept of wheel-free mobility and emulated the propulsion mechanism of tumbleweed, a dry, root-detached plant that rolls in the wind and spreads its seeds, often seen on the side of roads in desert areas. A vehicle without wheels has an advantage in moving over sandy and non-flat terrain. The rover resembles a rolling ball, and because of the different gravitational conditions on Mars (approximately one third of Earth's gravity), even a light breeze makes it move.[143]

NASA is also developing an innovative spacesuit. NASA doctors have observed that after astronauts return from space missions, they tend to be weak and often faint. This problem is caused by changes in blood pressure due to differences in gravity between space and Earth. To solve this problem, NASA studied how giraffes cope with rapid and grand changes in their blood pressure, since their hearts are about two and a half meters above the ground. One strategy that was identified is the tight skin around the giraffe's legs, which applies pressure on the blood vessels like compression stockings from all directions and helps return blood to the heart. Inspired by this design principle, MIT Labs with support from NASA developed an innovative spacesuit called BioSuit, which exerts counter pressure on the legs using a semi-elastic polymer that forms a structure that counters low blood flow on other planets. The BioSuit functions as a second skin that allows for more freedom in movement than traditional spacesuits that produce pressure on the body with gas.[144]

DARPA, the branch of the United States Department of Defense that handles technological developments, some of which are also intended for civilian use, has established the Biological Technologies Office (BTO). One of its most well-known funded developments is Big Dog, a robot developed by Boston Dynamics and other partners for the United States Army, which will follow soldiers and carry their equipment for them. The robot dog successfully walks through mud, snow, smooth ice, and steep slopes.

Rafael, which develops advanced combat systems, understood, like other defense companies around the world, that the defense industry can adopt mechanical and material solutions as well as mechanisms and principles from nature. A complex battlefield requires complex capabilities, as there are in nature. For example, the concept of a swarm of independent drones was developed, moving like a murmuration of starlings in the sky, in coordination and without collision. On the future battlefield, drones will be able to embark on missions, observe, track, and attack on enemy territory, while combat soldiers remain behind protected. When a command is given to a single drone, all others follow suit, just like in nature, where one bird spots a tree suitable for a night's rest and moves toward it, and all the others follow.

When the ability to carry out in-house R&D processes is limited, the quickest route for introducing bioinspired innovation to the organization is scouting existing technologies that have innovation potential. HP Indigo, which develops digital printing presses, has begun several projects in this manner. For example, lotus-effect technology was tested as a hydrophobic coating to repel ink contamination on internal machine parts, and structural color technologies were incorporated into inks to prevent counterfeiting. As in nature, ink containing structures that reflect different wavelengths at different angles has a color-shifting effect that can be used to detect counterfeit brands.

Other organizations are bringing biology to the design table through targeted innovation processes. The processes are carried out by innovation teams, with each team working on a different challenge that has been marked as significant to the organization. The teams are supported by biomimetic experts, who also supply them with the methodologies required for the process.

One could say that organizations are part of an ecosystem, just like in nature, and they draw from it and nourish it. The biomimetic ecosystem also has key players, initiatives, and organizations that provide the necessary knowledge and funding to support the growth of the ecosystem. Competitions, conferences, global networks, and funding channels are available to organizations interested in developing on this path.

Organizations that engage in bioinspired innovation often venture out to look for solutions in nature and find it with added benefits they didn't expect to find. For example, positioning yourself at the forefront of innovation, like what happened with Festo in a way that I will immediately demonstrate. An added value can even be redesigning the organization in the image of nature as a living organism, operating according to the design paradigm and ethos of nature. The amazing story of Interface, which I will describe below, is an example of this.

A Playground, a Bionic Safari, and the Cutting Edge of Innovation

Festo, a leading global manufacturer for industrial automation, established the Bionic Learning Network in 2006 – a multidisciplinary group of professionals from the fields of design, engineering, biology, computer science, and robotics, as well as partners from research institutions and academia. The motivation behind starting the group was the realization that the tasks the company deals with, such as gripping, propulsion, control, and regulation, are tasks that are performed efficiently in nature.

The group works on several projects at once that are not intended for sale, but to test new technologies. They are essentially the company's "playground." The insights and conclusions from the projects are later transferred to the company's R&D department for implementation and application. The group's projects also aim to show Festo's expertise in an appealing way. The projects are released online as videos and amass great interest, amazement, and innovative discourse. They attract the attention of customers and potential employees and position the company at the forefront of innovation. The group's projects also touch on social responsibility: they are designed to excite young people, ignite their imagination, and attract them to study technology and science. Project proposals come from company executives, colleagues, team members, and academics. Each proposal is evaluated according to the technologies they want to test, the messages they wish to deliver, and the mix of projects already being tested. Each project is worked on for about two years.

A quick tour of Festo's bionic safari reveals an impressive array of projects. The arthropod section has a bionic dragonfly, butterfly, ants, and spider. The bionic spider mimics one of the strangest defense mechanisms ever observed in the wild and reported in scientific literature: flic-flac. Flic-flac spiders quickly roll on the hot sand to escape from their predators. This light and elegant movement is reminiscent of the flexible Olympic gymnasts (*see 16). The bionic model is much bulkier than its natural role model, but it can roll on its own and move in impassable areas. Maybe we will see it rolling around on Mars someday. Their bionic ants act like colonies of ants in nature through self-organization. The constructed ants are small robots that work cooperatively using control algorithms that follow clear rules just like in nature, with the purpose of solving common tasks.

In the reptile section is a chameleon with a never-ending tongue. In nature, chameleons use their tongues to grip objects of varying forms and pull them toward their mouths, like an all-encompassing glove, wrapping, and pulling them into its mouth. Inspired by the chameleon tongue, the group developed the FlexShapeGripper, based on an elastic silicone cap capable of picking up several objects in a single gripping process without the need to manually consolidate them. Once the elastic cap encloses the objects, they attach to it via suction and are transported to their destination.

The bird section houses a bionic herring gull called a Smart-Bird and a bionic penguin. The SmartBird is an aviation model that looks just like a bird from a distance and can be used for imagery intelligence missions. The penguin is an underwater vehicle that mimics the propulsion mechanism and streamlined body characteristics of penguins which I described in detail in the chapter "Nature's Structural Language." The robot, which resembles a penguin in every way, has autonomous mobility and energy efficiency, and can be used for underwater missions, handling ports, and gathering intelligence.

A bionic kangaroo dwells in the mammal section. In nature, kangaroos advance by hopping and can even cover a distance of around 9 meters in a jump and reach a speed of around 40 kilometers per hour. Extremely strong tendons and powerful calf muscles contract and release like a spring while storing and preserving kinetic energy for the next jump. The bionic model mimics the natural kangaroo's jumping mechanism using pneumatic cylinders and springs. The result looks a bit clunky compared to the elegance of the natural model, but responds nicely to the operator's hand gestures. The flying fox, which belongs to the bat family – the only mammals that can fly – is also found in this section. The bionic model boasts stretchy elastic wings, and controlling their curvature increases lift force, similar to the natural model.

From Tile to Carpet: Company Redesign in the Image of Nature

Interface is the world's leading manufacturer of carpet tiles (modular flooring). In the 1990s, the company's executive team started getting asked: "What do you do for the environment?"

330 | WILD IDEAS

The late Ray Anderson, the company's founder and chairman, realized that he had no real answer to this question. In those years, the company's production system was take-make-waste, that is, taking raw materials from nature, using them, and returning them as waste. The company used petroleum-based raw materials (nylon fibers) and energy produced in carbon dioxide-emitting processes, and did not take responsibility for removing carpets at the end of their life cycle to landfills. Waste was actually viewed as a marker of business success: more waste meant more orders. The company's conduct was not unusual in the industry. It didn't violate any environmental regulations, but did carry out the minimum required by regulations.

Ray began searching for answers and found them in nature. He was determined to start a revolution and formulated a vision that led to reshaping the company in nature's image. The change included handling all stages of the Interface value chain. A value chain encompasses the full range of activities needed to create a product or service. The purpose of value-chain analysis is to improve each step in the process at which value is added, in order to deliver the maximum value to the customer. Changes were performed at various stages in Interface's value chain, including R&D, material resource management, production processes, and even the drafting of business models. The methodology that led the change was biomimicry.

• **A new series of carpets:** The R&D team began searching for sources of inspiration for carpets in nature and ventured out into natural wooded areas. A quick glance at the forest floor revealed a beautiful colorful carpet of leaves. The team was instructed to identify design principles behind creating this forest cover. Imagine you are walking on such a beautiful forest floor right now. The leaves cover the ground. Each step leaves a tiny mess. The leafy surface consists of many individual parts that are not identical. The appearance is alluring despite the great variation between the leaves in color, size, and shape. This diversity produces a harmonious feeling in nature, while in the industrial world, diversity is often seen as an imperfection. The design principle identified by the team was organized chaos. A chaotic combination of components that don't resemble each other produces an organized and harmonious pattern. If a red or orange leaf falls at any moment, large or small, smooth or jagged, nothing would change the harmonious sensation given off by the forest floor.

The analogy to the world of carpets is clear. The principle of organized chaos was translated into a successful carpet tile series called Entropy®, like the physics term 'entropy,' the degree of disorder in any complex system. The previous series were based on a predefined and pre-designed layout, but the Entropy series is based on a combination of unidentical tiles, just like leaves on a forest floor. The advantages of this series from an operational point of view are enormous. Installation is simple, quick, and uncostly; there is no need to arrange all the carpet tiles in a certain way before attaching them to the floor; less waste is created in the production process because there are fewer rejected parts; each tile is accepted as is, even if the shade is slightly different from the original design; maintenance is easier because damaged tiles can be substituted without replacing the entire area; and most significant is that there is no need to hold inventory. Tiles that need to be replaced or repaired can simply be taken from another series, just like any leaf is welcome on the forest floor. This revolutionary series was released in 2000 and changed the carpet industry. Customers loved the product and may have experienced the sense of harmony they get from nature. This was the breakthrough that led to a change in the company's design philosophy. Skepticism gave way to the next challenge.

• **A revolutionary adhesive solution:** Attaching carpets to floors uses a ton of glue. Adhesives emit volatile and toxic substances that are released into rooms, and also make recycling processes much more difficult. At the end of their life, carpets are removed with great effort and the bare floor is left with adhesive marks that are difficult to remove. The R&D team inquired about bioinspiration sources for adhesion and found the gecko's dry adhesion mechanism based on electrical connections. It seemed like a perfect role model, but soon the complexity of the mechanism became apparent. The question of adhesion, which led to a dead end, was replaced by the question of how surfaces in nature remain covered. There is no need for glue in nature, naturally. Leaves stay on the forest floor by gravity. This insight led to the development of TacTiles™, an innovative installation method that utilizes gravity. Instead of gluing the tiles to the floor, they are connected to each other using small removable square stickers placed at the shared meeting point of every four tiles. This creates a uniform surface with a significant amount of weight pressing between the walls, providing lateral pressure. The connected tiles don't budge, and there is no need to apply adhesives to the floor. The stickers themselves contain a minimal amount of glue and can be recycled at the end of their use. Installation is easy: there is no need for carpet experts and they can even be installed alone. Removal when needed is also easy, leaving the surface under the carpets undamaged.

• **Material resource management:** At the start of their journey, material resources efficiency was extremely low. Less than 5% of raw carpet materials were returned to the industry through recycling processes. Interface was confronted with the huge process of setting up the ReEntry® program, which reclaims carpets after use. Nature returns its components to the cycle of matter and Interface strived to do the same. But what's the point of collecting carpets at the end of their life if they can't be broken down into their constituents and reused? At this stage, Interface established ReEntry plants around the world that received carpets from the industry and recycled them, thereby reducing their dependence on virgin raw materials, most of which are petroleum-based, and reducing the waste that winds up in landfills. The ReEntry plants served the entire ecosystem and even recycle carpets of competitors. Interface shared its expertise with other carpet recyclers to establish similar operations. Although the company lost a competitive advantage in this process, it operated in the spirit of nature, serving nature and the environment, and in the process, established a micro-industry of carpet recycling.

• **Production processes:** Since Interface assembles raw materials and doesn't manufacture them itself, the most significant impact the carpet production process has on the environment is the energy consumption during assembly. The company began implementing small changes, which have had a cumulative effect, on the production floor, but wasn't satisfied and strove to increase their use of renewable energy sources. Toward this end, they operated in surprising ways: they invested in wind and solar energy projects to own means of production of renewable energies, and even collaborated to erect a biogas plant that converts landfill methane into energy. When waste decomposes in a landfill, it produces methane gas and other greenhouse gases that get released into the atmosphere. Interface has set up a facility in the landfill next to their production plant to collect gas to replace the fossil fuels used during production. Today, Interface is one of the most sustainable manufacturing systems in the world.

• **Business models:** Interface's carpet leasing program of the '90s is a coherent business model. Instead of customers buying the carpet, they buy the right to use it and also receive cleaning, maintenance, and removal services from the company. The benefits for both sides are apparent. Unlike a car that follows a price list, it was difficult to determine the residual value of a carpet at the end of the leasing period before the ReEntry program was introduced. In fact, 95% of carpets ended up in landfills, so it was hard to argue that the carpet's value was worth more than nil – on the contrary, its removal still had to be paid for. This fact made it difficult to suggest a viable financial leasing model. After the success of the ReEntry program, Interface launched a leading program. At that point, the company was able to easily prove that the residual value of a carpet at the end of the leasing period is much more than nil.

• **Innovation:** One by one, the links of the value chain were unraveled: R&D, material resource management, production processes, and drafting business models, and a new value of innovation was created inspired by nature, according to its principles. Nature's imprint could now be felt in the organization's DNA. Rebirth.

Innovation was now associated with profit. Ray Anderson said that "Through the inspiration of biomimicry and the wellspring of innovation that has come out of the idea of sustainable design... has made our products better than ever... this is about a way to make a bigger profit."[145]

Interface has become a key player leading and feeding its ecosystem rather than acting solely for itself. Continuing with the spirit and ethos of nature, Interface generously shares its knowledge with the industry, and has begun mentoring other companies and encouraging them to establish their own sustainability agendas. It is a circular economy of knowledge: knowledge returns to feed the ecosystem. As in nature, ecosystemic behavior yields prosperity. These are the laws of nature, and they are also exhibited in industries that operate this way. Interface is now considered the standard-bearer of sustainability in the industry, and its founder, the late Ray Anderson, who led the effort, was named a 'Hero of the Environment' by *TIME* magazine as a visionary who succeeded in getting the management team to follow in his footsteps, stood by his words, and provided the necessary resources for real change.

• **Ethos:** When an organization is reborn, new employees are born. Ray Anderson said that one day he attended a sales meeting. The meeting wasn't going smoothly and the client was acting resistant. During the meeting, the client asked to go to the bathroom and she passed by the production floor on her way. She encountered a particularly energetic forklift driver and asked him, "What are you doing?" to which he replied without a stutter, "I get up every morning to save the planet." Stunned by his response, she returned to the conference room calmer and more appreciative, and the deal was signed. The Interface story is one of ethos, culture, goodwill, and values that were cast by one person and permeated through to every employee.

Biomimicry in the Pedagogical Field: Learning and Teaching from Nature

The one concerned with days, plants wheat; with years,
plants trees; with generations, educates people.

Janusz Korczak

One day, I was sitting in my garden beside the wadi near our house. A mother and child were hiking in the wadi. The mother showed her son the kingfisher on the telephone wire near my garden. "Oh," said the boy, "that is the kingfisher that inspired the solution for the train noise problem in Japan." I didn't know the child or mother. That's when I realized that this story, and the other stories I've been telling for over a decade as stories of bioinspired innovation, have a life of their own. This is because the field of biomimicry has already been extensively researched all around the world, including in Israel, in formal and informal education.

The seeds of bioinspired innovation are sown in childhood. Around 40 years ago, as a child, Marc Meyers went for an evening stroll with his father in the forest on the edge of the small village where he grew up in Brazil. As they sat down to rest among the forest trees, they came upon the skull of a toucan lying on the ground. The distinctive giant bright yellow beak was already faded, yet it was hard not to notice the puzzling discrepancy between the size of the beak and the tiny weight of the toucan body. The beak was rigid and tough, yet incredibly light, reported Meyers, who as a child, wanted to understand how this unique combination of strength while remaining light could come about.[146] Meyers is now a material scientist and professor of mechanical and aerospace engineering at the University of California, San Diego. He fulfilled his childhood dream and studied the toucan beak as well as other structures in nature, in order to develop biomimetic materials with miraculous properties.

Pedagogy affects all of us – our children, the children in us. Though not all of us are teachers, we are all students who learn and develop, and we have at least one teacher in common: nature. So what makes nature such a good teacher to learn from and through?

• **Knowledge base:** Nature is a unifying factor in many fields that are studied separately today, but whose roots lie in it. Technology is constrained by laws of nature, such as gravity, and therefore many principles taught today in science and technology can be learned through similar phenomena in nature. For example, work with mathematical series can be illustrated using the Fibonacci sequence, which is found in sunflower flower heads and in the structure of pine cones. Newton's laws can be demonstrated using the jet propulsion mechanism that propels squids and is based on Newton's third law, the law of action and reaction. Adhesion forces can be demonstrated through the lotus effect, and mechanical joints – through the operation of joints in the human body. The combination of examples and analogies from nature contributes to understanding the phenomenon being studied and strengthens the connection between the phenomenon and daily life, and its possible applications.

Biomimicry as a discipline is an excellent platform for dealing with issues of innovation, invention, and entrepreneurship. One can tackle the question of how an inventive process looks when it begins with observation and study of nature. It is also an excellent gateway for engaging in issues of sustainability and environment by studying the principles of sustainability in nature. In contrast to other approaches in environmental education, which highlight what is lacking (running out of water and energy sources), working on environmental issues from a biomimetic standpoint instills a sense of security and hope regarding humanity's ability to cope with environmental challenges.

• **Emotion and experience:** In the presence of nature, we wake up, get curious, are amazed, and often relax and find peace. These emotions support the learning processes. The playfulness and joy provided by nature make it an excellent teacher. "The most effective kind of education is that a child should play amongst lovely things," said Plato. Nature is an experiential laboratory of research and discovery. One can spend hours in nature observing, experimenting, and discovering, investigating mechanisms and understanding relationships between structures and functions. Nature is full of wonderful things, no less than the best of children's games that have been designed by game designers.

• **Values:** Nature is a window to ethos and values, the assimilation of which leads to a better life, resilience, and prosperity. Learning from nature promotes respect for nature and sensitivity to the diversity of species. Even "small" organisms like ants and other insects can serve as our teachers. Another value is slowing down and observing. In the days of information flooding and technological temptations, it is very important to practice processes that allow us to stop, observe, and ask.

• **Reasoning:** Nature in general and biomimicry in particular are platforms for developing high-order thinking, which is required in STEM fields (Science, Technology, Engineering, and Math) and in the technological-scientific world.

1. **Interdisciplinary reasoning** – If there is one factor that can unite so many fields, it is nature, which bridges between the disciplines: biology, chemistry, physics, engineering, design, and others, and ties together concepts, theories, and knowledge bases. Biomimicry makes it possible to experience this nexus.

2. **Analogical reasoning** – Biomimicry, by definition, is an analogical process of transferring knowledge from one content domain (biology) to another (technology). Learning the field encourages analogical reasoning that can identify connections and similarities between solutions in nature and human challenges. The more developed the student's analogical reasoning, the deeper the process of imitation. For example, when biomimicry was taught in elementary schools, students were presented with a variety of biological systems and were asked to come up with ideas for inventions inspired by them. Third graders used formal analogical reasoning: one student saw a mushroom and suggested inventing an umbrella inspired by it. In higher grades (5th–6th), students presented ideas based on more complex analogies. They referred to material properties (strength and density) and proposed, for example, a structure mimicking the strength of a beehive.

3. **Systemic-functional reasoning** – Students learn to observe organisms through a systemic-functional lens, to distinguish between structures and processes, to separate function (what the system does) from strategy and mechanism (how it does it); They learn to distinguish between the components of the system and identify the interaction between them that produces the mechanism.

4. **Entrepreneurial-inventive reasoning** – Entrepreneurs wake up in the morning and cannot remain indifferent to the problems they encounter. They "collect" problems and identify possible solutions. If exposed to a solution, they actively strive

to reach it. In biomimicry studies, students develop a sensor for identifying problems and a radar for reviewing solutions. This is the awareness that leads to entrepreneurial-inventive reasoning. Children love inventing, and learning biomimicry shows them that this ability is accessible to them at all times.

• **Investigative skills:** The field of biomimicry promotes investigative skills, i.e., identifying research questions, formulating hypotheses, gathering information, observing and experimenting, refining and abstracting, and drawing conclusions. The object of study is the functional mechanism in nature. These research skills can be cultivated systematically, through experiential learning from nature.

• **Meaningful learning:** Nature as a teacher leads to meaningful learning, which is defined as learning that is relevant to the students' lives and touches their souls, while involving diverse aspects of mental, emotional, physical, artistic, productive, and other experiences. This type of learning calls for the development of reasoning, excellence, and in-depth study of topics that interest the learners and meet their needs through activities conducted alone and together.

Biomimicry is made from children's favorite materials: nature, animals, and inventions. Biomimicry programs involve going out into local nature, exploring local organisms, experiential learning that integrates play and activities, practicing biomimetic reasoning, and developing an invention inspired by nature as part of a project (PBL: Project-Based Learning). The students choose a project that attracts them and that stimulates them emotionally, and through it they deepen their reasoning. For example, inspired by chameleons, who change color in response to temperature changes in the environment, students invented a safety mechanism for detecting water temperature to prevent getting burned in the shower when the water gets too hot. Other students presented biomimetic projects including a friendly syringe that reduces fear of injections, knee pads for cyclists, and the "fastest" water slides in the world. Topics that are close to the students' worlds enhance the learning process and turn it into meaningful learning.

Tips and Ideas for Teaching the Field or Self-Study

• **Examples and case studies:** Narrative examples become etched in memory. When students in my children's classes see me, they know that it's almost vacation time. Every year, toward the end of the year, I come to their classes and conduct biomimicry activities. It always amazes me how, even though a year has passed since our last meeting, that they remember the invention stories I'd told them. Each story is an opportunity to strengthen the students' intuition about identifying possible innovation. For example, when students are presented with a snake locomotion mechanism and they suggest developing a robot inspired by it, it is worth presenting them with the existing solution on the market and showing them that they'd thought like the engineers who built the robot – this demonstrates to them that their intuition for identifying the application was good. It is also recommended to include a meeting with an inventor or biomimetic researcher in the learning process, someone to serve as a living example and tell their story. In my personal experience, these meetings have left a mark for many years.

• **Practicing BIO-WOW questions:** An important part of teaching is fostering curiosity and awe over nature. This can be done by practicing awe questions. For example, why don't birds get wet in the rain? Why don't ants get stuck in traffic? How does nature produce shiny things? Inventor and entrepreneur Roger Johnson spent many hours in the Amazon forest as a child, inquiring as to how nature makes shiny things like fish scales and cat eyes. As an adult, after studying a degree in engineering, he returned to investigate the glittering structures, delving mainly into lobster eyes. He turned into a biomimetic inventor when he discovered that inside lobster eyes is a structure of compound mirrored lenses that focus incoming light on points on the retina. Inspired by this structure, he developed a method to channel heat from a radiant heater efficiently, ensuring that it reaches the person sitting next to the stove and is not spread throughout the room.[147]

• **Analogy practice:** My youngest son was born after I had already entered the world of biomimicry, during my PhD. As befits a son born to older parents, he is endowed with the quality of kindness and personal charm. Every now and then he brings me something he found in nature and says, "This is for your biomimicry." Even when he didn't understand what it was, he understood two things: that it had to do with nature, and that his mother loved it. The road to my heart was shorter than ever. In the spirit of his gifts, I highly recommend encouraging students to collect interesting things from nature: fallen seeds, acorns, pods, leaves with special structures, dry cactus tissue, and everything that can and is permitted to be collected. This is a box of solutions. It is also a good idea to encourage students to note problems they encounter in daily life and write them down in the problem box. The ability to identify problems can also be practiced. A nice game I play with my kids while traveling instead of 'I spy' is the 'what's the problem' exercise. We think about a product and the children need to identify the need or problem it answers. Another nice exercise is to send students to walk around a natural environment holding a note in their hands with a challenge written on it and to encourage them to find something in nature that solves this challenge. For example, raising water vertically (tree), transporting over a long distance (seeds), and more.

• **Turning nature into a narrative:** An experiential way to study nature's inventions is to understand them as stories. Like any good story, nature has a hero (the organism), a problem (a missing function needed to survive), tension between the desired and existing situations, and a solution in the form of a functional mechanism. The narrative pattern helps us understand: What is the story about? Who is the hero? What is the hero's problem that is causing distress? And how is the problem solved? The following is an example of describing a mechanism in nature following a narrative structure:

1. **Exposition – background:** Place, time, main character, cause or problem disturbing the peace. *In the deserts of Namibia lives a small beetle who needs water to survive, but there is no water available.*
2. **Inciting incident:** Plot twists, meetings between two opposing elements, a special day or a special event. *One morning, the beetle woke up early in the morning and could barely see anything. The sky was full of fog.*
3. **Climax:** The most suspenseful part of the story, a struggle between opposing elements, someone getting lost, and so on. *The beetle realized that the water was very close to it, right in the air, and thought: If only I had a way to reach it!*
4. **Resolution:** The key to solving the plot is reached, expressed in a miraculous figure, idea, object, etc. *The beetle raised its hind legs, and water droplets began condensing on the bumps of its back.*
5. **Conclusion:** A return to peace, a new understanding, a lesson or a moral. *The drops slipped straight into the beetle's mouth and quenched its thirst.*

Another option is to suggest that students "dub" the organism and tell its story: if the organism could speak, what would it say? It should be noted that, as a rule, personification is not acceptable in the world of biology, but it serves as a pedagogical means to understand the mechanism when it comes to children of young ages.

Main Challenges in Learning the Field

The difficulties and challenges that students encounter in the learning process are not much different than those encountered by adults, but are intensified by their young age.

• **Difficulty finding biological information:** Searching for solutions is a challenge I explored in this book. The challenge escalates when information in a foreign language is needed. For some languages, information is not yet widespread, and students who are not fluent in English will find it difficult to access international databases. The solution is to make knowledge accessible in other languages, such as the Hebrew database developed by Taasiyeda – an association dedicated to advancing education in the changing world of technology that runs biomimicry programs in Israel.

• **Difficulty in abstracting the functional mechanism:** Understanding a biological mechanism requires abstraction and analytical abilities, which generally develop at a later age. The solution is templates adapted to the students' reasoning and abstraction abilities, such as system modeling tools from the engineering world for older students and the use of narrative templates for younger students.

• **Lack of professional knowledge to understand the mechanism:** It is important to direct students to choose mechanisms that they can really understand, even without in-depth knowledge of mechanics, chemistry, or physics (if they lack knowledge in these areas). One should choose mechanisms that are more intuitive, structural, formal, and principled. When the pedagogical process is not successful, the students are left with a gap between nature and the invention, and present the invention in too general a manner. For example: "Here's a bird and I thought about inventing an airplane from it." The analogy remains superficial, because the students don't have the ability to understand the mechanism, and the whole process of refining and abstraction is nonexistent.

Vision: Nature for Every Student

Nature is the greatest teacher and biomimicry is a platform for meaningful learning. A teacher who transmits knowledge, imparts values, and sculpts reasoning all in an experiential and exciting way, is a teacher I would choose for me and my children. In my vision, I see such teachers everywhere, teachers who instruct like and through nature, teachers of youth and adults, in formal schools and in the school of life.

I see schools beginning to speak the language of nature, a language of collaboration among teachers who teach science and technology and those teaching other subjects, such as art or even literature. Nature is a unifying factor for all professions.

I see schools cultivating the cradle of innovative culture, through an "invitation to invent," for example: each month a biological mechanism will be presented and students will be invited to conduct investigations, come up with ideas for inventions inspired by that mechanism, and present their ideas to the school as part of a rotating exhibition.

I see schools operating according to Life's Principles, nourishing the community and being nourished by it, treating resources and nature with respect. Schools in antiquity started in nature. The first academy established by Plato was located in a grove of olive trees. Perhaps it is time to return to nature and learn from its wisdom.

HIGHER EDUCATION AND EMPLOYMENT

Natural abilities are like natural plants;
they need pruning by study.

Francis Bacon

"My name is Tamir, and I'm 20-years-old. I have recently become interested in the world of biomimicry and would love to consult with you to understand it in more depth." I am always happy to receive such inquiries from young men and women who have fallen in love with the field and want to work in it. Sometimes they are still serving in the military, or completing their scholastic studies, and are already preparing for their next phase. This chapter was written for Tamir and his friends; it was also written for anyone who dreams of changing their career or who suddenly discovered a passion within that had not existed for a long time, and one morning woke up to discover they wanted more; for those who want to cultivate their natural talents through study, to go deeper and turn this field into a profession.

What is it about this field that makes it so fascinating? In my opinion, it's a mixture of several ingredients, each of which separately arouses passion, sparks imagination, and invites us to dream. Passion joining passion becomes a great fire. Biomimicry is about innovation, technology, inventions, nature, animals, and plants; it's an invitation to open the book of nature and walk among its pages, an innate yearning for nature in all of us described as biophilia. There is an opportunity here to change, if not the world, then at least our immediate surroundings, and to connect science with values of sustainability. The practice of biomimicry gives us meaning, pleasure, interest, and even happiness, stemming from love for the profession. "If we can except those isolated and miraculous moments fate can bestow on a man, loving your work (unfortunately, the privilege of a few) represents the best, most concrete approximation of happiness on earth," said the writer Primo Levi.[148]

Many dream of working in a company like Festo – to get up in the morning, look at nature's inventions, research them, and come up with "crazy" inventions. While there aren't a lot of biomimicry-labeled jobs today, and the chance of starting a job tomorrow in a bionics department like the one at Festo is low, this could very well change in the future. If you wish to work in biomimicry right now, you will need to be proactive and create opportunities, for example, by taking initiative and introducing the field to the organization where you work.

Biomimicry as a Field of Study

I'll start with the basics. Where and what do you study? The discipline of biomimicry is still being formed. As it matures and develops, it begins to enter academia as well, first as individual courses and over time, as longer training programs. Studies include theory and a lot of practice. A quick search on the web will yield educational institutions and training opportunities. There are also several study tracks available for master's and doctoral students. The list is constantly being updated.

The manner of study and curricula are adapted to the "habitat," similar to how tofu absorbs the flavors it's marinated in.

Some programs emphasize design, some emphasize biomechanics, and some emphasize sustainability. When choosing a place of study, it is important to examine the academic environment and see if it suits your goals. I have met people who made an effort, left to study abroad, and were ultimately disappointed.

Beyond the comprehensive studies programs, there are also stand-alone courses that offer extensive training. For example, over the past decade I have led a course in Israel called "Biomimicry: Innovation Inspired by Nature" on behalf of the Israeli Biomimicry Organization and in cooperation with the Association of Engineers. The course consists of 48 academic hours, including a walking tour in nature. The course focuses on the theoretical foundations of the biomimicry discipline alongside the best tools and methodologies available, and includes practical and hands-on experience in developing biomimetic solutions in multidisciplinary teams.

In many universities around the world, biomimicry is integrated into courses, workshops, and laboratories spanning various disciplines. Biomimicry courses taught at schools of environmental or sustainability studies focus on aspects of sustainability in nature, while courses offered at schools of mechanical engineering deal with mechanical solutions and include content from the world of biomechanics.

Design and Architecture

The connection to studies of architecture and design is organic, natural, and traditional. Since the dawn of architectural history, architects have observed structures in nature to gauge aesthetic and functional truths and principles. For example, the golden ratio, which represents many dimensions and sizes in nature, is embedded in various architectural designs. When I entered the field in 2008 and considered doing a PhD, I looked at what had already been studied. I found a wide variety of theses and studies specifically in the context of architecture, drawing knowledge and inspiration from structures and design principles in nature.

The field of biomimicry provides architects and designers with access to a wide world of solutions and ideas, reflecting a way of thinking that differs from the familiar and known. The purpose of biomimicry courses offered to architects or designers is to enrich their world of conceptual resources through principles that underlie solutions in nature.

For example, the Holon Institute of Technology offers a course that is run like a research laboratory. The goal is to enable aspiring students of design to feel the materials of life and challenge the obvious, as those who will be working with the material world later on. For example, for years researchers have been working with round petri dishes and when the students asked why the dish is round and flat, the petri dish exercise was born in the course. Petri dishes were designed in different forms to investigate whether there is a connection between the design of the petri dish and the way bacteria form the colonies. They found forms that were more preferred and others that were less preferred.

At the Bezalel Academy of Arts and Design, students are exposed to the field in various departments while emphasizing the extraction of design principles. At the Shenkar College of Engineering, Design, and Art, textile and fashion design students explore mechanisms in nature and are asked to translate biological knowledge into wearable design. Students are instructed not to settle for visual inspiration, but to also learn from how nature solves problems and to translate these solutions into the world of fashion. One student designed an evening dress inspired by the handicap principle in nature. According to this principle, an organism must bear a costly signal to demonstrate a trait reliably. For example, the large and heavy tail of a peacock incurs costs in flight, and only strong ones will be able to carry them. The student designed a dress in which the center of gravity has excessive fabric, thus it looks immense and conveys a signal of strength. Another student studied defense mechanisms and focused on the phenomenon of caudal autotomy, the self-amputation of the tail, as a defense against an attacker. The mechanism is based on fracture planes, weakened areas that allow quick detachment. The idea of fracture planes led to a search for new techniques for connecting elements and for designing a modular garment, in which many parts can be detached and reattached.

Tel Aviv University's School of Architecture has a bioinspired design studio offered to fifth year students. The students are asked to examine new ways of thinking that are based on natural patterns and find creative, efficient, and sustainable solutions to implement in their final projects. Design today lives and breathes at the points where different fields of knowledge meet and calls for an interdisciplinary approach. According to architect Moti Bodek, who leads the workshop, designers and artists are searching for new leads of inspiration, whether they turn to nature to draw models from it or collaborate with it; whether they work with synthetic biology experts to blur the line between natural and artificial, or combine design with biology, chemistry, robotics, and nanotechnology. What all these have in common is operating in the range between organic and inorganic, between nature and technology. The research includes both theoretical aspects and real-life experience. It provides students with professional design and research tools to cope with complex architectural challenges in the future.

Engineering and Biology
It is only natural that there be a connection to engineering and biology studies, the two disciplines that make up the bridge of

biomimetic innovation. However, I have found that there are more elective courses on biomimicry in engineering schools and less so in biology programs. Beyond the courses, active collaborations exist between engineers and zoologists who are conducting joint research, following the trends of interdisciplinary research. For example, a mechanical engineer and zoologist collaborated and created a new model for caterpillar propulsion, which, although they drew inspiration from the biological caterpillar in order to improve propulsion of robots, also provides new insights into how caterpillars move in nature. Both sides learn from the process. In recent years, as the field has been developing, collaborations have become more institutionalized. Research institutes and laboratories are being established all around the world to promote biomimetic research. They purchase equipment, raise research funds, and recruit graduate students.

Sustainability and Environment

The connection to sustainability and environmental studies is also natural and necessary, and biomimicry can usually be found in the courses of such programs, in various scopes and formats. Emphasis here is on studying the principles of sustainability in nature and gaining familiarity with nature's solutions for core environmental challenges: water, energy, and matter.

A Future Degree?

If I had to devise a degree program for biomimicry, I would formulate it in the form of two pillars connected by a bridge: a pillar of engineering knowledge and thinking, a pillar of biological knowledge and thinking, and a bridge connecting the fields through studies of design and systems thinking, functional view, and analogical reasoning. I always wished that I had studied more biology, and even toyed with the idea of earning a degree in biology. Although many years of observing nature and exposure to biological literature have expanded my knowledge, it does not substitute a degree.

There is a need for both the biological knowledge and the engineering perspective that presents the applications, and a way to connect between them. Such a program will foster new students who speak both languages of biology and engineering. This type of degree should strive to train people who think like da Vinci, interdisciplinary people who know how to dismantle and integrate, build bridges, observe, imagine, and invent.

How to Advance Even Without a Specific Degree

If you live in a country that doesn't offer biomimicry degrees, the best recommendation is to begin with one of the pillars – engineering or biology – and to acquire a good foundation for yourself. A good engineering foundation could be the study of mechanical engineering, aeronautics, or materials science, on which many biomimetic applications today are based.

During your studies, enrich yourself with courses from the second pillar. If you are studying engineering, take elective courses in the fundamentals of biology or biological thinking. The Japanese railway engineer shared his insights from the Shinkansen train innovation process and advised young engineers not to get stuck in their field but to be exposed to different fields of knowledge. He said that he studied engineering and regrets not studying biology more. Another engineer at Interface noted that the key is to bring a biological perspective to the company. The employees are exposed to biological principles, and some are even sent to school. It is rare today to find engineers who are also biologists. But the more biology you know as an engineer, the more advantage you will have in the future if you want to work in the field. If you choose to study biology, take enrichment courses from the world of engineering: engineering thinking and design processes, to get to know a bit about how engineers think.

Another piece of advice is to choose a final project or thesis based on biomimetic practice. As part of many degrees, students are required to participate in seminars, write research papers, and submit projects. Seek out a topic that will allow you to observe nature, study it, and experiment with implementing its solutions. As long as the topic is relevant, it is welcome, and you will gain irreplaceable experience. Even if you have not chosen to study engineering or biology and you want to get closer to and practice the field of biomimicry, this recommendation is appropriate for you too. If you study entrepreneurship, you can choose an entrepreneurial project with an idea stemming from nature. If you study management, you can choose a seminar topic that deals with the study of managerial issues in nature, for example, how nature behaves in a changing environment. If you study psychology, you can initiate a research proposal that covers, for example, strategies for coping with stress in nature. There is a lot to learn from migratory birds in this regard.

If you want to study an advanced degree, there are laboratories that offer a variety of biomimetic research areas depending on your background. Even if you can't find such a lab, you can always find an open and curious advisor and form a research proposal together. That's what I did. When I was looking for a doctoral advisor, the field was in its infancy, and there was no one who worked in it that could supervise. Yoram Reich, who worked in the field of design and innovation, brought all his experience as an advisor and tools he garnered from the world of design, and we defined the nature of the study accordingly.

The range of possible studies is huge. Any mechanism in nature that you wish to focus on is a subject of study. Beyond that, there are also meta studies that look at the field from a bird's-eye-view, focus on design principles in nature, or develop tools and methods for managing bioinspired innovation processes. In my opinion, anyone involved in the process of creating and designing products, processes, or organizations – engineers, executives, designers, architects, or entrepreneurs – will benefit immensely from being familiar with the field. Nature is a large reservoir of patents and solutions worth knowing.

Occupation

Graduates of biomimicry programs around the world engage in various fields. Some work in education, teaching, and research; some work in consulting and accompany biomimetic innovation processes; and some become ambassadors of the field and introduce it to their organization.

In one of the last courses I taught, there was a group of military personnel from a technology unit working in research and development. They told me about ideas for natural solutions that come up in their discussions and how these ideas enrich the discussions and design processes.

Some graduates of biomimicry training experience an expansion in their professional practice by bringing nature into the equation. Designers bring this practice into their studios. Business owners and freelancers modify and rebrand their business in the spirit of nature. For example, a graduate of the biomimicry program who owned a management consulting firm, marketed his uniqueness as a consultant who speaks the language of nature. Some of the program's graduates act as entrepreneurs with an added value: entrepreneurs who understand how nature works and how to learn from its inventions.

The New World

In the new world, which is changing at a rapid pace, there are new rules of the game. The Institute for the Future (IFTF) has identified a number of skills for success in the future workforce, among them **trans-disciplinarity**: crossing discipline boundaries to create a holistic approach; **novel and adaptive thinking**: Thinking 'outside the box' in response to unexpected situations; and a **design mindset** that connects process to outcome.[149]

Employees in the new world must be adaptable, entrepreneurial, creative, and flexible in their thinking. These skills are precisely the skills that biomimicry cultivates. Beyond receiving entry to nature's reservoir of solutions, working in the field also shapes mindsets, and is therefore particularly significant in the new world.

In the new world, there will be new students who speak nature's language and know how to build a bridge from the discipline they are studying to nature. In the new world, there will be new workers who have learned to build bridges and continue the construction work: connecting nature to the challenges of their organization. A system of interchanges and bridges is being built every day, an innovation highway under the auspices of nature.

BACK TO NATURE

The best way to predict the future is to design it.

Buckminster Fuller

At the dawn of civilization, man walked in the book of nature and lived among its pages, which were empty of written words. He was part of nature and shaped in its image. Nature was associated more than anything with progress and became a source of knowledge for the challenges that occupied humanity. Years later, technology developed. It soon became a source of knowledge and comfort for humanity's challenges, and stripped nature of the progress it was identified with. In the transition from nature to technology, humans also changed, along with their worldview, thinking, and values. The detachment from nature has led to the tearing of the network of connections that unites man and nature, a network that, even if invisible, is the cradle of our existence. In this context, the anthropologist Gregory Bateson claimed that we think in a way that does not acknowledge our delicate dependence on ecosystems. Bateson viewed all the elements of nature, including its human occupants, like jazz musicians improvising in unison, arguing that "the major problems in the world are a result of the difference between how nature works and how people think."[150]

In the new world, a new person is created, a narrow-viewed reductionist thinker, blind to the totality of the contexts of his actions. But the new challenges of humanity, such as those of sustainability, have begun overshadowing the achievements of technology. Is this the progress we were hoping for?

These challenges point us back to the book of nature, which now is riddled with text, and we are wiser, more knowledgeable and more sensitive to nature's solutions and genius. And so, equipped with a great deal of knowledge and the ability to understand nature's solutions, we can return to the fountain of wisdom, explore it in depth and with focus, and advance toward a much better future.

The trend of getting back to natural designs is already being felt today in architecture with the reviving metaphor of a building as a living organism rather than a building as a machine. Later on, it will not just be a building, but any system, organization, or product that will be designed like a living organism, according to nature's principles.

Further evidence of the return to nature's designs can be seen in the evolution of the material world, as described by Boaz Mizrahi of the Laboratory for Biomaterials at the Technion in a conversation we had. According to him, the first materials used by man were materials from nature. They were so significant that entire epochs were named after them according to the findings in archaeological excavations: the Stone Age, the Copper Age, the Bronze Age, and the Iron Age. One hundred and fifty to two hundred years ago, the "Polymer Age" began. Man ceased looking for substances in nature and began producing them. The following revolution in the material world occurred later, when man began producing composite materials (based on two or more constituent materials) to yield a variety of properties not found in other pure matter. The current revolution in the material world is that of materials that respond to various stimuli such as humidity, temperature, or electricity. In response to these stimuli, the materials change as predicted: change form, fold, open, and so on. The use of responsive materials in 3D printing adds a dimension of reaction to the printed material and is now called 4D printing.

My conclusion is that nature was the first to satisfy our material needs. Later we switched to synthetic materials, and since then we have returned to nature and are designing materials according to its laws – composite and responsive materials. Today nature is perceived as a treasure trove of novelty, and the ability to translate nature's solutions into commercial applications is growing. We no longer have to be in the right place at the right time in front of a kingfisher diving into the water. We can return to nature equipped with an organized methodology of innovation: biomimicry. Nature is once again carrying the torch of progress, in parallel to technology and together with it. The narrow reductionist view will expand to a holistic view, one that recognizes and appreciates the complexity of nature and the invisible connections among its details. The gaps between the way nature works and the way people think will shrink, and so will the problems that arise from these gaps. By then, we will also need to ask new questions, such as what does it mean to be a business organization, school, or family that operates according to the code of nature?

Technologies of the Future

Breakthroughs in the world of nanomanufacturing will allow us in the future to mimic a wide range of functions that are identified at the nanoscale. Biomimetic technologies that are now in their early stages will mature, and we will be able to reap the fruits and enjoy their applications. Technological development will allow us to better understand nature through new imaging and analysis methods that will be developed. With every passing day, our comprehension of nature will deepen, and we will find answers to questions we still don't know how to ask. Armed with a much broader interest in nature, we can now return to designing and creating the future. I will put on my futuristic hat for a moment and describe possible nexuses between humanity's challenges and nature's solutions.

• **Organizations in a changing and complex world:** COVID-19 came and devoured everything. It turned out that viruses don't need visas and we can't really control them. Today, more than ever, it is clear that we live in a changing environment, and those who don't change won't survive. These days especially organizations have much to learn from nature regarding managing complex systems under changing conditions, from the ability of organisms with swarm intelligence to organize themselves and spontaneously adapt to changing conditions, to flexible structures in nature that absorb vibrations and mechanical pressures. The range of solutions in nature is vast, and flexibility and self-organization are the name of the game in the coming years. Our ability to deal with a complex environment and complex issues will increase as we move from a reductionist perspective to a holistic outlook, which sees all the components of the system and the connections between them at the same time. Complexity lies in the relationships among factors and not in each factor separately.

• **Information:** The technologies of the future will deal with extracting information, deriving meaning from it, and transferring the information efficiently and quickly between many agents. The Internet of Things, big data, data mining, cloud technologies, and autonomous vehicles are just some of the technologies associated with the information management challenges of the 21st century. Models of communication in nature between many individuals can serve as a source of knowledge for solutions: How do bees transfer information efficiently between thousands of individuals? How does the brain work with the neural network, process information, and shape meaning? How do locusts move in swarms of tens of thousands of individuals and not collide with each other?

• **Material:** We live in a system closed off to matter, and the material challenges are undoubtedly the challenges of the future. In the future, we will strive to produce materials that emulate nature's chemistry, such that there will only be a few materials that form rich functionalities and that will be easily compostable and available for recycling at their end of use. Imagine being able to feed 3D printers such materials: we could print our future in the image of nature. The "take-make-waste" culture will be replaced by one that respects the material. In the future, we will be able to produce material in living environments, in energy-efficient processes, without heating up the materials, beating them with high pressure, and treating them with chemicals. Using reactive materials will bring us one step closer to nature's sensory abilities.

The world of biomimetic chemistry is still in its infancy. Over time, more and more proteins, enzymes, peptides, and molecules with incredible functionality will be discovered. At the end of 2020, an enzyme cocktail was discovered that succeeds in breaking down plastic into its elements – its original building blocks of oil and gas – at a particularly fast pace and without artificial intervention.[151] Perhaps this is the road to natural recycling plants? Or will we be able to mimic these enzymes in laboratories and produce biomimetic recycling plants? I wonder what the next discovery will be and what significant challenge it will solve. The 100 years of synthetic chemistry, during which synthetic materials were produced, are a blink of an eye compared to billions of years of evolution. In the future, we will see more and more materials that were first identified in nature which will be transferred for human use. We can imitate the miraculous properties of these materials through the use of nano-biotechnology and genetic engineering tools after appropriate industrial-scale production systems are developed. We can create many of the nanobiological building blocks that nature gives us, and with them we can design better machines and even produce artificial organs that will function better than organs derived from donors.

- **Energy:** Many challenges concerning humanity are related to energy. How can we best use energy? Nature uses less energy than technology. Many breakthroughs still await us in identifying novel solutions related to energy efficiency and energy harvesting. We live in an open energy system. Solar energy is available and renewable, and it is natural that we should strive to utilize it like nature does. In the future, we will see the maturation of technologies that make optimal use of sunlight, such as artificial photosynthesis. We may also see new engines, such as hydrostatic engines, capable of utilizing natural forces for propulsion instead of those that burn fossil fuels and consume non-renewable resources.

- **Water and Food:** How can we provide high-quality food and drinking water to a growing population? Water creation in nature doesn't involve pollution or massive energy investment. Biomimetic membranes have already been developed mimicking biological membranes, enabling purification and enhancing desalination of water. For example, Aquaporin, a company specializing in water purification solutions, developed a biomimetic membrane that emulates aquaporins, which are transmembrane proteins that prevent the passage of ions and protons. The MIGAL research institute in Israel is imitating desalination processes that occur in halophytes, plants that grow in saline conditions and store salts. These mechanisms are currently being investigated for their application in the desalination of industrial-agricultural wastewater. At this stage, nature is still being used, that is, the halophytes themselves. In the future, once the principles of desalination are understood, we may be able to build a biomimetic technological system that functions in a similar way. Today, substantial resources are also being invested in mimicking water harvesting mechanisms, similar to that of the Namib Desert beetle, in order to build giant facilities to be placed in populated areas that lack access to drinkable water sources.

The field of food science and food-tech technologies also has great potential for bioinspired innovation: optimized agricultural growth processes, food waste utilization, food packaging that provides protection without harming the environment, and even alternative protein technologies. These technologies are plant-based protein technologies seeking to recreate food products similar to meat, based on plant proteins, using biomimicry methods. An example of such a company is Beyond Meat, which offers an efficient and environmentally beneficial solution.

• **Medicine:** According to the assessment,[152] regenerative medicine and tissue engineering are the fields that will drive the market for biomimetic medical technologies. The study of natural healing processes for tissue reconstruction and understanding the function of biological tissues can lead to new healing technologies. For example, the discovery of a peptide that encourages remineralization of the enamel layer damaged by tooth decay has led to the development of a novel biomimetic tooth repair treatment.[153]

Another medical challenge that can be solved with the biomimicry approach is the need for minimally invasive technologies. Applications of bioinspired microrobots can address this need. For example, wood wasps are able to penetrate through different types of tissue (wood, leaves, etc.) to lay their eggs inside. Their unique drilling mechanism, which allows eggs to be inserted into the tree without rotary motion and with minimal force and impact, has been studied in the context of developing minimally invasive devices for neurosurgical procedures.[154] I believe that in the future, new bioinspired strategies will be found to fight bacteria – structural rather than material solutions. Will it be the end of antibiotics? Time will tell. The need to prevent and eradicate viruses, which escalated with the outbreak of the COVID-19 pandemic, may also find a solution in nature, for example through the development of antiviral surfaces. In my opinion, we will also find new drugs in nature's pharmacy due to the recent AI revolution, and we will be able to imitate them.

• **Urbanism:** Over the next hundred years, hundreds of millions of people are expected to move to cities, as part of a global urbanization trend. This figure requires reimagining and updating our thinking about the structure of the future city. The cities of the future will function like ecosystems, absorbing carbon dioxide instead of emitting it, allowing water to permeate and return to earth, and generating energy from sunlight instead of turning it into heat islands. The cities of the future, like nature, will cope well with floods, fires, and extreme weather changes. In recent years, we are starting to see more and more urban planning projects inspired by nature, while assimilating the principles of sustainability and viewing cities with the holistic view of being connected to their natural environment. The smart cities trend also has a lot of inspiration to take from nature: smart algorithms inspired by ants for optimal routing of traffic, means of reducing congestion and emissions, smart solutions for treating waste and turning it into a nutritious resource (waste = food), methods inspired by social insects for eradicating epidemics and preventing infection, and more. Will we live in innovative and smart cities in the future?

Leadership of the Future

The ability to utilize the potential human energy inherent in an organization is critical to its future success. A few years ago, IBM conducted a comprehensive study in 64 countries to examine the most vital leadership traits in executives.[155] Three top traits were found, one of which was the ability to inspire. The result is not surprising. A leader is supposed to move the organization to a better place, and inspiration is one of the most powerful human engines there is. Inspiration is associated with a flow of ideas and motivation to act. Inspiring is wonderful, but to me good leaders are those who not only inspire themselves, but also encourage employees to take responsibility for their own inspiration; to move from a passive place of receiving inspiration to an active place of seeking inspiration. Future leaders will know how to work with nature as an engine of inspiration and innovation, will instill nature's design paradigm in the employees, and teach them to observe nature's solutions. They will give them the rod and not just the fish.

A New Connection Between Man and Nature

A return to nature is not only a return to its reservoir of inventions; it is also a return to the human–nature connection that existed even before the Digital Age. Technology lies at our interface with nature today. We use technology to observe nature, using cameras, microscopes, and other means to study it. Technology has become an intermediary that shapes our relationship with nature.

There are two pictures that immortalize moments that teach us about our relationship with nature. In the first, man comes to nature, in the second, nature comes to man. The first image shows a nimble Japanese macaque monkey snatching an iPhone away from a tourist, and examining it curiously while standing in the middle of a hot spring. When the macaque decided to examine the new toy underwater, the owner of the phone most likely fainted. The Dutch photographer Marsel van Oosten, who was present at the scene, understood that there was an opportunity here to take one of the rarest photos of a macaque ever captured, and indeed the photo has been awarded one of the wildlife photographers of the year awards presented by the Natural History Museum in London. To me, this picture represents not only a photographic achievement, but also a rare moment of encounter between technology and nature. The Japanese macaque monkey is holding the phone in a manner extremely similar to how humans hold them. He is holding one of the symbols of 21st century technology with immense curiosity (*see 17).

The second image shows Yoina, a girl who lives in the rainforest, bathing in the river with an infant tamarin monkey on her head. The monkey, who hates bathing, spent most of the time on Yoina's head, away from the water. To me, this picture represents a moment when nature comes to humans, a moment of connection. I have already mentioned this picture in the context of observation (*see 7). Perhaps the path to connect the new with the old, between man and nature, passes through respectful observation while benefiting from the best of what technological observation has to offer. We need to leave room for both scientific investigation and for the heart to recognize and cherish the wonder of nature.

Traveler's Prayer

You have successfully reached nature's reservoir of inventions. It probably seemed far away at the beginning of the book, but you have progressed since then, you have gone through the what, the why, the how, and the where, you've circled the reservoir on all sides and are now ready to dive into it. What will you find inside? It depends on what you're looking for. Technological challenges are changing, and so are answers. Natural solutions are discovered every day through research that raises the water level of the reservoir. Some studies may turn out to be outdated, inaccurate, or irrelevant and evaporate from the reservoir. Seekers enter the reservoir each time with different questions. Learning from nature is endless, and therefore the passion and interest in nature are endless, too.

In the future, the ability to explore and mimic nature will break through the ivory towers of academia and move toward the individual. When the information and production capabilities (3D) are accessible to everyone, more and more curious people will turn to nature to explore and study.

When swimming in an actual reservoir in nature, you have fun and develop muscles at the same time. Nature's reservoir of inventions also offers, beyond the value of the inventions themselves, an opportunity to develop muscles and skills associated with both innovation and happiness!

A study described in the book *The Innovator's DNA*[156] examined the skills required to be innovative and identified five skills that are acquired and not innate. Among the skills were the ability to observe, ask questions, and associate seemingly unrelated problems or ideas from different fields. These are the exact skills that biomimicry cultivates. Studies in the field of positive psychology indicated that curious people are happier and can better unlock new opportunities for growth.[157] Curious people are viewed as open-minded and on a path of self-development that leads to happiness. Curiosity is another skill that can be developed by observing and finding awe in nature.

Once you have tasted nature's reservoir of inventions, you can't help but see it. Every time you go out into nature, every time you come across a scientific biological text, the reservoir of nature's inventions will reflect back at you. "Nature likes to hide," said Heraclitus. But from you it will no longer hide. Jump into the reservoir of inventions and derive pleasure from it. What would you like to find out?

ILLUSTRATION CREDITS

Pg. 19: Eden Project. Boaz Drori.

Pg. 36: Ear structure. Boaz Drori.

Pg. 37: The Eiffel Tower and bone structure. Boaz Drori.

Pg. 54: The gecko's foot: Liza Chepurko. Based on the photograph, "A micro and nano examination of the gecko's foot." from: "How Gecko Toes Stick." *American Scientist* 94, 124-132; in accordance with usage license CC-BY-SA-3.0. All rights reserved to Autumn, K.

Pg. 95: A spiral skyscraper. Liza Chepurko.

Pg. 95: Torso. Boaz Drori.

Pg. 160: Wild Carrot. Liza Chepurko.

Pg. 163: Helicone. Boaz Drori. Based on the photograph by John Edmark. All rights reserved.

Pg. 163: Carrota – Shading system. Boaz Drori. The illustration is based on the graphic design of Omro Keiser. All rights reserved. Carrota team: Yael Helfman-Cohen; Melanie Samson; Eliran Farhi; Ella Hassin; Roi Yosifoff; Tamar Vilnai; Saadia Sternberg; Omri Keiser.

Pg. 169: The Pine Cone Effect. Liza Chepurko. From: Mulakkal, M., Trask, R. Ting, V. P., & Seddon, A. (2018). "Responsive Cellulose - Hydrogel Composite Ink for 4D Printing." *Materials and Design* 160, 108-118. In accordance with usage license CC-BY-4.0.

Pg. 172: Namib Desert Beetle. Boaz Drori.

Pg. 178: Pangolin. Liza Chepurko. Based on the photograph by Darren Pietersen. All rights reserved.

Pg. 206: The fin ray effect. Liza Chepurko. Based on the photograph belonging to © Festo SE & Co. KG. All rights reserved.

Pg. 222: Geodesic dome. Liza Chepurko.

Pg. 225: Helicopter seed. Liza Chepurko.

Pg. 240: Barn Owl feather. Liza Chepurko.

Pg. 257: The Salvinia Effect. Based on: Barthlott, W., et al: "The Salvinia Paradox: Superhydrophobic Surfaces with Hydrophilic Pins for Air Retention Under Water." *Advanced Materials.* 2010. Volume 11, issue 21, Pages 2325-2328. Figure 1b. Copyright Wiley-VCH GmbH. Reproduced with permission.

Pg. 261: Rheum palaestinum (desert rhubarb). Liza Chepurko. Based on the photograph by Lev-Yadon. All rights reserved.

Pg. 263: Bird-of-paradise flower. Liza Chepurko.

Pg. 265: Layers of the tooth. Lize Chepurko.

Pg. 266: Dragonfly wings. Liza Chepurko.

Pg. 267: Bamboo. Liza Chepurko.

Pg. 267: Antelope horns. Liza Chepurko. Based on the photograph by Tom Junek, in accordance with usage license CC-BY-SA-3.0.

Pg. 268: Penguin. Liza Chepurko.

Pg. 269: Nepenthes pitcher plant. Liza Chepurko. Based on the photograph belonging to Mongabay. All rights reserved.

Pg. 299: Tiger. Liza Chepurko.

FURTHER VIEWING

1A 1B 2 3

4 5 6 7

8 9 10 11

12 13 14 15

16 17

References

1. Witt, R., & Lieckfeld, C. P. (Eds.). 1991. *Bionics: Nature's Patents*. Munich: Pro Futura.
2. Helfman-Cohen, Y. 2021. *The Nature that I Am*. Zichron Yaakov: Naturecode.
3. Benyus, J. M. 1997. *Biomimicry: Innovation Inspired by Nature*. New York: Quill.
4. "Advanced technology for leak location and sealing is launched." (2002, November 14). University of Aberdeen.
5. He, X., & Zhang, J. 2009. "On the Growth of Scientific Knowledge: Yeast Biology as a Case Study." *PLoS Comput Biol*. 5 (3), e1000320.
6. Full, R. 2009. "Learning from the gecko's tail [Video]." TED.
7. Ackerman, E. "MIT's Soft Robotic Fish Explores Reefs in Fiji." (2018, March 21). IEEE Spectrum.
8. Albo, J. 1930. *Book of Principles*.
9. Kook, A. I. 1978. *Lights of Holiness*. Paulist Press.
10. Mehling, M. "Da Vinci's Rule of Trees." (2020, January 27). COVE Editions.
11. Gleich, A., et al. 2009. *Potentials and Trends in Biomimetics*. New York: Springer.
12. Sadiq, S. "What Happens When You Put a Hummingbird in a Wind Tunnel?" (2015, March 31). KQED.
13. *Biomimetics* & Bioinspiration Journal, Design & Nature Journal.
14. STANDARDS BY ISO/TC 266, Biomimetics.
15. "The Da Vinci Index & Biomimicry." Point Loma Site.
16. "Bioinspiration: an economic progress report." 2013. Fermanian Business & Economic Institute, P.L.N.U.
17. "Global Biomimetic Technology Market is Anticipated to Reach $18.50 Billion by 2028." 2018. BIS Research
18. Beheshti, N., & McIntosh, A. C. 2008. "A Novel Spray System Inspired by The Bombardier Beetle." *WIT Transactions on Ecology and the Environment* 114: 13-21.
19. "A conversation with author Janine Benyus." Biomimicry 3.8.
20. Bateson, N. 2010. "An Ecology of Mind [Video]." IMDBPro.
21. Goodall, J. 2007. *"How humans and animals can live togethe*r [Video]." TED Global.
22. See reference 3, above.
23. Livio, M. 2017. *Why? What Makes Us Curious*. New York: Simon & Schuster.
24. "Gecko feet inspire amazing glue that can hold 700 pounds on smooth wall." (2012, February 16). ScienceDaily.
25. "Fly like a butterfly, sting like a bee, expensive like a fighter aircraft." (2020). Rafael Defense podcast.
26. Kalisman, P., et al. 2016. "Perfect Photon-to-Hydrogen Conversion Efficiency." *Nano Letters* 16(3): 1776-1781.
27. Ju, J., et al. 2014. "Cactus Stem Inspired Cone-Arrayed Surfaces for Efficient Fog Collection." *Advanced Materials* 24(24): 6933-6938.
28. Zhang, J., et al. 2019. "Robotic Artificial Muscles: Current Progress and Future Perspectives." *IEEE Transactions on Robotics* 35(3): 761-781.
29. Mueller, T. "Biomimetics: Design by Nature. What has fins like a whale, skin like a lizard, and eyes like a moth? The future of engineering." (2008, August 22). National Geographic.
30. Latty, T., & Lee, T. "How many species on Earth? Why that's a simple question but hard to answer." (2019, April 29). The Conversation.

31. Cohen, M. 2017. "Intellectual Property: Biomimetic Inventions." Biomimicry Academy & Industry conference, Tel Aviv.
32. Patterson, L. "Foxes Use Earth's Magnetic Field to Jump on Prey." (2011, January 13). Earthsky.
33. Baraniuk, C. "How do we know that animals can see, hear and smell?" (2015, October 19). BBC.
34. Andrew, J. P. & Sirkin, H.L. 2022. *"Innovating for cash."* Harvard Business Review.
35. Grant, A. 2017. *Originals: How Non-Conformists Move the World.* New York: Penguin Books.
36. Roach, J. "Microsoft finds underwater data centers are reliable, practical and use energy sustainably." (2020, September 14). Microsoft.
37. Chamovitz, D. 2012. *What a Plant Knows: A Field Guide to the Senses.* New York: Scientific American/Farrar, Straus and Giroux.
38. Zygourakis, C., et al. 2014. "What do hotels and hospitals have in common? How we can learn from the hotel industry to take better care of patients." Surg Neurol Int 14; 5(2): S49– S53.
39. Heath, D&C. "A Problem-Solver's Guide to Copycatting." (2009, January 11). Fast Company.
40. Herstatt, C., & Kalogerakis, K. 2005. "How to use analogies for breakthrough innovations." *International Journal of Innovation and Technology Management* 02(03): 331-347.
41. Johansson, F. 2004. *The Medici Effect: Breakthrough Insights at the Intersection of Ideas, Concepts, and Cultures.* Harvard Business Press.
42. Vincent, J. F., et al. 2006. "Biomimetics: its practice and theory." *J. R. Soc Interface* 3(9): 471–482.
43. BBC. 2012. "Can Cuttlefish camouflage in a living room? Richard Hammond's Miracles of Nature [Video]." YouTube.
44. American Chemical Society. 2015. "The secret to the sea sapphire's colors and invisibility [Video]." YouTube.
45. Yong, E. "A squid's beak is a marvel of biological engineering." (2008, March 27). National Geographic.
46. Benyus, J., 2009. "Biomimicry in action [Video]." TED Global.
47. Berkebile, B., & McLennan, J. 2004. "The living building: biomimicry in architecture, integrating technology with nature."
48. See reference 3, above.
49. Schoeppler, V., et al. 2017. "Shaping highly regular glass architectures: A lesson from nature", *Sci. Adv.* 3(10).
50. Rose, A. "Biomimetic shatterproof ceramics." (2008, December 8). Long Now.
51. Hawken, P., Lovins, A. B., & Lovins, L. H. 1999. *Natural Capitalism: Creating the next Industrial Revolution.* Boston: Little, Brown.
52. London, J. "Printing data-driven wearables that mimic nature." (2017, March 2), MIT News.
53. Watson, B. "The greenhouse that acts like a beetle and other inventions Inspired by Nature." (2016, April 10). The Guardian.
54. Alexandersson, O., 2002. *Living water, Viktor Schauberger and the Secrets of Natural Energy.* Dublin: Gill Books.
55. "IKEA Starts Using Biodegradable Mushroom-Based Packaging for Its Products." (2018, April 11). Medium.

56. Rosenberg, D. "In Kids' Rooms, Pink Is for Girls, Blue Is for Boys." (2013, April 9). Salte.
57. See reference 51, above.
58. Brondizio, E., et al. "Global assessment report on biodiversity and ecosystem services." 2019. IPBS.
59. Attenborough, D. 2020. "A Life on Our Planet [Video]." Netflix.
60. Undercurrentspaulo. 2010. "The Impossible Hamster (and economic growth) [Video]." YouTube.
61. "Waves of innovation of the first and the next industrial revolution." 2004. The Natural Edge Project.
62. "BioWave Port Fairy Pilot Wave Energy Project." Tethys.
63. Nidumolu, R., et al. 2009. "Why Sustainability Is Now the Key Driver of Innovation." *Harvard Business Review* Sep 09: 57-64.
64. "ECOncrete® Wins $100,000 Ray of Hope Prize®." (2020, August 25). Biomimicry Institute.
65. Wünsch, S. "Berlin Gold Hat: Calendar from the Bronze Age." (2019, June 17). DW.
66. Thoreau, H. D. 2006. *Walking*. Cosimo, Inc.
67. Goodall, J. 2003. "What separates us from chimpanzees? [Video]." TED.
68. Krishnamurti, J. 1997. *Touch the Essence: A Hebrew collection from J. Krishnamurti's writings*. Tel-Aviv: Keter Books.
69. Engel, C. 2002. *Wild Health: How animals keep themselves well and what we can learn from them*. Boston: Houghton Mifflin Harcourt.
70. Ehrlich, P., & Reed, J. 2020. "My Octopus Teacher [Video]". Netflix.
71. Ehrlichman, E. "It is impossible to stage nature". (2007, September 19). YNET. [In Hebrew].
72. Lindgren, A. 2005. Pippi Longstocking. London: Puffin Books.
73. James, C. H. "Yoina" Charlie Hamilton James.
74. Shapira, H. 2020. "About curiosity, wonder and the meaning of everything that surrounds us [Video]." Vimeo (In Hebrew).
75. Campbell, J. 1995. *A Joseph Campbell Companion: Reflections on the Art of Living*. New York: Harper Perennial.
76. Beau Lotto and Cirque du Soleil. 2019. "How we experience awe – and why it matters [Video]." TED.
77. Feynman, R. 2001. *What Do You Care What Other People Think? Further Adventures of a Curious Character*. New York: W. W. Norton & Company.
78. Simard, S. 2016. "How trees talk to each other [Video]." TED Summit.
79. Pianka, E. R., & Parker, S. W. 1975. "Ecology of Horned Lizards: A Review with Special Reference to Phrynosoma Platyrhinos." *Copeia* 1: 141-162.
80. "The anti-icing tricks of penguins." (2015, November 23). Science Daily.
81. Richman, K. "Kinetic Toy Transforms from a Pinecone to a Helix with the Simple Flick of a Wrist." (2018, December 26). My modern met.
82. ExtremeBio. 2015. "Renewable Energy from Evaporating Water." YouTube.
83. "1 in 3 people globally do not have access to safe drinking water." (2019, June 18). UNICEF.
84. Azad, A. K., et al. 2015. "Fog collecting biomimetic surfaces: Influence of microstructure and wettability", *Bioinspiration & Biomimetics* 10: 016004.
85. "Caltech Field Laboratory for optimized wind energy (Flowe)." Dabiri Lab.
86. Arnot, M. "All about airplane winglets and how to tell them apart." (2019, December 9). The points guy.

87. World Economic Forum. 2018. "Will the Future Be Human? -Yuval Noah Harari [Video]." YouTube.
88. Reynolds, C. 1987. "Flocks, Herds, and Schools: A Distributed Behavioral Model." *Computer Graphics* 21(4): 25-34.
89. Bradley, M., & Chohan, A. "Cardboard to Caviar." Algalbiomass.
90. Mercedes-Benz. 2013. "Mercedes-Benz 'Chicken' MAGIC BODY CONTROL TV commercial." YouTube.
91. Yarden, A., & Esterman, N. 2008. "The effect of disciplinary identity on interdisciplinary learning during scientific group meetings." *Proceedings of the Eighth International Conference for the Learning Sciences – ICLS*, Utrecht, The Netherlands 2: 475-482.
92. Life is Beautiful. 2018. "Travel with NASA from the biggest to the smallest distance of the universe." YouTube.
93. Bertalanffy, L. V.1969. *General System Theory*, George Braziller Inc.
94. Romeo, J. "The Truth About Woodpeckers." (2023, January 16). Science World.
95. Rockwood, K. "Biomimicry: Nature-Inspired Designs." (2008, October 1). Fast Company.
96. "Fin Ray Effect." Bionics4education.
97. Natan, E., et al. 2020. "Symbiotic magnetic sensing: raising evidence and beyond." *Phil. Trans. R. Soc. B*, 375 (1808).
98. www.asknature.org
99. www.findstructure.org
100. "BioM Innovation Database." Bioinspired.Sinet.
101. Nevo, E. "Ada Yonath – Unraveling the secrets of Life's Building Blocks." (2017, November 28). Davidson institute, educational arm of the Weizmann Institute of Science.
102. Nagel, J. K., et al. 2010. "An engineering-to-biology thesaurus for engineering design." *Proc. ASME IDETC/CIE*.
103. Yanai, Z. 2005. *Journey into the Consciousness of Nature*. Tel-Aviv: Am Oved (in Hebrew).
104. Evan. 2009. "World's first controllable MAV monocopter, Robotic Samara (maple seed)." YouTube
105. Oeffner, J., & Lauder, G. 2012. "The hydrodynamic function of shark skin and two biomimetic applications." *J Exp Biol*. 215 (5): 785–795.
106. Traugott, J., et al. "The Nearly Effortless Flight of the Albatross." (2013, January 28). Spectrum.ieee.
107. Fridenzon H. E. 2016. "From inspiration to sketches (FITS) methodology for students of product design." *Proceedings of the 18th International Conference on Engineering and Product Design Education (E&PDE16), Design Education, Collaboration and Cross-Disciplinarity*, Aalborg, Denmark: 386-391.
108. https://natureofform.com/
109. www.triz40.com
110. BBC. 2015. "The silent flight of an owl: Natural World: Super Powered Owls Preview - BBC Two [Video]." YouTube.
111. Petit de Meurville, M., et al. "Shop on the Go." (2015, February 15). Business Today.
112. Greenemeier, L. "Airless Tire Promises Grace Under Pressure for Soldiers." (2008, August 11). Scientific American.
113. Cassidy, J., & Shields, L. "Porcupine Barbs for Better Wound Healing." (2019, April 9). NPR.

114. Duque, E. F., et al. 2010. "Moonstruck Primates: Owl Monkeys (Aotus) Need Moonlight for Nocturnal Activity in Their Natural Environment." PLoS ONE 5(9): e12572.
115. Hasson, N. "Did King David's United Monarchy Exist? Naked Mole Rats Uncover Monumental Evidence." (2018, April 16). Haaretz.
116. Vogel, S. 2009. "Nosehouse: heat-conserving ventilators based on nasal counterflow exchangers." *Bioinspir Biomim* 4(4): 046004.
117. Schulson, M. "In Social Insects, Researchers Find Hints for Controlling Disease." (2020, July 22). Undark.
118. Thompson, D. 1917. *On Growth and Form*. Cambridge University Press (edition 1).
119. Vogel, S. 1988. *Life's Devices-The Physical World of Animals and Plants*. Princeton University Press.
120. Hwang, K. 2020. "Form Follows Function, Function Follows Form." *Journal of Craniofacial Surgery* 31(2): 335.
121. Büsch, J., et al. 2018. "Bionics and green technology in maritime shipping: an assessment of the effect of Salvinia air-layer hull coatings for drag and fuel reduction." *Philosophical Transactions of the Royal Society* A, 377(2138)
122. Botcharova, M. "A gripping tale: Scientists claim to have discovered why skin wrinkles in water." (2013, January 10). The Guardian.
123. Lev-Yadun, S., et al. 2009. "Rheum palaestinum (desert rhubarb), a self-irrigating desert plant." *Naturwissenschaften* 96(3): 393-397.
124. Stewart, I., & Golubitsky, M. 2011. Fearful Symmetry: Is God a Geometer? New York: Dover Publications.
125. Bejan, A. 2000. Shape and Structure, From Engineering to Nature. Cambridge University Press.
126. "ICD/ITKE Research Pavilion/University of Stuttgart, Faculty of Architecture and Urban Planning." (2013, March 6). Arch Daily.
127. See reference 54, above.
128. "World Commission on Environment and Development: Our Common Future." 1987. Report of the World Commission on Environment and Development, O.U.P, ISBN 0-19-282080-X.
129. McDonough, W., & Braungart, M. 2002. Cradle to Cradle: Remaking the Way We Make Things. New York: North Point Press.
130. Goldman D. "Apple recovered 2,204 pounds of gold from broken iPhones last year." (2016, April 15). CNN BUSINESS.
131. Bedford, C.B. 2024. "The next industrial revolution [Video]." Vimeo.
132. USC Stevens Center for Innovation. 2010. "Jane Poynter: Biosphere 2." YouTube.
133. Baumeister, D. 2013. Biomimicry Resource Handbook: A Seed Bank of Best Practices. Biomimicry 3.8: Missoula, MT, USA.
134. "Animal infobooks: Tigers Physical characteristics." Seaworld.
135. Shoseyov, O. 2016. "How we're harnessing nature's hidden superpowers [Video]." TED@BCG Paris.
136. Nevo, E. "The Cicadas that Jumped the Gun." (2021, April 26). Davidson Institute of the Weizmann Institute of Science.
137. "Genius of Biome Report." 2013. Issuu.
138. "Laws of technical systems evolution." Wikipedia.
139. "Harvesting Ancient Dates." (2021, August 25). Arava Institute
140. Rivera, J., et al. 2020. "Toughening mechanisms of the elytra of the diabolical ironclad beetle". Nature 586(7830), 543–548.
141. Harnish, V. "5 Trends to Ride in 2017." (2017, Match 17). Fortune.

142. "V.I.N.E. (Virtual Interchange for Nature-inspired Exploration)." Glenn Research Center, NASA.
143. Orcutt, M. "Researchers Test a Next-Gen, Wheel-Free Mars Rover." (2010, June 2). Popular Mechanics.
144. Newman, D. 2012. "Building the future spacesuit." Ask Magazine 45: 37-40.
145. Interface. 2016. "The Business Case for Sustainability - Ray Anderson [Video]." YouTube.
146. Graham, R. "Engineers Discover Why Toucan Beaks are Models of Lightweight Strength." (2005, November 30). UCSD News.
147. Ritter, S. "How Lobster Eyes Inspired a Radiant Heater." (2014, November 10). Makezine.
148. Levi, P. 1988. The Monkey's Wrench. New York: Summit Books.
149. "Future Work Skills 2020 Report." 2011. Institute for the Future for the University of Phoenix Research Institute.
150. See reference 20, above.
151. Marshall, M. "How 'super-enzymes' that eat plastics could curb our waste problem." (2022, February 5). The Guardian.
152. See reference 17, above.
153. Dogan, S., et al. 2018. "Biomimetic Tooth Repair: Amelogenin-Derived Peptide Enables in Remineralization of Human Enamel." ACS Biomater. Sci. Eng. 4(5): 1788–1796.
154. Vincent, J. F., & King, M. J. 1995. "The mechanism of drilling by wood wasp ovipositors." Biomimetics, 3(4):187–201.
155. Zenger, J., & Folkman, J. "What Inspiring Leaders Do." (2013, June 20). Harvard Business Review.
156. Dyer, J., Gregersen, H., & Christensen, C. M. 2011. The Innovator's DNA: Mastering the Five Skills of Disruptive Innovators, Boston, MA: Harvard Business Press.
157. Sun, J., et al. 2018. "Unique Associations Between Big Five Personality Aspects and Multiple Dimensions of Well Being." Journal of Personality 86(2): 158-172.